William Nelson Lovatt in Late Qing China

William Nelson Lovatt in Late Qing China

War, Maritime Customs, and Treaty Ports, 1860–1904

Wayne Patterson

LEXINGTON BOOKS
Lanham • Boulder • New York • London

Published by Lexington Books
An imprint of The Rowman & Littlefield Publishing Group, Inc.
4501 Forbes Boulevard, Suite 200, Lanham, Maryland 20706
www.rowman.com

6 Tinworth Street, London SE11 5AL, United Kingdom

British Library Cataloguing in Publication Information Available

Library of Congress Control Number: 2019951235

Library of Congress Cataloging-in-Publication Data Available

ISBN: 978-1-4985-6646-9 (cloth)
ISBN: 978-1-4985-6647-6 (electronic)

Contents

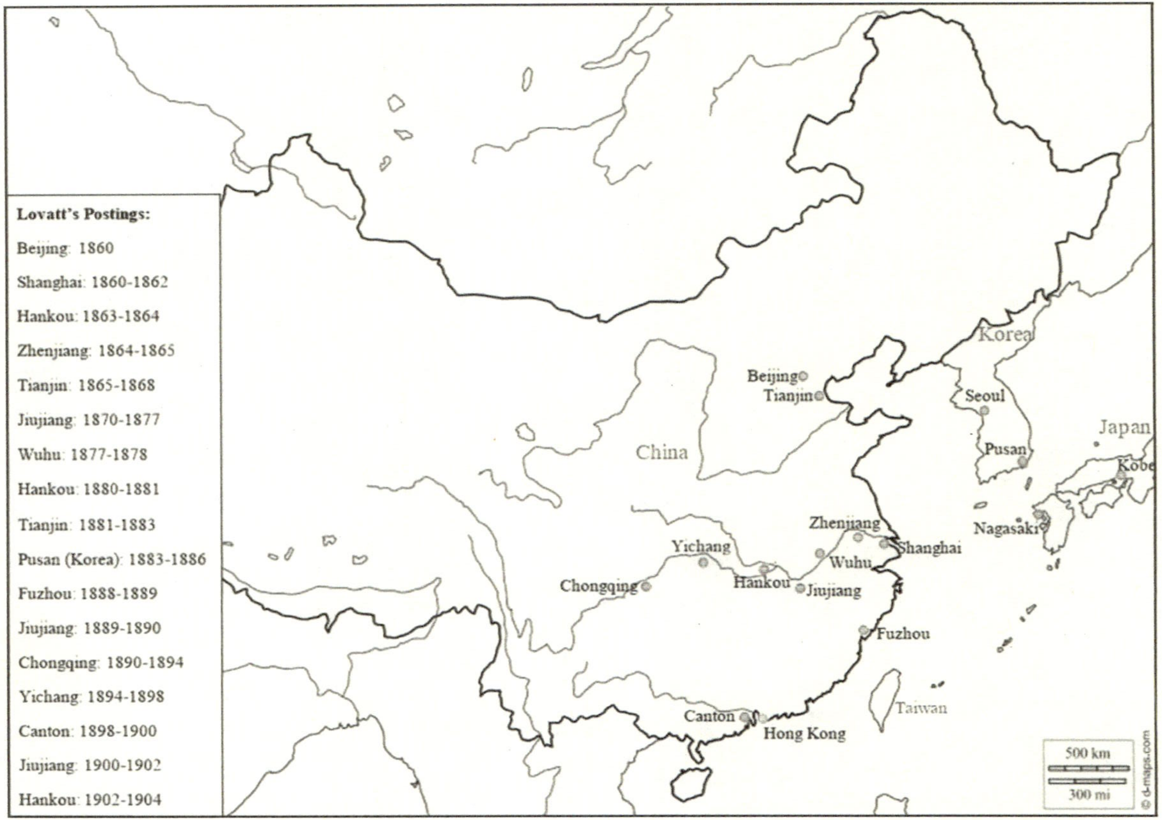

Figure 0.1 Lovatt's Postings.

Introduction

William Nelson Lovatt (*Lu Fu*) initially arrived in China as a British soldier in 1860, remained in China for most of the rest of his life as a tidesurveyor (*zongxun toudeng*) in the Chinese Imperial Maritime Customs Service (*Zhongguo haiguan*), and died there in 1904. Although he cannot be considered a major figure, he is nonetheless significant because he was on the scene during the last half-century of the Qing (Manchu) dynasty (1644–1911), leaving photographs and detailed accounts in his journals and letters that provide us with a unique view of that period. After marrying a woman from Minnesota, for most of his adult life he identified as an American.

The Customs Service for which he worked was a product of the Unequal Treaties forced on China beginning with the conclusion of the First Opium War (1839–1842), establishing treaty ports and authorizing the collection of customs duty. Customs houses were originally established and staffed by Chinese, but these were seen as corrupt and inefficient by both the Chinese government and Western merchants. In 1854 British consul Rutherford Alcock in Shanghai established a system of duty collection staffed by Westerners that gave the Chinese government a regular and predictable source of income. Horatio Lay became the first inspector general (IG) in 1859, but after a falling out with the Chinese government, Robert Hart (1835–1911) assumed interim control of the Customs in 1861 and in 1863 was named IG. Hart would control the Chinese Customs as a civil servant employee of the Chinese government for the next half-century until his death in 1911.[1]

Contending views dominate the historiography of the Customs Service and Hart, and tend to cluster around the binaries of Chinese backwardness and Western oppression on the one hand versus Western progress and benevolence on the other. For nearly a half-century after the founding of the People's Republic of China in 1949, historians in China as well as some Western historians viewed the Customs and Hart as spearheads of Western imperialism (*diguo zhuyi*). In this view, China endured semicolonial domination by the West, and the Customs served as "the executive organ of th imperialists' aggressive policies," not only harming the Chinese people but also propping up a corrupt and dying Qing dynasty. As for Hart, he was "a sly colonizer" who "committed many crimes against the Chinese people."[2]

Others see the Customs in more favorable terms, as China's first modern civil service and an exemplar of incorrupt efficiency, with Hart as a loyal civil servant, strengthening rather than harming China. This view notes that the Customs provided a stable and steady income to the government, promoted reforms, funded Western military training, established institutions like the Interpreters College, and developed infrastructure like a postal system and navigational aids such as buoys, beacons, lighthouses, and wharves. Hart and the Customs, in other words, "did a service to China that is difficult to estimate."[3]

Still other historians have taken a more nuanced approach, recognizing that historical reality rarely falls into neat dichotomies, and that the Customs defied easy categorization. Some see it as a compromise between China and the West, a "synarchy" benefiting both. Others acknowledge that while the Customs was certainly centralized, highly organized, and disciplined, it was nonetheless an institution dominated by foreigners and thus representative of a sort of informal empire. Increasingly, historians in China have adopted this more nuanced approach.[4]

This brief overview is not meant to suggest that those issues will be put to rest by this volume. Nor does this study represent an economic history of trade at the treaty ports of China. Rather, this study provides the context in which the Customs and Hart (and Lovatt) operated. While most historians approach the subject from the top down and from the outside looking in, concentrating on the twentieth century for which there is abundant documentation, fewer accounts employ an insider, bottom-up approach focusing on the nineteenth century, when documentation is less abundant. This study falls into the latter category.

Observers also differ on Hart's leadership of the Customs. Some, including many former employees, see the IG in positive terms, as efficient and impartial, but other former employees are less positive. Because Lovatt aspired to rise to the rank of commissioner, he was keen to do whatever it took to win Hart's favor and reach that goal. Some rose quickly to that rank in the Service, like Harvard graduates H. B. Morse and Edward B. Drew. Drew, for example, joined the Service in the same year as Lovatt and within three years had risen to the rank of commissioner, an ascent that normally took twenty years.[5]

While Lovatt could not claim an Ivy League pedigree, he was nonetheless a hardworking and competent tidesurveyor who had, moreover, not only mastered Chinese but also continued his study of the language to improve his prospects for promotion. Failure to master Chinese was one of the reasons, as Hart explained to Drew, why some did not advance: "complete ignorance of China and the Chinese language, than which ignorance nothing can better qualify a man for working in China—nothing better entitles him to rapid advancement in the Chinese service! I can meet any complainant and tell him why I did not advance him: I have had a Service reason for all I have done or left undone."[6]

But Drew and Morse were Americans, and Lovatt was nominally British. According to Paul King, Hart was an "unpredictable autocrat" who held grudges and whose "impartiality" masked a bias against British subjects. Hart had

> a habit of only taking active steps against people he disliked when quite sure they could not retaliate. With his British employees he always had a free hand, and could treat them well or badly just as he pleased. It was not so with the American and European members of the Customs Service. Watchful Consuls at the ports and jealous Plenipotentiaries at Beijing saw to it that their nationals got their due in the matter of promotion, and even sometimes rather more. But British representatives—Ministers and Consuls alike—exercised from the very first days a 'self-denying ordinance' in regard to interference with the internal concerns of the Customs Service, which, whatever its ethical beauty, in practice too often resulted in unredressed wrongs to the British employees.

Lovatt's career in the Customs will illustrate, at least in this one instance, whether Hart was impartial and unbiased, unpredictable and biased, or somewhere in between. That is, if this study says less about Hart's place in late nineteenth-century China, it can speak more to his management style through the eyes of one of his Anglo-American subordinates. It will conclude that Hart's leadership fell somewhere between the binaries of biased and partial on the one hand and unbiased and impartial on the other.[7]

The work of the Customs took place in the treaty ports, where customs houses, Western diplomats and diplomatic missions, businessmen, gunboats, Christian evangelizing organizations such as the China Inland Mission, hongs such as Jardine and Matheson, banks such as the Hong Kong and Shanghai Banking Corporation, and European-style residences created discrete islands a world apart from that of the average Chinese. Lovatt served in nine of these treaty ports, some more than once, most of them on the Yangzi River. If these treaty ports represented outposts of Western imperialism, did its inhabitants manifest an "imperial mentality," and was Lovatt a willing participant? This study will show that Lovatt was in many respects a product of the times who enjoyed the privilege of extraterritoriality, who approved of Christian evangelizing and the timely use of Western gunboats. At the same time, Lovatt showed extraordinary appreciation for the Chinese and things Chinese, and was quick to criticize Western foibles in China.[8]

Connecting these treaty ports were steamships that carried Lovatt not only between his postings but also across the Pacific more than a dozen times. More than simply means of transport, they also represented "social spaces," bringing not only passengers and cargo but also captains and crew, mail, rumors, newspapers, and dispatches from Hart in Beijing. Additionally, native junks were part of the transportation network, serving a crucial role in opening new treaty ports, such as the voyage Lovatt made to Chongqing in 1890, tracking upriver and which he documented. In short, steamships and junks were central to treaty port life, and much of Lovatt's story involves travel to and from these ports of call.[9]

In these treaty ports, Lovatt provides a firsthand look at life on the ground, where he interacted with a wide variety of Westerners, foremost among them his customs colleagues. Although Lovatt met the man at the top, Hart, only a handful of times throughout his career, Lovatt interacted on a daily basis with customs personnel, at the apex of which at every treaty port was the commissioner. Lovatt as second in command as tidesurveyor and harbormaster occupied a unique vantage point to observe the various commissioners and how they comported themselves. He was also strategically placed to take the measure of those he supervised in the outdoor staff (*waiban*), such as the tidewaiters. Lovatt thus provides an inside look at the nuts and bolts of the customs enterprise.

Aside from customs personnel, Lovatt cast a critical eye on missionaries in the treaty ports, perhaps the most influential group of Westerners in China at the time. Lovatt, an Anglican himself, counted many missionaries as his friends. While generally approving of mission work in China, Lovatt was nonetheless able to critique the missionary enterprise, providing chapter and verse to the personalities and actions of individual missionaries and revealing their follies. While there exist many accounts of missionaries and mission work in late nineteenth-century China, Lovatt provides a fresh perspective.[10]

The third group of Westerners that Lovatt interacted with on a consistent basis in the treaty ports was diplomats. His relatively high status in the Customs hierarchy caused him to be a frequent guest at diplomatic social functions where international politics were regular topics of conversation, giving Lovatt insight into the policies and personalities of the major Western players in China. These functions were not always purely academic, however, as evidenced by one instance when Lovatt faced arrest by British consular officials during the Japanese invasion of Taiwan.

In addition to Westerners, Lovatt also had extensive interaction with Chinese of all stripes, from officials and merchants to ordinary citizens. Because he was fluent in Chinese, not averse to mingling with the local population, and a frequent traveler outside the confines of the treaty ports, Lovatt was a keen observer of daily life and customs. He overheard their conversations and listened in on their gossip, so little esçaped his attention. Although he occasionally referred to the Chinese as "heathen," this did not materially skew his observations of Chinese people and society. In short, he was able to see firsthand the fault lines of late Qing China.

One of those fault lines, related to Westerners generally and missionaries in particular on the one hand and the Chinese citizenry on the other, was the rise of antiforeignism in the late nineteenth century. Those looking for antecedents of the 1900 Boxer Rebellion will find no shortage of evidence in the numerous situations that Lovatt observed and participated in—events that increased in number and intensity as the end of the century approached. His eyewitness accounts of antiforeign incidents are particularly instructive. For example, was Lovatt sympathetic to the view that foreigners were disruptive of the traditional social harmony? Or was "foreign devil" Lovatt himself a target or a cause of antiforeign sentiment? This study will demonstrate that while Lovatt himself did not precipitate antiforeign sentiments and blamed much of the antiforeign sentiment on false rumors, he was alive to the roots of antiforeignism due to the actions of Western missionaries.

Military affairs play a significant part of this story, particularly early on. The mid-nineteenth century saw China defeated in two Opium Wars (1839–1842 and 1856–1860 [the Arrow War]), enduring massive and simultaneous rebellions (1851–1868), including the Taiping and Nian, and facing an invasion by Japan (1874). Traditionally, since rebellions are signs of dynastic decline, it certainly appeared that the Qing was close to being overthrown. That is, in traditional Confucian terms, the dynasty seemed about to lose the Mandate of Heaven. Lovatt was an active participant in each of these four conflicts, once against the Qing and three times on the side of the Qing. His eyewitness accounts supplement earlier accounts of these conflicts, adding to our understanding. And his participation on the side of the Qing contributed to the Cooperative Policy that emerged in the 1860s when Western powers supported the Chinese government in suppressing rebellions. Since he was also engaged in training Chinese artillerymen and cavalry, Lovatt was a significant contributor to the military aspect of the Self-Strengthening Movement. Was he a competent drillmaster? And, more broadly, were the efforts of Lovatt and other Western trainers to modernize the Chinese military successful? This study will demonstrate that while Lovatt himself was successful, the larger project of which he was a part remained stillborn.[11]

In short, more than simply a story of one expatriate's experience, Lovatt's career in China provides a rich and original inside look not only at the last half-century of the Qing dynasty but also at the inner workings of Hart and the Imperial Maritime Customs Service, treaty ports, missionaries, diplomats, and Chinese society.

This study had its origins in the early 1980s while leading a student trip to China when I had the good fortune to meet Lina Sharp who, upon learning my occupation, mentioned that she had acquired the correspondence of a man who had worked in China in the late nineteenth century, given to her by a friend before he died. When she asked if I would be interested in the letters, I replied in the affirmative. The letters were those of William Nelson Lovatt. Although some letters are illegible, missing, incomplete, or lacking in dates, leaving gaps in the documentation, the collection is complete enough to allow the themes identified above to be fleshed out. Although this book rests largely upon Lovatt's correspondence to his wife, research on three continents added significantly to the picture. At each location, I was aided immeasurably by many institutions and individuals.

Work began in earnest first in the United States in 2000 at Harvard University, first as a visiting scholar at the Fairbank Center for East Asian Studies and then as visiting professor of Korean History, enabling me to make use of that university's library and archival collections, in particular the Harvard-Yenching Library and the Houghton Library, containing the correspondence of Sir Robert Hart. I was able to return to Harvard in 2008 for additional research, thanks to a grant from the China and Inner Asia Council of the Association for Asian Studies, which I gratefully acknowledge. While at Harvard, I also began to locate the descendants of Lovatt and his wife for additional information, many of whom I met at a Lovatt family reunion in Minnesota in 2004, the centennial year of his death. Several of them had additional letters and photographs that they were kind enough to share with me.

At the University of California—Berkeley in 2009–2010, simultaneous appointments as visiting professor of Asian Studies and Visiting Scholar at the Institute of East Asian Studies gave me the opportunity to locate at the Bancroft Library Lovatt's photo album and journals donated by his grandson, Henri de Carbonel. Also in the San Francisco Bay area was the great-grandson of Lovatt, Frank de Carbonel, who provided additional letters and photographs.

Other research locations in the United States included Nevada, Arizona, Minnesota, and Wisconsin. Nevada was not only the home of Lina Sharp who had acquired Lovatt's correspondence but also the home of two fourth-generation descendants of Lovatt, William de Carbonel and Susan de Carbonel Schultz, who shared additional letters and photographs. Dorothy Shaw Gillette of Arizona, a descendant of Lovatt's wife, shared additional correspondence and photos. In Minnesota, the State Historical Society in St. Paul and the Stillwater Historical Society helped me locate the site of Lovatt's house and that of his in-laws, his marriage license, and the graves of his wife and daughter. In Wisconsin, at my home institution of St. Norbert College, I am indebted to the Faculty Development Committee for summer grants to conduct additional research and to the Faculty Personnel Committee for a sabbatical leave for this research. Thanks for technical support go to Lois Velicer, Sean McIlheran, Rachel Jensen, Jenna Kempen, Jonathan Kent, and Leah Hennick. My greatest thanks, however, go to Peggy Schlapman, Humanities Division secretary, who spent long hours conscientiously transcribing Lovatt's often illegible handwriting. Without her invaluable assistance, this study would not have been possible.

Research for this project also took me to Europe. In Andorra, I interviewed Michael Lovatt, Lovatt's only surviving grandson. In England, the Public Records Office and the library of the School of Oriental and African Studies at the University of London yielded valuable information. I was able to access Robert Hart's nearly indecipherable diaries in the Special Collections of Queen's University, Belfast, Ireland, assisted by its curator, Deirdre Wildy.

Finally, the research trail led to China. While affiliated with the Hopkins-Nanjing Center at Nanjing University, I was able to use the material in the Number Two Historical Archives. In Beijing I consulted with Zhang Zhiyong at the Chinese Academy of Social Sciences, and in Shanghai with Zhan Qinghua at the Shanghai Customs.

As this project took shape, earlier versions of some chapters appeared initially as conference papers. The first was at a conference on "Robert Hart and the Chinese Maritime Customs Service: Reassessments" at The Queen's University—Belfast in December 2008. Another was at the conference on "Treaty Ports in Modern China" at the University of Bristol in July 2011. At these venues, I was able to sharpen my focus thanks to the comments by the discussants and the audience.

Thanks also to Adrian Bennett for his useful comments and suggestions, and to my editor Eric Kuntzman, who skillfully shepherded the manuscript into final book form.

Final thanks go to my wife, Marlene, for her support throughout. And my canine and feline research assistants, Spencer and Bogart, were always eager to help. Although I would like to blame them for any errors of fact or interpretation, in the end, I am solely responsible.

In reconstructing Lovatt's career in China, I have attempted wherever possible to use his own words, with only minor changes in punctuation. The spellings he uses are a combination of Wade-Giles, Postal Service, and his own idiosyncratic spelling, often in illegible handwriting. As a result, some of the names and places are difficult to identify. Except when Lovatt or others are quoted directly, I have used pinyin romanization. Many of the citations, noted at the end of each paragraph, are Lovatt's letters to his wife, Jennie Shaw Lovatt, and appear as WNL to JSL. In keeping with East Asian convention regarding name order, family names appear first, followed by the given name.

NOTES

1. Hart was born in Ireland, studied classics at The Queen's University in Belfast, and in 1854 became a student interpreter in Ningbo where he learned Chinese and joined the British consular service. John King Fairbank, *Trade and Diplomacy on the China Coast: The Opening of the Treaty Ports, 1842–1854* (Cambridge: Harvard University Press, 1953). See also John King Fairbank, Richard J. Smith, and Katherine Frost Bruner, eds., *Entering China's Service: Robert Hart's Journals, 1854–1863* (Cambridge: Harvard East Asian Monographs, 1986). The most recent treatment of Hart and the Customs is Hans van de Ven, *Breaking with the Past: The Maritime Customs Service and the Global Origins of Modernity in China* (New York: Columbia University Press, 2014). Hart reported to the Zongli Yamen, a subcommittee of the Grand Council. In 1901, the Zongli Yamen was abolished and replaced by a Foreign Office.

2. *Preface* (Huang Xiang) and *Introduction* (Chen Xiafei) in Chen Xiafei and Han Rongfang, eds., *Archives of China's Imperial Maritime Customs Confidential Correspondence between Robert Hart and James Duncan Campbell, 1874–1907*, Comp. The Second Historical Archives of China and the Institute of Modern History of the Chinese Academy of Social Sciences. Four Volumes (Beijing: Foreign Languages Press, 1990). An example of a Western historian sharing this negative view is Joseph Esherick, "Harvard on China: The Apologetics of Imperialism." *Bulletin of Concerned Asian Scholars* 4 (1972), 9–16.

3. See, for example, Juliet Bredon, *Sir Robert Hart: The Romance of a Great Career* (London: Hutchinson, 1910). See also Stanley F. Wright, *Hart and the Chinese Customs* (Belfast: Wm. Mullan and Son, 1950). Preface to John King Fairbank, Katherine Frost Bruner, and Elizabeth MacLeod Matheson, eds., *The I. G. in Peking: Letters of Robert Hart, Chinese Maritime Customs, 1868–1907*. Two Volumes. (Cambridge and London: Belknap Press of Harvard University Press, 1975).

4. Fairbank coined the term "synarchy" to describe the Customs. For an account of how Fairbank came to study Hart and the Customs, see Robert A. Bickers, "Purloined Letters: History and the Chinese Maritime Customs Service." *Modern Asian Studies*, 40 (3) (2006), 691–723; Donna Brunero, *Britain's Imperial Cornerstone in China: The Chinese Maritime Customs Service, 1854–1949* (New York: Routledge, 2006), especially 1–19; Jurgen Osterhammel, "Semi-Colonialism and Informal Empire in Twentieth-Century China: Towards a Framework of Analysis," in W. J. Mommsen and Jurgen Osterhammel, eds. *Imperialism and After: Continuities and Discontinuities* (London: Allen and Unwin, 1986), 290–314. See also Catherine Ladds, *Empire Careers: Working for the Chinese Customs Service, 1854–1949* (Manchester: University of Manchester Press, 2013), 2–7. Recent works by historians in China include: Chen Shiqi, *Zhongguo jindai haiguan shi* (*China's Modern Maritime Customs History*) (Beijing: Renmin Chubanshe, 2002); Dai Yifeng, *Zhongguo haiguan yu Zhongguo jindai shehui: Chen Shiqi jiaoshou jiuzhu huadan zhushou wenji* (*The Chinese Maritime Customs and Modern Chinese Society: Essays Commemorating the 90th Birthday of Professor Chen Shiqi*) (Xiamen: Xiamen University Press, 2005); Zhan Qing-hua, *Quanqiuhua shiye: Zhongguo haiguan yangyuan yu ZhongXi*

wenhua chuanbo (*A Globalization Perspective of Foreign Staffs in the Chinese Maritime Customs Service and Trans-Cultural Communication between East and West (1854–1950)*) (Beijing: Zhongguo Haiguan Chubanshe, 2008); Zhang Zhiyong, *Hade yu wanQing ZhongYing waijiao* (*Hart between China and England in the Late Qing*) (Shanghai: Shanghai Shudian Chubanshe, 2012).

5. John King Fairbank, Martha Henderson Coolidge, and Richard J. Smith, *H. B. Morse: Customs Commissioner and Historian of China* (Lexington: University Press of Kentucky, 1995), 12–24. Another was Henry F. Merrill, who graduated from Harvard in 1874 and entered the Service the same year.

6. Hart to Drew, August 22, 1875, *Hart Letters*, Houghton Library, bMS Chinese 4.

7. H. B. Morse, *The International Relations of the Chinese Empire. Volume Two. The Period of Submission, 1861–1893* (London and New York: Longmans, Green, and Co., 1910–1918); Paul King, *In the Chinese Customs Service: A Personal Record of Forty-Seven Years* (London: T. Fisher Unwin, 1924), 22, 26, 66, 238, and 246. King described his unpredictable nature thusly: "No one really knew how to take Robert Hart. His likes and dislikes reminded one of the celebrated Blondin Donkey. The expected was always met by the unexpected."

8. Overviews of treaty port society can be found in Robert Bickers, *The Scramble for China: Foreign Devils in the Qing Empire, 1832–1911* (London: Allen Lane, 2011), and *Britain in China: Community, Culture and Colonialism, 1900–1949* (Manchester: Manchester University Press, 1999); see also Par Cassel, *Grounds of Judgement: Extraterritoriality and Imperial Power in Nineteenth Century China and Japan* (Oxford: Oxford University Press, 2012). There are also descriptions of specific treaty ports. See, for example, William T. Rowe, *Hankow: Conflict and Community in a Chinese City, 1796–1895* (Stanford: Stanford University Press, 1989).

9. Anne Reinhardt, *Navigating Semi-Colonialism: Shipping, Sovereignty, and Nation-Building in China, 1860–1937* (Cambridge: Harvard Asia Center, 2018), 133–178.

10. For an overview, see Dan Bays, *A New History of Christianity in China* (Oxford and New York: Wiley and Blackwell, 2011). For an example of one missionary, see Adrian Arthur Bennett, *Missionary Journalist in China: Young J. Allen and His Magazines, 1860–1883* (Athens: University of Georgia Press, 1982).

11. See, for example, Andrew Wilson, *The "Ever-Victorious Army": A History of the Chinese Campaign under Lt.-Col. C. G. Gordon, C.B. R.E. and of the Suppression of the Tai-Ping Rebellion* (Edinburgh and London: William Blackwood and Sons, 1868; reprinted Arlington: University Publications of America, 1976); and Henry B. Loch, *Personal Narrative of Occurrences during Lord Elgins's Second Embassy to China in 1860*, Third Edition (London: John Murray, 1900).

Chapter 1

Entering China

The Siege of Beijing, 1860

EARLY LIFE IN ENGLAND

William Nelson Lovatt was born in Southampton, England, on January 10, 1838, into a military family. His father, John (1805–1871), had been in the Royal Fusiliers, and his two younger brothers, Tom and John, enlisted in the British navy. He also had a sister, Sarah. Although we know little about his childhood, one month after his fifteenth birthday, in February 1853, the self-described "young and weak" teenager enlisted in the Royal Artillery and underwent basic training, complaining that "I hardly ever remembered being so tired," adding "I thought soldiering hard work then. How little I knew what was before me." After seven months of training, Lovatt's unit embarked for Bermuda, but because of Yellow Fever there, his ship was diverted to Nova Scotia in the fall of 1853. After ten weeks, Lovatt's troop ship again set sail, arriving in Bermuda on Christmas Eve, 1853. Although his stay in Canada was brief, he was destined to return to North America fifteen years later under much different circumstances.[1]

BERMUDA, ENGLAND, AND INDIA, 1853–1860

Lovatt kept a journal, and some of his earliest entries concerned the chief local product—rum—labeling it "the soldier's curse." But in fact the teen-aged Lovatt was a rowdy lad with a taste for booze himself, characterizing his eighteen months in less-than-hazardous Bermuda as "duty and dissipation." During another stopover in Nova Scotia on his way back to England, "I got into trouble a couple of times through drink." Back in England in the fall of

1855, "again, I got into a scrape." Visiting his family during the Christmas furlough, "I was inclined to drink and amusements of different sorts. I ought to have behaved better for I think I must have pained my dear Father." In February 1856, he was promoted to Acting Bombadier, "although I little deserved it for my conduct was anything but what it should have been." Aware of his shortcomings, Lovatt attended school and "greatly improved myself," and "my brother John was quite an example for me." But neither seemed to have much of an effect, as he "got into another scrape, and lost my stripe in June, and afterward I got into a second [scrape], but again got off with a few days drill."[2]

Perhaps he would have continued along that low road, except that when his unit boarded the troop ship in Portsmouth for the eighty-five-day voyage to India in August 1857 to quell the Sepoy Rebellion, a preacher gave him a small Bible and told him to read it. Lovatt replied carelessly that "I would read it to please him some day." The preacher replied, "read it for yourself alone." Lovatt took the advice to heart, writing, "thank God I have done so." Looking back, he noted that "I was always more or less impulsive, but I know I led quite a religious life when I was a young man."[3]

In India, Lovatt's new-found faith transformed him on the question of alcohol. "I do not *drink*," he wrote, and moralized about its effects on his comrades: "What generally makes India so unhealthy to European soldiers is their own fault. I noticed a Corporal and two of his guards laying drunk in the sun at nearly 11 o'clock in the day." He later recorded, "the first death occurred this day [when a soldier with] eleven years service, greatly given to drink, and having been drinking this country's liquor to excess, found himself not able the next morning to march, and on reporting himself sick was admitted into hospital, where he died that afternoon. Surely that instance carries its own lesson."[4]

His Christian faith also colored his initial reaction to Asians. A year in India convinced him that Christianity, Western civilization, and the British imperial mission were exactly what the locals needed, characterizing the Indians as "a weak feeble race of people, lazy and indolent," and hoping that "the time may come when all will be Christians." The justness of the British colonial cause toward those "poor people" elicited the comment that "I wish they would surrender [to England] and go back to their work again," and he prayed for "our safe deliverance from the hands of the enemy [the rebellious colonial troops] and restoration of our authority over India."[5]

While critical of the character of the Indians, he was equally hard on himself—"my whole conduct lately has been disgraceful"—despite his rejection of alcohol. His rowdy behavior led to his being "brought up" before the captain, resulting in a severe reprimand and cancellation of one month's leave. Peccadillos aside, he saw combat for the first time in the spring of

Figure 1.1 Lovatt with Medals and Sword, 1860. *Source*: Dorothy Shaw Gillette.

1858. Acquitting himself well in this and subsequent engagements, he was promoted in August of 1858 to Bombadier, earning the British War Medal and the Clasp for Central India (figure 1.1).[6]

HONG KONG AND NORTH CHINA, APRIL–NOVEMBER 1860

After two years in India, Lovatt's unit received orders to deploy to China in the spring of 1860. Marching to Calcutta, Lovatt boarded a troop ship, passed through the straits of Malacca, and arrived in Singapore in early April. There, in his first exposure to East Asians, he found "the inhabitants mostly Chinese, a strange looking race of people" and their ships "a quaint-looking craft called a Chinese Junk." From Singapore, Lovatt's unit proceeded to Hong Kong in late April 1860, where he was billeted in Kowloon near a group of Chinese "wanting to gamble after supper until past midnight." Comparing them to the Indians he had just left, Lovatt recorded that "the Chinese appears to me a sturdy sort of people, but nothing of the grace of the Hindoo about him." The "very civil and kind" gamblers offered him his first taste of Chinese tea, which "had such a strange flavour, much weaker than our own." They also offered him the strong and fiery *mao tai* which he sampled, despite his claim to be a teetotaler, and found that "not being used to it, only took two glasses, but that was two too much." And he continued to rail against excess consumption by his British compatriots: "Oh, what a Sabbath day, with drunken sailors and soldiers cursing and swearing all the afternoon and singing songs by professing Christians; what an example to the heathen!"[7]

After two months in Hong Kong, in June of 1860 Lovatt and his unit again boarded a ship bound for north China. Events in Beijing had made a renewed clash between China and the West increasingly likely, as Prince Yi, the leader of the antiforeign party opposed to complying with what they considered the distasteful 1858 Treaty of Tianjin, had achieved temporary ascendancy in the Chinese court. That treaty called for the stationing of resident ministers in Beijing, the opening of ten new treaty ports, the opening of the Yangzi River to foreign commerce, and freedom to live and travel in the interior, particularly for missionaries, all provisions that would affect Lovatt's future. When the Chinese government refused to ratify the treaty, the British and the French were determined to press the issue.

Upon disembarking, Lovatt's unit was among those ordered to take the Dagu forts blocking river access to the capital. On August 12, three years to the day that he had left England for Asia, Lovatt had his first taste of combat in China, dragging 8-inch mortars through "knee-deep" mud in the assault. Although the allies suffered no casualties, 400 Chinese were killed, in the aftermath of which, while noting the inferiority of their rockets and referring to them as heathen, Lovatt paid them grudging respect: "There is no mistake in these fellows; they fought well, and that against two crack armies of France and England during the storming of the fort."[8]

When not engaged in combat, Lovatt began what was to be a lifetime of keen observations of Chinese life and customs. Aboard ship en route to north China, the death of one of the Chinese bullock drivers gave him the opportunity to observe differences between East and West: "What a solemn thought—a soul ushered into eternity, a dark and benighted heathen; his comrades took him on deck, no burial service or anything, just thrown over like one of our dead bullocks would be." And after disembarking he noted the differences in gender roles: "From the number of men I saw, their women I suppose they keep confined to their houses, for they seldom show themselves."[9]

Meeting mostly men in the villages, Lovatt found them to be friendly and their homes attractive: "We passed many villages, clean and well built, and met some of the inhabitants, fine noble-looking men, some of them, and well dressed in good silks. They have generally been very civil and kind to us." One group was interested in his watch and "when I showed them the watch they were highly pleased and astonished." In the mostly deserted village he first encountered, Lovatt and his comrades occupied the mud and thatch vacant houses, inside of which "I was taken by surprise at the beautiful furniture many of them contained; they seem to be very much in advance of the Indians." The streets, by contrast, were "very narrow and in wet weather they are very dirty and filthy."[10]

Lovatt was equally impressed with the countryside. As he sailed up the Peiho toward Tianjin, "the country improved in appearance and beauty as we passed a large number of villages on both sides of the river, looking prosperous and happy, with their nice green gardens and orchards very nicely laid out and cultivated." Moving further inland, he observed that "I never saw a more fruitful country. We generally had an abundance of vegetables by going to the fields and gathering them, sweet potatoes, onions, cabbage, in abundance."[11]

Given that abundance, Lovatt had no problem finding enough to eat. After taking the forts, Lovatt's unit helped themselves to the tea, sugar, and pigs left behind to make sausage, and "the Chinese supplied us with fruit, vegetables, mutton, fowls, eggs, and other articles, and sell them generally at a reasonable price." What was not available at a reasonable price was alcohol, which "is very dear, but them who love it will buy it at whatever cost." On the other hand, clean drinking water was scarce, and disease stalked the troops. One soldier in his unit contracted cholera, many had diarrhea and dysentery, and Lovatt himself came down with a fever, which he blamed on the water (figure 1.2).[12]

Lovatt's unit had now been ordered to proceed to Tianjin in early September to prepare for the final assault on the capital while other units were ordered to Shanghai, for reasons yet unknown to Lovatt. At Tianjin, Lovatt and his unit disembarked from the steamer and marched northwest for about

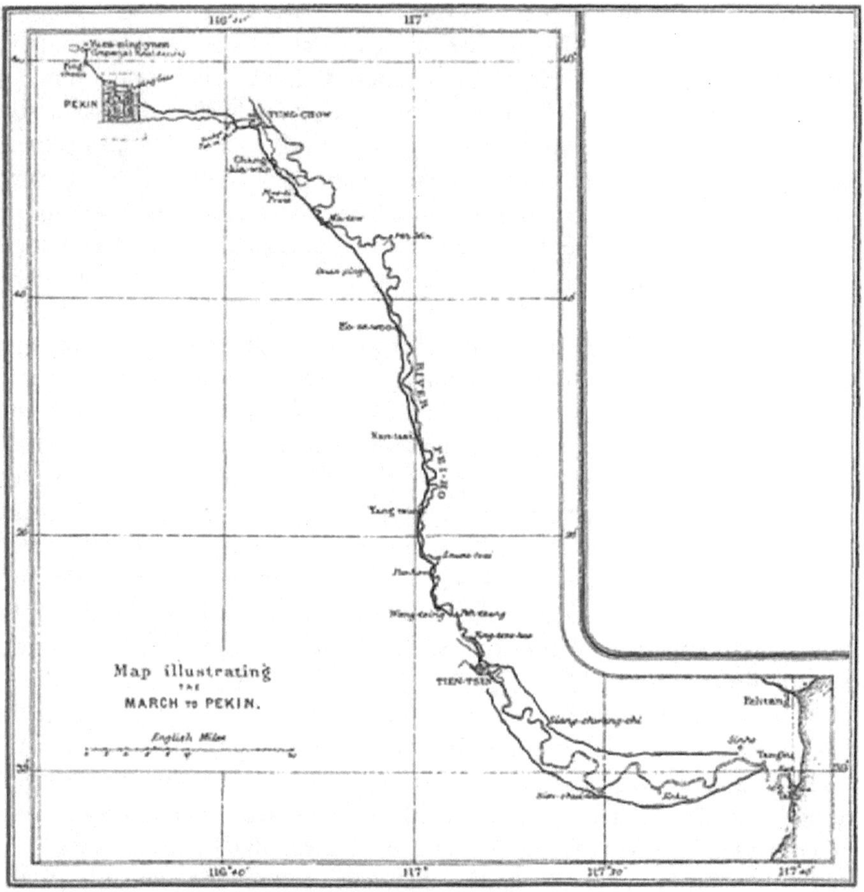

Figure 1.2 Lovatt's March from Dagu to Beijing. *Source*: Henry B. Loch, *Personal Narrative of Occurrences during Lord Elgin's Second Embassy to China in 1860*. (London: John Murray, 1900 (Third Edition)).

100 miles on a "dusty and very difficult" road that took him through Yangcun, Hexiwu, Matou, and finally to Tongzhou, in the eastern suburbs of Beijing, the staging area for the assault. Lovatt described Tongzhou as "a town of considerable size and walled in, under a mandarin who remains neutral, and [who] sends his people with provisions to the army to sell." Just before arriving in Tongzhou, Lovatt's unit learned that the Manchu general Sankolinsin, a member of the antiforeign faction, had captured thirty-nine British and French officers under a flag of truce, and murdered twenty of them. Waiting in Tongzhou was the British representative Lord Elgin, there to insist that, in Lovatt's words, "the proud and vain Chinese" admit foreign ambassadors to the capital.[13]

But first the Chinese had to be subdued. From Tongzhou, Lovatt's unit took the stone-paved road toward Beijing, its ruts causing his shells to fall off the carts, and camped about four miles away. His artillery battery was prepared to blow open the gates in the northwest section of the city wall if they were not opened, but the peace faction headed by Prince Gong had achieved ascendancy, and "the Chinese like good sensible people opened the gate at the time appointed and thereby saved their town from ruin and destruction, much to the disappointment of the French and many of our own people." And so on October 12, the allied troops entered without resistance, clearing the way for Elgin to sign the Convention of Beijing, ratifying the Treaty of Tianjin and winning for Lovatt yet another medal. With no more fighting to be done, Lovatt pitched his tent near a temple whose "carving of the interior is very beautiful indeed and shows great skill and ingenuity." Lovatt was clearly developing an appreciation for Chinese culture.[14]

With the successful conclusion of the operation, Lovatt and his unit returned to Tongzhou and boarded a gunboat back to Tianjin, marking his second visit to that city. On his initial visit, Tianjin had not impressed him, with the streets "narrow and dirty." Now, two months later, in early November, he went for a walk on the main street, named by the English High Street, which was "very narrow, and the shops and houses are very irregularly built. There is no footpath, neither is the street paved in any way. Kept clean in dry [weather], they are in a dreadful state in wet weather. Some of the shops are very fine indeed." While in Tianjin, Lovatt received orders to depart for Shanghai, and so, on November 9, 1860, Lovatt embarked for that city where a new and confusing situation awaited him and the other British forces.[15]

NOTES

1. WNL *Journal.* This and all subsequent entries for the next seven years were written from memory when he was stationed in India between December 1859 and January 1860. As a result, there are no discreet daily entries for most of the 1850s. There is no record that Lovatt ever became a naturalized American citizen. The Lovatt family did have an earlier American connection when a member of the "old central England family" emigrated to Massachusetts in the seventeenth century. *Biographical Memo* written by Lovatt on April 21, 1901. In that memo, Lovatt spelled the surname as Lovett. Courtesy of Frank de Carbonel. WNL to JSL, March 4, 1882, and October 17 and November 16, 1888.
2. WNL *Journal.*
3. WNL *Journal*; WNL to JSL, December 16, 1891.
4. WNL *Journal.* Emphasis in the original.
5. WNL *Journal*, December 12, 1858, July 28, 1859, and January 18, 1860.

6. WNL *Journal*, January 23, May 9, and June 6, 1859.

7. WNL *Journal*, January 7, March 9, April 5, 9, and 24, and May 4, 10, and 31, 1860.

8. Wright, *Hart and the Chinese Customs*, 145; WNL *Journal*, August 12, 1860.

9. WNL *Journal*, June 9 and September 6, 1860.

10. WNL *Journal*, June 9, August 4, and September 18, 1860.

11. WNL *Journal*, September 6 and 18, 1860.

12. WNL *Journal*, August 9 and 12, and September 5 and 6, 1860.

13. WNL *Journal*, September 17 to October 12, 1860; Wright, 146; see also map on page 192 of Fairbank, Smith, and Bruner, eds., *Entering China's Service: Robert Hart's Journals, 1854–1863* .

14. WNL *Journal*, October 12–20, 1860. The Summer Palace (*Yuan Ming Yuan*) was destroyed in retribution for the killing of the Western emissaries by the Chinese, who had ignored the white truce flag. Concluding that such an action could not have occurred without the assent of the highest authorities, the Allies sought to punish those at the top lest the Chinese hand over low-level scapegoats. Lovatt took no part in its destruction and railed against the plundering of Chinese property by allied troops. Lord Elgin signed the Convention of Beijing on October 24, 1860, concluding what is often termed the Second Opium War.

15. WNL *Journal*, September 6, October 30, and November 6 and 9, 1860.

Chapter 2

Fighting the Taiping

Shanghai, 1860–1862

ARRIVAL IN SHANGHAI

Even before docking in November 1860, Lovatt was impressed: "I like the appearance of Shanghai very well from the river. It has fine noble buildings and very large mansions from several of which the different Consulate flags are flying." Five months in, he was still "very fond of Shanghai," and after a year, his admiration continued: "One is struck with the large improvements that are continually taking place even in a foreign settlement like this is and so far from old England. New houses and new streets are springing up in every direction, and fresh faces meet you at almost every turn, such is the energy of my country." Clearly, the British imperial project in Shanghai won Lovatt's approval, but his admiration for the city rested on more than architecture and city planning.[1]

Shanghai had been one of the first five treaty ports established in 1842 after the First Opium War by the Unequal Treaties, along with Canton (Guangzhou), Ningbo, Amoy (Xiamen), and Fuzhou. Making its reputation as a trading entrepot, there were more than 100 foreign firms in place by 1860. Westerners, other than the 5,000 soldiers like Lovatt, made up about 2,000, the most numerous being British, many of whom were traders with their Chinese compradors. The Unequal Treaties had removed the prohibitions against Christianity, and missionaries saw China as a vast field for proselytizing. The missionaries in Shanghai were mostly Protestants (like Lovatt, who was Anglican) from England and the United States, who also benefited from the extraterritorial rights granted to Westerners by the Unequal Treaties.

Up to this time, Lovatt's religious activities had consisted of Sunday services and Bible meetings in tents in the field and exclusively among soldiers. But now, Lovatt for the first time began to make the acquaintance of missionaries. Within days of his arrival, he went to the London Mission Chapel and afterward had tea with one of the missionaries. "It quite takes me by surprise to have such kind friends who take an interest in soldiers and give us such a warm welcome to their houses," he wrote, noting, "how kind and attentive the missionaries are to us, their houses always open, and a hearty warm welcome ready for us whenever we chose to visit them."[2]

Lovatt liked the company of missionaries also because they preached against alcohol. For example, he attended "a very nice tea-party, well attended with missionaries, sailors, and soldiers, the temperance question was brought prominently forward and had numerous advocates." In fact, one of his first duties was to guard a soldier about to be court-martialed for trying to shoot a fellow soldier: "[He] tells me he was in the horrors of drink. Is this not one of the fearful effects of drink in our army?" Even professing Christians were not immune: "On my arrival I was informed of the sad fate of our Scripture Reader McCruickshanks, all through *Drink*, that curse of our country." To avoid the drinking attendant upon Christmas, Lovatt instead went sightseeing, visiting a temple, stopping at a teashop, and traveling to nearby Bubbling Well Village to observe burial practices, where the "graves [are] like mounds of earth, for the coffin is placed generally on the level of the ground and the earth thrown up over it" due to the high water table in the area.[3]

In addition to their hospitality and opposition to alcohol, Lovatt also approved of missionary work to convert the Chinese. On Chinese New Year (February 10, 1861), he observed that the Chinese will mostly stay home and "address the idols and offer sacrifice to their lords. May the day speedily come when all shall know thee, the true and only God." He came to appreciate the challenges faced by the missionaries when he "spoke this evening to our Chinese interpreter of the true and living God [and] experienced the difficulty missionaries do in explaining the plan of salvation to the heathen."[4]

Now that the right of missionaries to travel and reside outside the treaty ports had been affirmed by the Convention of Beijing, some began to depart for the interior—a movement that also won Lovatt's admiration: "Many of our missionaries of Shanghai have gone to the west and north of this country and are establishing missions. Oh what vast field of labour [is] this dark and heathen land, where so many millions of thy creatures grope in darkness and have no light." Other missionaries departed for health reasons, leaving Lovatt to lament that they were not being replaced, and to note wryly that there was no shortage of businessmen:

> Alas, how few have been the new missionaries who have arrived to take the place of those who, unable to withstand the climate, are obliged to leave. How very few who are willing to give themselves to the work of the Lord. While the ranks of the merchants are being continually recruited, none are found to labour in this heathen vineyard.[5]

Figure 2.1 Lovatt's Engagements with the Taiping, 1860–1862. *Source*: Caleb Carr, *The Devil Soldier* (New York: Random House, 1992).

Lovatt continued to socialize with those missionaries who remained in Shanghai. He regularly attended the Bible class run by John Hobson, the chaplain to the British community from the Church Missionary Society, until Hobson departed for Japan. Thereafter, his circle expanded to include, increasingly, American missionaries. In February 1861, for example, he spent "a happy evening" at the home of Reverend Matthew T. Yates, a Southern Baptist who had been in Shanghai since 1847. The next month, he attended a tea-party at Yates' chapel where "I greatly enjoyed myself." And a month later, Lovatt led a prayer session at the home of Reverend Tarleton Perry Crawford, an American Baptist missionary, for crewmen on the United States Frigate *Hartford*, calling it "a very happy meeting." Lovatt was becoming increasingly comfortable in the company of Americans.[6]

ENGAGING THE TAIPING

But Lovatt's main purpose was not religious but rather military. Now a corporal, having been promoted in March 1861, he and his artillery unit were there to protect the resident foreigners who "are afraid of an intended attack upon the city of Shanghai by the [Taiping] rebels. We are prepared for them." And the threat appeared serious enough that "we are likely to remain here till next winter (figure 2.1)."[7]

The Taiping Rebellion had broken out in southern China in 1851 to overthrow the Qing dynasty and replace it with a regime based on equality of land ownership and social relations. Many poor peasants became adherents, and even some Westerners were initially supportive because its ideology contained elements of Christianity and because it came at a time when the West and the Qing were enemies in the Arrow War/Second Opium War in the late 1850s. The leader of the rebellion, Hong Xiuquan, had even declared that he was the younger brother of Jesus. After a decade of fighting, the Taiping had succeeded in conquering a great deal of territory and had established a capital in nearby Nanjing, about 100 miles away. But beginning in 1860, successful campaigns by Zeng Guofan forced the Taiping eastward toward Shanghai and Ningbo, two treaty ports dominated by Western interests. In May of 1860, they took Suzhou, 60 miles from Shanghai, and Jiading, only 25 miles away, in June. The threat seemed palpable by the summer of 1860.[8]

To protect Shanghai, the American Frederick Townsend Ward in June 1860 established the Foreign-Arms Corps, the forerunner of the Ever-Victorious Army, with another American as second in command, Henry Burgevine. Composed of foreign residents serving as officers over local Chinese recruits, it was supported by the *daotai* (Circuit Intendent) of Shanghai, Wu Xu, and

British minister Frederick Bruce, who vowed to defend the city. When the Taiping approached in August, Allied troops took up defensive positions on the periphery of the city and at each of the seven gates along the 4-mile-long city wall. Initially, the British had been reluctant to take sides in this civil war and, to remain neutral, Admiral James Hope in February 1861 negotiated an agreement with the Taiping not to come within 30 miles of Shanghai. Despite the fact that the British were technically at peace with the rebels, Lovatt had little sympathy for them.[9]

By early 1861, accounts of Taiping cruelty reached Lovatt's ears: "A dire calamity rages here in this country—civil war. The Taipings or *chang-maw*—meaning long-haired men who are in opposition to the imperial government—are fighting and devastating the country wherever they go, which is daily driving hundreds from their peaceful homes to perish in want and misery." He noted that "the havoc and depredations the lawless robbers, for I can call them nothing else, commit upon the poor defenceless inhabitants of the country, is horrible in the extreme, murdering indiscriminately men, women and children without reference to either age or sex, and burning and destroying all property they can lay their hands on." Seeing through their supposed Christianity, Lovatt noted that "These people profess to read and carry out the doctrines of the Bible and so deceive other men and nations, but I now think the veil is lifted." In the face of such cruelty, Lovatt castigated British neutrality: "But we can only look on. Our Government can not or will not help to establish peace or quietness."[10]

Although Lovatt had made up his mind about the Taiping, he was aware that some of his missionary friends had mixed feelings: "There are many conflicting opinions, some for the rebels, and others against them." Missionaries who had visited the Taiping in Suzhou during the summer of 1860 brought back glowing reports, and one Baptist missionary in Shanghai, Issachar J. Roberts, even became the Taiping vice-minister of Foreign Affairs in the fall of 1860. Lovatt acknowledged that "many missionaries' sympathies were with them at first," and that divisions still remained: "Public opinion in China among foreign residents is very much divided, missionaries also." But by 1861, opinion had turned decidedly against the Taiping: "[Missionaries] for the most part now utterly abhor their doings and practices, since they have been enabled to enter the country and see their depredations." The few Taiping sympathizers were now distinctly in the minority, as "all generally tend to disapprove of the rebel movement."[11]

Even as Lovatt was bemoaning the lack of a proactive policy, Britain was beginning to tilt toward the Qing government. Ever since the ratification of the Convention of Beijing in 1860, Chinese relations with the Allies had begun to improve, and what was to be known as the Cooperative Policy began to take shape—a policy that would last for most of the 1860s and which would signally affect Lovatt. This included, among others, the establishment of the *Zongli Yamen*, a foreign office for dealing with the West, and a declaration that self-strengthening (*ziqiang*) along Western lines would be undertaken.[12]

When it became increasingly clear that the Taiping were not abiding by their agreement not to intrude within 30 miles of the city, Admiral Hope went to their capital in Nanjing in December 1861 and warned them, only to be told that "Shanghai was a little place [and] we have nothing to fear from it; we must take it to complete our dominions." And in a disquieting report, British intelligence indicated that the 30,000 Qing forces defending Shanghai were almost all ineffective or disloyal. This news changed British policy from a neutral defensive policy to an active one of helping the Chinese government suppress the Taiping, a major aspect of the Cooperative Policy.[13]

One of the opening salvos of this new more active policy occurred when Hope sailed up the Huangpu River, spoiling for a fight. It had the desired outcome: "A party has gone up the river of our men with our Captain to drive the rebels from the position they occupied when they fired upon the Admiral." Lovatt was pleased to note that the next day, "the party has returned all well after accomplishing their purpose." Given Lovatt's low opinion of the Taiping, he welcomed this change in British policy, and yet at the same time he grappled with the contradiction inherent in this more active policy: "The present government is certainly rotten and bad, but the rebels [are worse], for between two great evils it's wisdom to choose the lesser one." But even the lesser of two evils was barely palatable, given the behavior of Qing troops: "Our men speak in strong language of the gross brutality of the imperial soldier."[14]

Meanwhile, the Taiping rebels came ever closer, and by the fall of 1861 Shanghai was awash with rumors: "A large body of the insurgents (rumour says 60,000) have gone to the eastward of Shanghai and are expected to attack the city. The authorities appear to place some confidence in the reports and are getting ready to give them a warm reception when they choose to visit us." A week later there were "again rumours of a large body of insurgents coming to take Shanghai. We hear guns occasionally firing a long distance off. The imperialists [Qing troops] have been beaten." Not surprisingly, Lovatt's journal noted that "we are again to winter in Shanghai."[15]

By the end of October, the fighting between the Taiping and Qing troops came so close that Lovatt and his compatriots were confined to their barracks:

> We could hear the reports of their guns quite distinct and see large villages on fire. We got our guns out of the barracks into position and laid them on a bend in the river, intending to give them a warm reception if they were so imprudent as to attempt to come this way. A very heavy cannonade was kept up during the day by the insurgents and imperialists and toward evening it drew to a close.

The next day, "the firing has been kept up during the day, but the imperialists have gained a slight advantage and are now changing their position and attack their left. Toward evening the firing gradually ceased, the imperialists having forced them to retire. We are all quiet again." Lovatt closed that day's journal entry with "May it please thee O God to overrule the present sinful and evil war for good."[16]

But the Taiping soon reappeared. One group burned several villages near Wusung, 8 miles downriver from Shanghai. Another unit from Suzhou captured towns to the west of Shanghai. So devastating was their offensive that the horizon was obscured for days by the smoke, and thousands of refugees poured into the foreign settlement, causing the inhabitants of Shanghai to become increasingly jittery, with Lovatt using phrases as "very disturbed" and "panic is again spreading." Additional defensive measures by the foreign residents, such as the creation of the Shanghai Volunteers to stand guard at night and act as sentries on the roads, were undertaken, a development that Lovatt supported: "I have not been able to see them drilling yet, but to all appearance they are a very fine smart lot of fellows with few exceptions."[17]

As 1862 began, Lovatt caught his first real glimpse of the Taiping:

> For the first time I got a sight of them from the Stone Bridge Lookout. They certainly are coming rather close than to be agreeable to His Excellency the Taotae [Wu Xu]. A foraging party came quite close to the Stone Bridge yesterday and some of my comrades saw them cut down several women and one man and rob and plunder them. In fact, a few of my comrades acted so imprudently as to go quite up almost to the village they occupied. In the afternoon we turned out with our three guns to defend the Settlement in case of an attack and took up positions on the race course. Our men are all employed in throwing up earthworks at the back of the Settlement for its protection where guns are to be mounted.[18]

As British policy tilted toward the Qing as part of the Cooperative Policy, the Chinese government began to allow its soldiers to be trained by foreigners. In Shanghai, Admiral Hope supplied thirty British gunners to teach Ward's troops "the art and mystery of using artillery." One of those gunners was Lovatt: "I am at present in charge of 150 coolies and drilling them generally every day. There could be a very fine regiment raised here and would answer very well. The coolies we have are very attentive to their drill, and they are not near so good as might be got." That opinion was shared by William Henry Sykes, who wrote that the troops Lovatt was training "proved most apt pupils and they fire with astonishing accuracy." After only a month of training, Lovatt was able to write: "It is rumoured that we are to attack the rebels (I don't think we will). My Chinese Brigade are, I think, improving greatly." Like Ward, Lovatt had discovered that "the Chinese are capable, under European supervision, of being good soldiers," a sentiment that would be echoed eighty years later by General Joseph Stilwell during the Pacific War. Lovatt was obviously a skilled instructor.[19]

While training Chinese gunners, Lovatt made the acquaintance of a fellow Briton, William Mesny, who had arrived in China in 1860 to help the Chinese army, and who observed Lovatt's training: "I had the good fortune of making the acquaintance of Mr. W. N. Lovatt of the British Royal Artillery, [who] gave me many a useful hint on guns and gunnery. I was a frequent witness of the instructions imparted to Chinese artillery men at the British Artillery Barracks in the Honan Road." Armed with Lovatt's training, Mesny departed for Hankou in the summer of 1862 as an instructor in the use of Armstrong breech-loading field guns and 32-pound siege guns. While he was in Hankou, he told its commissioner of Customs Thomas Dick about Lovatt.[20]

More than simply training soldiers, Lovatt now began to engage in combat in that spring of 1862. His unit's initial engagement, preceded by an inspection by General Charles Staveley, was Wangjiasu, a Taiping stronghold 15 miles to the southwest that had been "causing a great deal of uneasiness to our merchants and plundering the country in all directions." Lovatt's artillery barrage breached the city wall: "Our guns quite astonished the rebels and soon made them beat a hasty retreat" 5 miles further inland to Longquan. The rumor mill indicated that there would be more such sorties: "I hear the English Commanders, naval and military, have decided on putting down the rebel movement in any place where it affects our trade or threatens the security of our merchants and their property. Our Minister at Peking (the Hon F. Bruce) is most decidedly against them."[21]

In the fight against the Taiping, the British were now allied with Ward's Ever-Victorious Army, but Lovatt had little respect for Ward, who he first encountered when, with 500 of his "disciplined Chinese," Ward attempted to take Longquan to which the Taipings had retreated the day before:

> In the afternoon a fellow calling himself Col. Ward (but I am proud to say no countryman of mine), serving under the Taotae of Shanghai with his Chinese Brigade, were very roughly handled by the rebels when attempting to drive them from a second entrenched position named Lung-chuan. They had I think 80 or so wounded without taking the place after all. We also turned out to a false alarm and got into position, but I think it was owing to Col. Ward's mob coming back beat.

Longquan was attacked again the next day, this time by a combined French and English force of 700, assisted by 100 of Ward's men. Lovatt was an eyewitness to that engagement and noted the ineffectiveness of the Ever-Victorious Army: "This morning got our [guns] into boats and sent them down by the river. The naval brigade, both French and English, moved up to attack the rebels where Ward's Brigade were beaten and after firing a few rounds, took the place, and then pursued the rebels for some distance."[22]

In another engagement a week later with Ward's "disciplined Chinese" Ever-Victorious Army, Lovatt and his unit successfully attacked a "strong" rebel position at Zhoupu, 18 miles east of Shanghai, killing 300. In that assault, Lovatt again castigated the "Ward mob" and their reprehensible behavior: "I entered the place with our Captain and saw a great many horrible and disgusting signs; a great deal of looting went on and many made a good round sum." One interested observer of that battle was Viceroy Li Hongzhang, the governor of Jiangsu Province, who had just arrived in Shanghai and who reported to Zeng Guofan on the accuracy and power of Lovatt's artillery, whose "shells bloomed upon touching the ground." Li and Zeng would soon adapt Western weaponry and training to their own troops, including the establishment of arsenals to produce the type of weapons used by Lovatt.[23]

Lovatt's next engagements were at Nanxiang and the walled town of Jiading about 25 miles northwest of Shanghai at the end of April and the beginning of May. Jiading was symbolically important because the Allies had held the city earlier only to be forced out. In a combined assault with 700 British troops, 800 French troops, and 1,000 of Ward's Ever-Victorious Army, preceded by artillery barrages from Lovatt's unit, the town was taken, leading to a carnival-like atmosphere and more widespread looting by Ward's Chinese troops. The pillaging was so bad that it finally was prohibited, although Lovatt noted otherwise: "No person was allowed to loot, although many did; a large sum of money was taken and a great many ponies and silk and other things." Lovatt laid the blame for the Ever-Victorious Army's behavior in part to its Western officers, a mixture of Americans, British, and French, who were described as rowdy, uncouth drunkards by Chinese and foreigners alike. Even Ward acknowledged that his officers were impossible to control. At the same time, Lovatt acknowledged that his fellow British soldiers were little better: "It is drink (the curse of the British Army) that is doing its work in our midst. Our Cap says 'I will put a stop to the drunkeness.' Well, let us see how he stops it." For example, at Nanxiang, "the party we sent out was in a sad state—they found a small cask of rum on their arrival, and it may be easily guessed in what state they were—disgraceful in the extreme."[24]

Lovatt fought in two final engagements before the summer lull. The first was in mid-May at the walled town of Qingpu, 30 miles west of Shanghai, and the second at Cholin, where he fought alongside three howitzers manned by Chinese soldiers who he had trained. In Cholin, Lovatt found a large quantity of grain that the Taiping had stolen from the peasants, but "now that the place was ours, [the peasants] were turning [out] in large numbers to get what they could of it, poor, famished, half-starved creatures they looked."[25]

As these campaigns came to an end, Lovatt began to consider mustering out, despite the fact that he had been promoted to sergeant. In addition to his earlier complaints, he cited the practice of flogging: "One thing disgraceful and beastly always accompanies the British army—the cat-o-nine tails. If I am spared, I shall leave the army for that reason." By June he had made up his mind: "I am very desirous of obtaining my discharge and by the last mail sent letters home for that purpose."[26]

But it would be months before his discharge, and as the summer of 1862 wore on, Lovatt picked up rumors of a renewed offensive: "I hear we are going to take the field early in September, [and] a blow will be struck at [the Taiping capital of] Nanking." Other reports picked up by Lovatt indicated that the threat to Shanghai was by no means over: "Rumours again of the rebels coming from Kading to attack Shanghai," followed two days later by reports that "rebels are in our immediate vicinity again." A visit to the nearby town he had visited the previous Christmas confirmed the proximity of the threat: "Marched to the Bubbling Well Village, which was quite deserted by its inhabitants, several of whom were laying about with their throats cut and hacked in a most dreadful manner. We then started in several small parties to hunt the rebels, but did not succeed in catching any of them."[27]

Jiading and Nanxiang, which had changed hands several times, now became the focus in the fall of 1862 in what would be Lovatt's final two engagements. His unit, along with Chinese troops, was sent first to Jiading and then to Nanxiang, where Lovatt once again beheld how Chinese armies on both sides dealt with civilians:

> Marched to Nanhsiang, villages in ruins, and villagers which are generally a few old women in a dreadful state of starvation. Nothing can be more horrid to look upon: a few old decrepit women in a state of starvation, two or three ragged children whose sunken eyes and hollow voice with outstretched hand plainly denote their sufferings, numerous dead bodies lying about, some burnt by fire, some starved to death, others with their heads off, show the work of some Chang Maw or Imperialists, for they deal with each other in the same way. Horrid, horrid indeed was the spectacles which these villages presented.[28]

As Lovatt awaited his discharge papers that fall, instead of planning to return to England, he instead saw his future in China. For one, he started learning the language, and his teacher "tells me I am very quick at it, but it will at the least take six months to learn to speak it in any degree fluently, but I am determined to persevere." Additionally, he contemplated joining the Ever-Victorious Army that he had early disparaged but that was now led by the American Henry Burgevine because Ward had been killed in September. That option attracted Lovatt because it was expected to attack Nanjing, the capital of the Taiping that Lovatt had come to hate. But Lovatt also had other options.[29]

In December, Lovatt finally received the news he had been awaiting since the summer that "my career in the British Army is near its close, for the last mail has brought my discharge from England." Instead of joining the Ever-Victorious Army, he decided to remain in a civilian capacity: "Having heard of a situation in the Imperial Customs at Hankow, I have determined in taking that at 70 taels per month in preference to joining Burgevine on the same [salary], and the army is not quite permanent." Lovatt's discharge was effective on December 28, 1862, allowing him to write on New Year's Eve that "I stand once more a free man, never, I hope, to have again to look upon men being flogged as most decidedly has been done in Shanghai and on the various expeditions. I was much affected in bidding my old comrades farewell. But farewell to army and my comrades. This ends my military career in the British Army." After two years in Shanghai a new career awaited Lovatt.[30]

NOTES

1. WNL *Journal*, November 14, 1860, April 11, 1861, and November 16, 1861. For a thumbnail sketch of Shanghai in the early 1860s, see Bennett, *Missionary Journalist*, 16–19.

2. WNL *Journal*, November 14, 1860.

3. WNL *Journal*, October 30 and November 14, 1860, and March 6, November 24, and December 24, 26, 27, and 30, 1861, and January 1, 1862. Emphasis in the original

4. WNL *Journal*, February 10, 1861 and March 12, 1862.

5. WNL *Journal*, August 1, 1861 and November 16, 1861.

6. WNL *Journal*, February 25, March 15, and April 22, 1861, and April 8, 1862. Matthew T. Yates (1819–1888) was a scholar of China, a contributor to the *Chinese Recorder*, and served as a translator and American Vice-Consul. Tarleton (1821–1886) and Martha Crawford arrived in Shanghai in 1852 and departed in August, 1863. For more on Crawford, see Irwin T. Hyatt, *Our Ordered Lives Confess: Three Nineteenth-Century American Missionaries in East Shantung* (Cambridge: Harvard University Press, 1976), 3–24. Lovatt's interaction with missionaries may have inclined him toward charity, and he briefly considered adopting an orphan: "I got a little rebel boy fifteen years of age. He has been with the rebels about three years. His father and mother are both dead. I could not get him into school, he being rather too old, [so] I have given him to a dear friend of mine who will take care of him." WNL *Journal*, October 16, 1862.

7. WNL *Journal*, January 18, March 26, and April 11, 1861.

8. For a full account of the Taiping Rebellion, see Steven R. Platt, *Autumn in the Heavenly Kingdom: China, the West, and the Epic Story of the Taiping Civil War* (New York: Knopf, 2012). For a contemporaneous account, see Hosea Ballou Morse, *In the Days of the Taipings: Being the Recollections of Ting Kienchang, Otherwise Meisun, Sometime Scoutmaster and Captain in the Ever-Victorious Army and*

Interpreter-in-Chief to General Ward and General Gordon: An Historical Retrospect (Salem: The Essex Institute, 1927).

9. Wilson, *The Ever-Victorious Army*, 80–81; Richard J. Smith, *Mercenaries and Mandarins: The Ever-Victorious Army in Nineteenth Century China* (Millwood, NY: KTO Press, 1978), 7, 17; Caleb Carr, *The Devil Soldier: The American Soldier of Fortune Who Became a God in China* (New York: Random House, 1992).

10. WNL *Journal*, July 1 and October 27, 1861. Those who rebelled against the Qing wore their hair long rather than in a queue to signify their opposition.

11. WNL *Journal*, October 27, 1861, and January 16 and April 1, 1862; Smith, *Mercenaries and Mandarins*, 19. Roberts (1801–1871) is known as the only Westerner to have taught Hong Xiuquan, the leader of the Taiping. For more on Roberts, see John Rapp, "Clashing Dilemmas: Hong Rengan, Issachar Roberts, and a Taiping 'Murder Mystery'." *Journal of Historical Biography,* 4 (Autumn, 2008), 27–58.

12. Smith, 22–23. For background on the decision of the British and other Western powers to support the Qing, see Masataka Banno, *China and the West, 1858–1861: The Origins of the Tsungli Yamen* (Cambridge: Harvard University Press, 1964), 42–53.

13. Smith, 7, 15–16; Wilson, 81.

14. WNL *Journal*, January 16, February 26 and 28, and March 1, 1862; Smith, 50.

15. WNL *Journal*, September 25, October 1, and October 4, 1861.

16. WNL *Journal*, October 27 and 28, 1861.

17. WNL *Journal*, November 24 and December 13, 1861, and January 14, 1862; Wilson, 81–82.

18. WNL *Journal*, January 10, 13, and 16, 1862.

19. WNL *Journal*, February 26 and March 1 and 27, 1862; Smith, 58–59, 61, 69–70, and 83; William Henry Sykes, *The Taeping Rebellion in China, Its Origins, Progress and Present Condition* (London: Warren Hall and Co., 1863), 61. Lovatt would again be drilling Chinese troops a few years later under a different set of circumstances.

20. William Mesny, *Mesny's Chinese Miscellany: A Textbook of Notes on China and the Chinese*. Volume One (Shanghai: China Gazette Office, 1896), 403, 484.

21. WNL *Journal*, April 1 and 3, 1862.

22. WNL *Journal*, April 3 and 8, 1862; Wilson, 83–84.

23. WNL *Journal*, April 11, 1862; Wilson, 83–84; Smith, 95. Li and his 40,000-man Anhwei Army had just arrived in Shanghai in April 1862.

24. Smith, 63, 81–85; Wilson, 83–84; WNL *Journal*, April 11 and 26, and May 1, 1862.

25. WNL *Journal*, May 6 and 20, 1862; WNL to JSL, October 11, 1890.

26. WNL *Journal*, May 1 and June 15, 1862.

27. WNL *Journal*, July 15, and August 2, 18, 20, and 26, 1862; Smith, 78–79.

28. WNL *Journal*, October 15, 20, 21, and 31, and November 3 and 4, 1862.

29. WNL *Journal*, August 17 and December 20, 1862.

30. WNL *Journal*, December 20, 25, and 31, 1862. Lovatt was hired as an assistant tidesurveyor. At the time one *tael* equaled $1.60. The salary for a foreign artillery sergeant in the Ever-Victorious Army was 96 Mexican dollars per month. Burgevine was dismissed two weeks later and replaced by the British colonel Charles "Chinese" Gordon.

Chapter 3

Entering the Customs Service

Hankou and Zhenjiang, 1863–1865

HANKOU, JANUARY 1863–MARCH 1864

By 1861 there were 11 treaty ports, one of which was Hankou, on the northern bank of the Yangzi River 600 miles upriver from Shanghai, part of a tri-city nexus that included Wuchang and Hanyang, now known collectively as Wuhan. Robert Hart, the interim inspector general of the Maritime Customs, and the Zongli Yamen had agreed in October 1861 to establish a customs house in Hankou, after it had been opened by the 1858 Tianjin Treaty, and in December, Hart made his first trip to open the port to foreign commerce, with Thomas Dick as the first commissioner of Customs. Soon, foreign firms opened business houses, a Foreign Settlement was established, and missionaries began to make their appearance, one of the first being Reverend Griffith John of the London Missionary Society, who held services for the small foreign community.[1]

Lovatt is silent on how he came to be hired, and because Hart, who had been named inspector general in 1863, destroyed his own journal covering the period December 1858 to June 1863 to obliterate any reference to his Chinese paramour, there is no information from that quarter. It is likely, however, that Lovatt's friend William Mesny when in Hankou had recommended him to Commissioner Dick who then passed on that recommendation to Hart. At that time the expanding Service needed additional outdoor staff and Lovatt had the requisite qualifications: he was British, the nationality that dominated the Customs; he had acquired a modicum of a classical education; his Chinese was improving; and he was healthy, of high moral character, under thirty, and unmarried. As an assistant tidesurveyor, he assisted the tidesurveyor who supervised port activities as harbormaster, controlling shipping and cargo, and examining and appraising goods. Underneath assistant tidesurveyors were boat officers, examiners, assistant examiners, tidewaiters, and watchers. Only the tidesurveyor, the commissioner, and his assistants in the Indoor Staff were above the assistant tidesurveyor.[2]

New Year's Day 1863 saw Lovatt "anxious to leave Shanghai and get to my destination at once." Only the year before, Russell and Company had established the Shanghai Steam Navigation Company to ply the route between Shanghai and Hankou twice weekly with a four-day layover at each end. Using this service, Lovatt departed on the morning of January 3 aboard the *Firequeen* along with two other customs officers bound for Jiujiang, where the boat stopped en route and where Lovatt would be posted seven years later. Arriving in Hankou on the morning of January 8, he immediately reported to the "kind, gentlemanly" Commissioner Dick. A friend of Lovatt's from Shanghai, Robert J. Goldspink, put him up for the first few nights while he arranged for lodging. Although the Customs provided housing for foreign staff either by a subsidy or by purchasing houses for their use, Lovatt found himself initially "roughing it" in the cold with just three blankets and no bed. Within a few days, he moved to "more comfortable" quarters on the other side of the Han River.[3]

Lovatt found that he was able to carry out his new duties "very well," but found the hours "long and tiresome." By February, Lovatt had settled into a routine—during the day, attending to the customs duties, and in his spare time studying Chinese, in which "I think I am improving a little"; in the evening, reading or writing, and occasionally calling on a friend. On Sundays he attended services at Griffith John's house. His only diversion in those first few months was Chinese New Year when all business was suspended for a week.[4]

Given the relative isolation of Hankou, visitors or newcomers of any kind were rare and cause for comment. Some were unwelcome, such as the robber gang that approached and caused a "slight panic," such that many left in boats for Wuchang on the other side of the river for a few days until the danger passed. Others were more welcome, such as Richard F. Littledale, a British missionary from Singapore, who Lovatt described as a "very zealous warm-hearted Christian man [who] I like very much." Also arriving was twenty-three-year-old William Mesny, who was hired as a tidewaiter. Mesny had met Lovatt the previous year in Shanghai and had been held captive by the Taiping in Nanjing for four months after his initial visit to Hankou. Mesny's facility in Chinese caused Lovatt to reflect on his own language study: "I continue to plough away at Chinese and trust I am making a little progress."[5]

After five months in Hankou, Lovatt's Chinese language skills had progressed to the point that Commissioner Dick sent him on a solo mission to [illegible] down the Yangzi to discuss the tea trade. Upon arrival, he found that the inhabitants were "generally civil [and] mostly collect to stare at me."

As this was Lovatt's first trip dealing directly with a Chinese official, he chronicled the meeting in some detail:

> At 3:30 in the afternoon I went and called on this blue-buttoned gentleman who was dressed and had his hat and button on. I Chin Chinned [greeted] him as I walked in and he done the same, both of us bowing. A Chinese gentleman came in at the same time who had likewise come from Hankow. We all three walked to a chair and sat down all at the same time. This mandarin being a country gentleman, I did not understand his dialect, but the Chinese gentleman who walked in with me and looked to be very anxious to get a situation commenced a conversation with the mandarin. It must have been mostly flattery, for he was continually bowing and smiling. In fact, our seedy-looking friend must have layed the soft soap on pretty thick at times for it would make the old gentleman rise from his seat and smile and give a very low bow. Tea was at length brought in and we all took the cups of hot water tea, at each other smiled and sipped, and then smiled and laid them down. I hope I looked pleased, but the stuff was boiling hot and very nearly burned my lips. I then got up and through another gentleman explained what I had come to do, bowed, and retired. [Upon leaving, I] was stared at by the people of the village and called foreign devil [*yanggweizi*] by [people] who had never seen a foreigner before and even now while I write many of them stand gazing at me as if I was a tiger.[6]

Lovatt would often find himself an object of curiosity, especially to those who had never before seen a Westerner. Before he left, a detachment of Hunanese soldiers flocked to see

> the _______ as they politely call me. They had to shut the front doors to keep the lawless soldiers out. And then they knocked at the door and made so much noise the mandarin had to go out to them and promised to let them see me, so they opened the door and I let them look at me. They passed a great many not very flattering remarks about me. When I passed out they opened a way for me to pass and laughed and joked at me.[7]

Back in Hankou, Lovatt found himself mainly weighing tea and examining cargo. Because his position brought him into contact with foreign businessmen, he found that many of them were unscrupulous in their dealings with the Chinese, "which I think is very bad." His position required that he deal courteously with the Chinese employees in the customs, as Hart had admonished, a lesson that his friend Goldspink learned the hard way when he was suspended for striking a Chinese tidewaiter. His work also carried with it physical risks: "On returning from the steamer *Fire Dart* with her papers to the customs [house] in one of the customs boats pulled by three men, we came across a line that was holding a junk with one end fastened to a buoy. My boat was capsized and I thought I should be drowned." In addition to his duties, to advance in the Service, "I still carry on my study of the Chinese language, but under great difficulties from the heat, but I must not give up." As a result, the commissioner "has been very kind to me and has increased my salary ten taels per month." But that fall, Hart transferred Dick to Shanghai, so before he left, Lovatt requested a leave of absence so that he and his friend Littledale could make an overland trip to Yichang.[8]

The two had become good friends by the summer of 1863, holding a prayer service together every Tuesday that attracted an average of but five of the 150 foreign residents. Now in November they were about to embark as traveling companions deep into the interior of China—a veritable no-man's land where there were few foreigners, as most were concentrated in the sizeable treaty port cities. Moreover, the Taiping Rebellion was still in progress to the east, and armed bandits were capable of making an appearance at any time. But Lovatt had been studying Chinese for over a year, and was young, healthy, adventurous, and adept at the military arts.[9]

They set out in mid-November, and their first stop on the way west was a temple, whose priest was "very civil and obliging." When they paid a courtesy call at the local *yamen* (government office) and sent in their cards, the official asked where they were going, their business, names, and ages. The two gave answers, "none of which he appeared to believe." Throughout the meeting they were besieged by the locals who had never seen a foreigner, so upon leaving, the official "turned out a very noisy rabble of young men and boys, for which we were very thankful." On the second day, they covered 75 *li* (25 miles) and stopped for the day in the late afternoon at a tea shop along the Han River, where they observed that the people "live in wretched hovels, but appear to have sufficient of the necessaries of life. They are very anxious to see us, but civil and respectful."[10]

On the afternoon of the third day the two arrived at a town whose one main street doubled as a market, through which the two travelers had to pass. "A noisy crowd followed us of roughs and boys. The old men of the place frequently called out to them to be quiet, but they all stopped following us at the first bridge." The following night was spent at a temple where the people were "civil but *very* inquisitive." On the next day, however, before stopping at a tea shop for the night, the inhabitants at the local market were not quite so civil: "the scamps and boys of the village were very noisy and occasionally threw stones or pieces of earth or brick which seldom struck us." On the following night, they again put up for the night at a roadside tea shop, where the locals were "very civil, but their intense curiosity very annoying."[11]

Their first brushes with danger came a week into their trip. As they passed through another market town, "a very large crowd turned out to look at us and in their haste very near pushed us into the river. A little patience and forbearance brought us through all right." A second close call came when they stayed the night at another tea shop that also housed "a fellow whom we both very much disliked, [so] I got my revolver in order in case during the night he might think he had a better right to any of our things than we had."[12]

While there were no more threats from robbers, the constant problem of rowdy crowds intensified as they continued. Soon after entering one town,

> we passed two or three very large tea shops when someone unfortunately saw us and gave the word that two foreigners had arrived. Such a howling noisy crowd I have seldom met with, some hundreds of the roughs of the town followed us, and I could hear many shouts of *yanggweizi*, which was very unpleasant to hear. In a distant town on a dark night the roars and howlings from the mob in these places was something horrible indeed.

Since he was an employee of the Chinese government, and since the Zongli Yamen had issued edicts obligating district magistrates to protect foreigners, the two sought out the local *yamen* for protection: "The mob was still very noisy and rioted outside so we sent our cards and my passport to the mandarin and requested him to send soldiers to guard the house, which he very kindly did, saying also he would call on us tomorrow." When the local official did come the next day and "asked the usual questions," it was clear that he was unprepared for the variation in appearance between Westerners:

> He was very much surprised at the contrast between me and Littledale, him quite fair with light hair and no whiskers or moustache, and me the very reverse, and only a slight difference in our ages. I think no one believed us when we told them we were both Englishmen. They of course never said so, but they certainly looked their thoughts which was unbelief.

The magistrate provided an escort of four soldiers upon their departure the next day, which was fortunate because when "a very large crowd follow[ed] us clear of the town, the soldiers at once stopped them whenever they made use of any improper language." They put up for the night at a temple that was "very comfortable" and the "inhabitants very civil."[13]

As the two traversed the country, the reception they received varied. In the mountain regions, it was mostly curiosity, as "very many of the country people came to see us," including an old man of eighty. They "looked contented, none appears to work hard, their clothes are all warm, but the cottages wretched in the extreme, miserable hovels." As for female pulchritude, he allowed that "the women I have seen since I left Hankow are all hideous. I have not seen one pretty girl yet." In the larger valley towns, the reception was often rude. Going through two such towns in one day, Lovatt remarked that "both these places are large market villages where we were much annoyed by large crowds of roughs and boys throwing pieces of clay and calling out Foreign Devil and other disagreeable things of which it is best to take no notice." When they put up for the night at a teashop, the only uninterested people were four gamblers who "just stopped to look at us and then resumed their game." Because they attracted so much unwanted attention, when they reached the Yangzi River they decided to take a boat the rest of the way to Yichang, 45 *li* (15 miles) distant, to "avoid any large crowds."[14]

When they arrived in Yichang, they went to a temple where they were "very kindly" received by an old man who had a school in the temple. On the next two days, they went sightseeing in the Yangzi River gorge, and, guided by the old temple schoolmaster, set out for a temple in the mountain, having been invited by its head priest. When they arrived, the priest "led us into a cave [that] contained about fifty wooden images. The temple is cut out of solid rock and must have took the Chinese a long time to do it."[15]

As they began the return trip to Hankou, they had to go through the usual market where they were "annoyed by a crude mob of roughs," but Lovatt put a culturally sensitive spin on that, noting that Western countries were not immune from the same unruliness: "prudence [is] the best part of valour in these cases which often take place in Christian countries who boast a higher civilization." In a countryside town two days later, when many people crowded around them, Lovatt remarked that "if you want them to go away, it must certainly be done by politeness, otherwise they would not go." But politeness often did not work in the larger towns, for on the next day in just such a town, the local district magistrate arranged for a six-soldier escort that turned out to be needed because there was "a great crowd of men and boys outside in the street [who] were continually shouting and, when the door was opened to admit anyone, they made a rush in, but our guard of soldiers were quite on the alert." They faced a similar raucous crowd the following day after visiting a pagoda when

> we were followed by a crowd whom our feeble guard could scarcely keep in order and from crowding upon us. The roughs were very noisy and threw a few stones and bricks. I think it would have been impossible to go through the place without the soldiers, who certainly tried to keep the crowd in order and us from annoyance and insult.[16]

One of the highlights of their return trip was an invitation by some local merchants in one of the towns to lunch and dinner. Up to this point, their meals had come from jars of preserved meats, ham, cheese, chocolate, sauces, and curried fowl. On the way to the lunch,

> we were followed by a dense crowd who, soon after we sat down to tiffin [lunch], forced their way in. Many of the ladies of the establishment were

peeping through all manner of nooks and corners at us, but the crowd was so riotous we made a hasty tiffin and in getting to the door our kind host who was trying to see us out got borne down by the crowd and lost.

Later that day, they "returned to the hong [company] and sat down to a grand Chinese dinner." Since the meal was to be eaten with chopsticks, it was clear that despite Lovatt's familiarity with China, "I could not manage the chopsticks very well but got through all right." His merchant hosts

were very civil and very curious, which is very natural in any people to see two strangers whose appearance, manners, dress, and customs, are so entirely different from their own, and whom they had heard no doubt of in exaggerated reports. Our visitors were very anxious to [learn] about England, our customs, etc. I hope we set them right in many things, as well as our knowledge of the language would permit.[17]

On the road again, the two ran into more raucous crowds, where the "people [were] not very civil, calling [us] disagreeable names," and by now, Littledale's patience was wearing thin. At one such town, "the people turned out and pelted us with stones and bricks without hurting us, and [we] got out of the scrape as soon as possible. I think the reason the villagers were enraged was somebody throwing a stone, and Littledale, turning round, struck a fellow with his stick which rather enraged the people." On the next day in another market town, "Littledale gave a boy who was very rude a crack with his stick and made his head bleed; when the roughs of the town set on us and we were likely to fare bad, I pacified the youngster with a thousand cash."[18]

The two intrepid travelers finally arrived back in Hankou in mid-December after their monthlong adventure, having covered a total of 1,731 *li*, or 577 miles, and expending 40 taels each. In a section of his journal entitled "Summary of the March," despite the commotion and antiforeignism occasioned by their presence, Lovatt saw the trip positively:

The people are everywhere in favor of us. They treated us kindly and were always very polite and civil. Of course the boys are the same in China as in England [who] mock and make fun with the strangers. Anyone going who cannot speak a little of the language would find [the country] very dull indeed. It was the occasional roadside chat with the people which made it pleasant. I should strongly advise everyone never to resort to arms or force in any way (of course excepting when for life it is the last chance). There is no retreating when in the interior. Talking civilly will in all cases be the best. The mandarins will as far as they are able protect foreigners, but they cannot do much. They have so little power or force to carry out their orders. We avoided all large places, and put up for the night generally at solitary temples or little roadside teashops, the inns of China. The country people were in all cases very civil.[19]

Lovatt remained in Hankou for 15 months, until March 1864, when he was transferred to Zhenjiang, replaced in Hankou by his friend Mesny. His first assignment had been a positive one, persuading him that he had found his career. Central to that determination was the influence of the commissioner, Thomas Dick. When Lovatt learned 13 years later that he was very sick at Chefoo with abscess on the liver and not expected to recover, he wrote that "I am very sorry indeed, for he was always my friend, when a friend was urgently needed." Dick passed away soon thereafter.[20]

ZHENJIANG, APRIL 1864–OCTOBER 1865

Zhenjiang, located at the junction of the Yangzi and the Grand Canal, had been opened as a treaty port in 1858 and to the Customs three years later in 1861, after Hart's initial visit. Lovatt was now just a one-day steamer ride away from Shanghai, where he had been stationed for two years fighting the Taiping. Nine months after arriving in Zhenjiang, he visited Shanghai "partly on my own pleasure" in January 1865 where he encountered Hart, perhaps for the first time. The IG was on his second inspection tour of the customs houses in the treaty ports, and it was Lovatt who conveyed him between ship and shore: "In the afternoon the *Fire Queen* with ship *Silver Eagle* in tow arrived down. [I] boarded them, and brought over Mr. Hart, the Inspector General, who looked round on this side and boarded the *Swallow* when he afterwards returned." Hart, who had just turned thirty, was en route from Shanghai to Hong Kong that day, but his diary makes no mention of meeting Lovatt.[21]

Lovatt's journal is quite sparse for his nineteen months in Zhenjiang, indicating that his work and life there were uneventful. In addition to the occasional trip to Shanghai, for diversion he went pheasant hunting with his commissioner, and was cheered when his friend Goldspink was transferred there from Hankou as a tidesurveyor in the summer of 1865. His circle of friends consisted mostly of American missionaries, and his reading was increasingly on American topics, including one book about the Civil War that caused him to sympathize with the North.[22]

Except for the antiforeignism that he and Littledale had experienced first-hand, up to this point Lovatt had rarely commented on the phenomenon. The only time had been during his army years a few years earlier in Shanghai, when news from Japan caused him to address the topic for the first time. That news was the killing of two Britons in Tokyo in July 1861 by a group of *shishi* (men of high purpose) espousing *jōi* (expel the barbarian): "[Samurai] attempted to kill the whole British embassy. From what I hear, they are a proud haughty race of people, something like the Chinese, and very much dislike foreigners." Several months later, he heard more "sad news from

Japan [of] the murder of another Englishman," Charles Richardson. Lovatt favored retaliation: "I think we cannot long refrain from going to war with the Japanese. Insult upon insult is thrown upon us and it's time some active steps were taken in the matter. The Japanese Government is like the Chinese. They cannot give us protection, not having authority over their own subjects."[23]

Now in Zhenjiang in the summer of 1865 antiforeign violence struck closer to home:

> This morning horrified to hear that during the night some Chinese soldiers broke into a house in which three foreigners were living and nearly hacked them to pieces. One died in two hours, one is mortally wounded and not expected to live, and the other is badly cut in several places. It appears that a foreigner who keeps a Chinese girl crassly insulted a high mandarin whose soldiers, seeing it, in the night visited this house and, out of revenge, nearly killed three innocent men.

As the wounded were being evacuated by the *Szechuan* to Shanghai for treatment, Lovatt hoped that, absent retaliation, Britain's diplomats would at least make the necessary representations, but he was not optimistic: "I hear H[is]. M[ajesty's]. Consul is taking the matter up, but from the well-known apathy of consuls in China not much is expected. There can be no doubt if the Consul don't press the Chinese authorities for satisfaction, the lives of the foreign community will be in great danger, with some 8 or 10,000 [Chinese] troops encamped in this vicinity." Lovatt would encounter similar antiforeign episodes throughout his career in China.[24]

Another entry of note in Lovatt's journal that summer was brief but, like antiforeignism, would also provide a glimpse into his future in China, and sooner than he could anticipate: "Fell in with two old comrades today who had been trying to get military service with the mandarins." Less than two months later, in October 1865, Lovatt was "sudden[ly]" transferred and promoted to the rank of tidesurveyor: "Commissioner sent for me today and told me I was to prepare to go to Tientsin, as the Inspector General [Hart] had ordered me to do so. I am glad in one way to get north." Lovatt departed Zhenjiang two days later for Shanghai en route to his new posting, unaware of why Hart wanted him to go to Tianjin, and why he was wanted there so quickly.[25]

NOTES

1. Fairbank, Smith, and Bruner, 248–249; Alfred Broomhall, *Hudson Taylor and China's Open Century. Volume Three: If I Had a Thousand Lives* (London: Hodder and Stoughton and the Overseas Missionary Fellowship, 1982), 262–264, 361. John had arrived in the summer of 1861 from Shanghai with his wife and children. For more on Hankou in the early 1860s, see Britten Dean, "Sino-British Diplomacy in the

1860s: The Establishment of the British Concession at Hankow." *Harvard Journal of Asiatic Studies*, 32 (1972), 71–96. For a thumbnail sketch of Hankou, see Robert Nield, *China's Foreign Places: The Foreign Presence in China in the Treaty Port Era, 1840–1943* (Hong Kong: Hong Kong University Press, 2015), 97–102.

2. King, *In the Chinese Customs Service*, 22–23.

3. WNL *Journal*, January 1, 3, 8, and 12, 1863.

4. WNL *Journal*, January 12 and 21, February (no date), and March (no date), 1863.

5. William Mesny, *Mesny's Chinese Miscellany: A Textbook of Notes on China and the Chinese*. Volume Two (Shanghai: China Gazette Office, 1896), 520; WNL *Journal*, April (no date), 1863.

6. WNL *Journal*, May 26 and 31, 1863.

7. WNL *Journal*, June 10, 11, and 19, 1863.

8. WNL *Journal*, July 19 and 31, August 1, September 22, and October 7, 1863. Dick was replaced by William MacPherson.

9. WNL *Journal*, June 30 and August 1, 1863.

10. WNL *Journal*, November 13 and 14, 1863.

11. WNL *Journal*, November 15, 16, 17, and 18, 1863. Emphasis in the original.

12. WNL *Journal*, November 19, 1863.

13. WNL *Journal*, November 20 and 21, 1863.

14. WNL *Journal*, November 22, 23, and 24, 1863.

15. WNL *Journal*, November 24, 25, and 26, 1863.

16. WNL *Journal*, November 27, 29, and 30, and December 1, 1863.

17. WNL *Journal*, December 1 and 2, 1863.

18. WNL *Journal*, December 7 and 8, 1863.

19. WNL *Journal*, December 11, 1863.

20. WNL *Journal*, March 18, 1864; WNL to JSL, August 9, 1876, July 4, and September 12 and 14, 1877, and December 21, 1891; Mesny, *Mesny's Chinese Miscellany*, Volume Two, 520. Mesny (1842–1919) departed Hankou in October, 1862, was captured by the Taiping, and was not released until the following year, when he returned to Hankou. He would remain there until 1868. He later commanded the Guiyang arsenal, and as an officer under Zuo Zongtang participated in the campaign to suppress Yakub Beg and the Moslem Rebellion in Xinjiang. He later married the daughter of a Chinese official.

21. Nield, *China's Foreign Places*, 68–71; WNL *Journal*, January 11, 1865. Although Hart's diary makes no mention of meeting Lovatt, their chance meeting in Shanghai no doubt reminded Hart of Lovatt's military background and contributed to his decision to transfer him on short notice from Zhenjiang for duty that was distinctly military in nature.

22. WNL *Journal*, January 23, July 16 and 28, August 14, and September 20, 1865.

23. WNL *Journal*, September 1, 1861, and May 12 and October 1, 1862.

24. WNL *Journal*, September 2, 5, and 18, 1865.

25. WNL *Journal*, August 24, and October 15, 17, and 18, 1865. When he arrived in Shanghai the next day, Alfred Burt Stripling put him up. Eighteen years hence, Lovatt and Stripling would serve together in Korea.

Chapter 4

Training the Cavalry and Taming the Nian

TIANJIN, 1865–1868

After a week stopover in Shanghai, Lovatt boarded the *Gerard* for the trip north, arriving at Dagu on October 31, 1865, where he had engaged in combat just five years earlier against the Qing, and noted the irony now that he was an employee of that government: "How different now to when I was last here on hostile intent." When he arrived at Tianjin, one of the tidewaiters "kindly" put him up until Reverend W. G. Hale, who Lovatt had known from Shanghai, "very kindly offered me a bed." When the "conceited cotcomb" of a tidesurveyor he was replacing departed two weeks later, Lovatt took occupancy of his permanent living quarters. His "very simple and easy" duties at the customs house commenced on the morning of November 6. But he would soon be called upon for duties of a far different sort—duties that would explain his recent sudden transfer from Zhenjiang.[1]

After 1860, China's leadership included several important figures who believed in military "self-strengthening" (*ziqiang*), having witnessed the performance of the Western-trained forces of Frederick Ward, Henry Burgevine, Charles Gordon, Prosper Giquel, and Lovatt himself against the Taiping. Heading this group in Beijing was Prince Gong, head of the Zongli Yamen. Also in the Zongli Yamen was Grand Councilor Wenxiang. In nearby Tianjin was Chong Hou, superintendent of the Three Northern Ports of Tianjin, Chefoo (Yantai), and Niuzhuang. Finally, there was Li Hongzhang, the nationally prominent governor of Jiangsu Province, who embraced the ideas of Feng Guifen of training Chinese troops along Western lines and who had witnessed Lovatt's artillery fire.[2]

Among the foreign powers, it was the British who took the lead in proposing military reforms to these leaders as part of the Cooperative Policy. At the diplomatic level was the British minister Frederick Bruce, his successor Rutherford Alcock, and Thomas Wade, secretary to Alcock who would later serve as British minister. Equally important was Hart, who had already helped finance the Interpreter's College (*Tongwenguan*) and had also funded improvements in harbors, buoys, and beacons. Now, Hart, who had long been critical of the Qing army, offered not only customs revenue but also *customs personnel* to establish military training camps.

British general Charles Staveley had established one such camp in Tianjin in 1862, with British officers serving as instructors, leading one observer to comment that "the Chinese army is being regenerated." Two years later, at the initiative of Hart, Gordon, and the British consul in Shanghai Harry Parkes, another foreign-training program was established at Fenghuangshan near Shanghai, financed in part by the Customs. Originally headed by Gordon, in 1865 the camp came under the direction of William Winstanley, a British officer who had served under Gordon, training remnants of the Ever-Victorious Army.[3]

Hart's inspection trip to the treaty ports in central and southern China between October 1864 and June 1865 (including Shanghai where he had met Lovatt in January 1865) included Fenghuangshan in May. Impressed, Hart returned to Beijing that summer determined to support similar training in the capital region. Hart found in Chong Hou an enthusiastic supporter because of the deteriorating military situation. Although the Taiping in southern China had been defeated, just to the north of Beijing and Tianjin in southern Manchuria, mounted banditry was increasing. And just to the south, the Nian rebellion, which had erupted in 1853 from a combination of bandit groups and peasant armies, threatened nearby Henan and Shandong Provinces, necessitating the transfer to Tianjin in July of 7,000 troops from Fenghuangshan. Finally, farther afield in the northwestern province of Xinjiang, a Muslim rebellion threatened to erupt.[4]

Chong Hou had initiated the expansion of Western-style training in Tianjin even before Hart returned from the south. After consulting with Prince Gong, in May 1865 Chong Hou memorialized that the region needed expanded training because of its strategic importance as the Grand Canal gateway through which grain shipments from the south to the capital passed. So when Hart returned to Beijing in the summer of 1865 to suggest an expansion of the Tianjin training center and to lend it financial support, Chong Hou had already put the process in motion. Accordingly, more Western instructors were hired, among whom was one of Lovatt's former comrades who "has been offered the situation of drill instructor to a battery of artillery, which he will accept."[5]

In addition to artillery, Chong Hou wanted a trainer for cavalry and asked Hart to recommend someone "at once." Hart was pleased by the initiative, remarking that the Chinese were "getting their backs up" as "a first sign of returning vigor." To comply with his request, Hart began to reassign ex-soldiers who were now customs officials to "temporary duty," beginning with Horatio Octavius Brown, who had served with Gordon. But Chong Hou wanted more than one drillmaster, for on the following day Hart received a note from him "asking about my *nominees* for cavalry-drill." Needing to recommend another instructor, Hart first submitted the name of Colonel John Kirkham, who had also served under Gordon, but Kirkham balked at the $200 monthly salary that Chong Hou offered and declined, a decision he would later regret. So, in early October, Hart submitted Lovatt's name as his second choice to fill the vacancy under Brown, and then told the commissioner in Zhenjiang to send Lovatt to Tianjin immediately.[6]

While Hart and Chong Hou were conferring on drillmasters, and Lovatt was about to leave Zhenjiang for Tianjin, the government selected the Beijing Field Force (*Shenjiying*) to receive the cavalry training. As a conquest dynasty, the Manchus wanted to maintain military supremacy, and the Beijing Field Force had been created in 1862 to reinvigorate the Manchu Bannermen. As the *Shenjiying* commander argued, if they mastered Western methods, the cavalry and other Western-trained units could coordinate more easily, they could return to the capital and teach others, and then "our army might not be less competent than the foreigners and we will be confident of winning in the future because the foreigners will lose their advantage."[7]

Meanwhile, the military situation continued to deteriorate. Thirty thousand mounted bandits were reported moving southward from Manchuria, causing Wenxiang to mobilize elements of the Beijing Field Force and Chong Hou's newly expanded training program at Tianjin. Knowing that Wenxiang and the Zongli Yamen wanted to accelerate cavalry training, in mid-October Hart went to the Zongli Yamen bearing letters from Chong Hou and Brown. Eleven days later, Hart returned and during the two hours he spent there observed that the "thin and worn" Wenxiang "is anxious about Cavalry Drill at Tientsin." To allay his concern, Hart asked H. O. Brown to come to Beijing to meet with Wenxiang. While waiting for Brown to arrive from Tianjin, Hart got the approval of Thomas Wade to employ British subjects as trainers. Brown arrived in Beijing on October 29, and the next afternoon Hart took him to the Zongli Yamen where for an hour and a half they discussed cavalry training and the employment of Lovatt. As this meeting was occurring, Lovatt, still unaware of what was in store for him, was en route to Dagu.[8]

On November 3, Hart from Beijing and Lovatt from Dagu converged on Tianjin, meeting for only the second time. Lovatt would now learn for the first time why Hart wanted him to come to Tianjin on such short notice—to train Chinese cavalry. When Lovatt agreed to do it, Hart went to Chong Hou's office that afternoon and "asked him to write to the [Zongli] Yamen to *chaou-huang* [communicate with] Wade relative to O. Brown and Lovatt as instructors for the cavalry." This was a necessary formality, because only the Zongli Yamen could officially ask Britain to use its subjects to train Chinese troops. With Lovatt now on board, the staffing for cavalry training was complete and Hart could leave, departing Tianjin the next day aboard the *Nanzing* for Shanghai where he briefed Li Hongzhang on the training program.[9]

On December 16, 500 bannermen and 200 horses departed Beijing and arrived three days later, camping in an open space outside Tianjin's South Gate to await the start of training. When Chong Hou inspected the new arrivals, he noted that while the men were all young and strong, the horses were another matter, as 12 had died en route and the remaining 188 appeared thin and tired. When Brown told Chong Hou that the horses were unacceptable and because the Tianjin area did not produce horses, on Christmas day Chong Hou requested strong horses to replace the weak ones. As for salary, Chong Hou fixed the monthly salary for the cadets at 7.5 taels, and Brown as instructor-general (*zong jiao*) and Lovatt as instructor (*fen jiao*) "will receive their monthly salary in the amount that we see fit." Hart would soon take exception to his employees receiving a salary from Chong Hou.[10]

Meanwhile, after his early November meeting with Hart, Lovatt had begun his normal tidesurveyor duties in Tianjin. As it would be two months before the start of drilling, Lovatt settled into the local routine. He lived in the foreign settlement of Tzuchulin (Red Bamboo Forest) and made friends quickly, beginning with the local missionaries who "all appear earnest and devoted men and exceedingly kind." On his twenty-eighth birthday in January, "my kind friend" Reverend Hale, who had given him a place to stay when he first arrived, "gave a dinner in honor of it to which the mission ladies all contributed something made by themselves." Nonetheless, he found that "foreign life here is dull, mostly spent in eating, drinking, smoking, and looking forward to the arrival of each mail. Some go hunting, but very few." As he awaited the commencement of training, he waxed philosophical on the hiring of former soldiers such as himself to augment China's military: "If 'coming events cast their shadow before,' great changes are likely to take place in this empire."[11]

Even before they began drilling, Lovatt and Brown were being eyed not only as military trainers but also as officers who might lead their charges against enemies of the realm. Because "a formidable body [of mounted bandits is] causing great alarm, Ching lin [Zhenglin, a Zongli Yamen official] has written to Tsung How [Chong Hou] for Yang Tseang tuy [*yangqiangtui*, foreign-trained troops]," Hart wrote. And Wenxiang "desires to send O. Brown *and others* [Lovatt] to take the field against [them]." Hart wondered if the British government would agree. It was one thing to have British subjects *train* Chinese soldiers but quite another for them to *lead* Chinese soldiers into battle. Although the subject was broached, it went no further at that time because a detachment from Fenghuangshan was sent to deal with these bandits, Hart noting with approval that "the disciplined troops commence to be appreciated." But the subject would soon resurface.[12]

Beginning in early January 1866, Lovatt's duties now became those of an instructor rather than a tidesurveyor, his journal reporting that he was "engaged in drilling nearly every day," drawing on his training experience in Shanghai. After a month, he had formed opinions about his cadets that were less than stellar: "These Manchus are a very tame, poor-spirited lot—nothing one would expect to find in the conquerors of such an empire." When fresh horses arrived from Mongolia, the pace quickened somewhat: "we are getting [the cadets] on rapidly in their drill. Whether they will fight is another thing." The fact that Lovatt was drilling at all was because Kirkham had turned the offer down. Lovatt of course had not been privy to the behind-the-scenes negotiations when he encountered him: "Col. Kirkham is here but unable to obtain military employment." Still adrift more than a month later, Lovatt felt sorry for him: "Poor (Col.) Kirkham called today—a complete wreck. He has returned from Pekin. He says Sir R[utherford]. Alcock will interest himself in trying to get him something from the Chinese Government."[13]

After two months of drilling, the issue of who Lovatt and Brown actually worked for arose, since "Chinese authorities again sent 30 taels for last month's drilling, but Mr. Hart will not allow us to accept it. I learn (from Mr. B[rown].) that it is to be paid into the Customs every month and remain there until such time as Mr. Hart chooses to dispose of it." Because his prerogatives were being questioned, Hart tackled the issue head-on, departing Beijing on March 7 for Tianjin where, on March 12, he met with Chong Hou and recorded in his journal that "Taels 150 [$250] a month to be issued by Tsung How on account of monies rendered by Brown and Lovett [*sic*], the sum to remain in the safe and somehow returned." Hart had thus reaffirmed that Lovatt and Brown were under *his*, rather than the Zongli Yamen's, authority. Just as this issue was put to rest in mid-March 1866, the first drilling cycle came to an end, and for the next six weeks Lovatt resumed his normal tidesurveyor duties.[14]

When the second cycle began at the end of April, "my old friend Goldspink" took over Lovatt's duties while Lovatt "took up my new quarters and commence drilling tomorrow," characterizing it as "taking over shot and shell for [the] Chinese government." A month into the second cycle, Lovatt remained unimpressed with his new group of students: "Drilling away at the Chinese. They improve slowly. Of the 500, there are at least 200 men too old to make soldiers of." Again in June, "we continue drilling. Many of the men improve and would get on rapidly if they had any internal discipline. They have *none*, and, considering that, the attention they pay to us is very creditable to them." This second cycle ended in early July, after which Lovatt received a leave to visit Hong Kong and Canton, a trip that would have life-altering consequences for him.[15]

Back in Tianjin, the third cycle began in late July the usual way, with Lovatt lamenting the lack of ability of his cadets: "Drilling away as usual. Swords arrived and issued to the men. I take them every evening to Sword drill. They improve very slowly. The great want of discipline is manifest in everything done." However, as he continued drilling, Lovatt became more optimistic: "Our Chinese dragoons are improving. We are taking them every day to jump a couple of ditches and two trunks of trees we have for the purpose. Many have been the fall, and some have severely hurt themselves." He also noted that some of his trainees were gentry, suggesting that for some, the requirements of nationalism were changing traditional elite attitudes against military service: "The mandarins are very shy of this kind of work, but shame makes them try."[16]

Lovatt's increasing optimism was paralleled by the support that he and Brown received from Chong Hou. In a memorial to the Zongli Yamen, Chong Hou recounted Brown's insistence that the cavalrymen should all be strong, and that those who are old, sick, or do not know how to ride a horse should be replaced. Complying with Brown's wishes, Chong Hou made regular inspections and sent the unqualified back to Peking. As a result, "now the newcomers are all young and strong." As for the Mongolian horses, those that were old, thin, or tired were replaced, such that "now the horses are all in good shape." And new swords and Enfield rifles were distributed. To give an incentive to the cadets, Chong Hou promised that "those who study earnestly and acquire outstanding skills will be promoted." As a result, "we expect a well-trained and powerful army with excellent equipment."[17]

As drilling continued into the fall of 1866, Lovatt's reading, in addition to his six years of residence, was transforming him into a seasoned China hand. And his language skills had progressed to the point where "I have finished a translation of the *Sword Drill* with the help of my teacher and one of the officers." He also took an interest in some of China's first returned students when his former commissioner in Hankou became his new commissioner in Tianjin:

> Mr. Dick has arrived and taken over office, and with him came three of the young Chinese students who have been visiting Europe. When I returned their call and asked them about the different countries they had been [to], they could hardly say anything. Their ideas appeared so confused—in fact, just what one might expect from such a hurried visit.[18]

The year 1866 ended on a good note for Lovatt. He still enjoyed his work: "I commenced another drill today on foot. Drilling every day as usual. Brown takes them to target practice with revolvers. I go to riding and sword drill." And his earlier cautious optimism continued: "The regiment improves very rapidly, and do sword drill, squadron drill, and several of the regimental movements very creditably. Some of them will be very smart fellows with the sword in time if they are taken care of in Peking (which is very unlikely)." The IG, who was at that time passing through Tianjin on his way back to Beijing with his new bride from England, Hester Bredon, was reportedly "pleased" by the skill of the cadets. As Lovatt looked back on his first year in Tianjin he mused "I think I can say that this has been one of my most pleasant and happy years."[19]

Having trained Chinese troops in Shanghai in 1861–1862 and now in Tianjin in 1866, despite his occasional criticism of them, Lovatt did not blame them for China's weakened condition. Rather, he blamed the leadership, both Chinese and foreign. The Chinese

> feel the foreigner's superiority and see it, but don't like it, for they see we are acting a part to them they would not do to us. It's a mistake to treat the Chinese as a poor, simple nation. They know what is right, but are dying for want of energy, indomitable energy, without which no two-legged creature can call himself a man. Alas, poor China. There is a shaking in shoes which will awaken thy rulers from their selfish slumber and which will only bring blessings on the country.

The passivity of Western diplomats was also to blame: "I think foreign officials are all acting wrong in not continually pressing for the country to be opened to one improvement after another. They seem to draw their salaries and live easily in Peking year after year."[20]

The year 1867 began much the same as 1866 had ended, with Lovatt, now 29 years old, "still drilling. Expect to finish the regiment about the end of February." As usual, training took the usual Lunar New Year break in February, during which, "I have been spending the week amongst my friends at the foreign settlement and enjoyed myself thoroughly." As the end of the winter training cycle approached that spring, a rumor circulated that he and Brown might return to Beijing with their trainees. While wondering if they would be going to the capital, in a surprise move, Beijing came to them.[21]

The Zongli Yamen had decided that after fifteen months of training, Brown and Lovatt deserved commendations: "Received a notice from Mr. Brown to be at his place at 9:15 a.m. to receive a commission from the Emperor through His Excellency Tsung Ho. About eleven of His Excellencies came and complimented us." Brown received the honorary Chinese rank equivalent of colonel and Lovatt that of major, and both received "mandarin dress"—the imperial yellow jacket (*Huang magua*). At the conclusion of the ceremony, Lovatt was free until the next training cycle two weeks later, so he departed for Beijing in part "to attend the [Zongli] Yamen to thank Tsung Ho for the honor."[22]

Now in Beijing in mid-April, Lovatt decided to do some sightseeing, with a Methodist missionary as a traveling companion. After visiting the Western Hills and the Marco Polo Bridge south of the capital, they arrived at a temple where they were "kindly received by the priest who showed us what he said was one of Buddha's teeth. I asked what evidence they had of it, [and] he said nothing but oral tradition." Skeptically, Lovatt observed that "one might truly exclaim in this case, man, great is thy faith," adding that "the Chinese are certainly not a religious people, for you may say anything about their idols and laugh at them, in which they will join you. All they care about is making money." After nearly two weeks of sightseeing, Lovatt departed Beijing and returned to Tianjin at the end of April, ready for another training cycle.[23]

His new group of trainees, "much younger men than the earlier lot," arrived on May 4, and five days later, Lovatt met them at muster for the first time, divided them into squadrons, and dismissed them until the beginning of training two days later. Training included sword drill, lance drill, and mounting guard, twice a day, once in the morning from 8 to 10 and again in the afternoon from 4 to 6. The cycle proceeded normally, although there were now indications that Lovatt was starting to tire of "the same dull routine of drill."[24]

Lovatt nonetheless continued to acquit himself well through the summer, and in October was rewarded with a promotion by Hart to second class tide-surveyor at 150 taels per month. The promotion was due in no small part to his drilling that Hart had himself witnessed the previous November. Thus, 1867, like the previous year, also ended well for Lovatt. To celebrate his promotion, he asked for and received a ten-day leave and combined it with the Chinese New Year to do more sightseeing in Beijing. And so, in mid-January 1868, he departed Tianjin with two missionaries as traveling companions. After stopping at Hart's office to leave his card, Lovatt and his companions set off to the Great Wall at Badaling, the Ming tombs, the emperor's exclusive hunting ground, and the *Yuanmingyuan* (Summer Palace), which had been destroyed by Allied troops seven years earlier. After this short visit to the capital, Lovatt returned to Tianjin to begin the winter training cycle, a cycle that would be anything but routine.[25]

Beginning in the summer of 1867, from nearby Shandong Province came reports of "unsettled" conditions and "very great dissatisfaction." Lovatt noted that "many of the poor people [are] suffering for want of food," and an eyewitness gave Lovatt "a deplorable account [of] people starving, and everywhere inclined to rise in rebellion from want of food." The reports implicated government officials: "Nothing [has been] done to obtain grain from the south," and the eyewitness pointed to "exactions of the mandarins [being] the cause." Lovatt observed that the people "have an indefinite idea that the mandarins are the cause of their sufferings, which is very true to a greater extent than they are aware of." Exploiting this dissatisfaction were the Nian rebels who threatened the foreign community at Chefoo. However, since Tianjin was not directly threatened, Lovatt continued to drill.[26]

But by the spring of 1868, the Nian had advanced northward, Hart noting that "they threatened Tientsin the other day, and Chung How has had quite enough to do with the Nienfei [Nian bandits] in the first instance and with Li [Hongzhang]'s troops, who arrived, of course, the day after." Unlike the Taiping, the Nian were highly mobile, utilizing primarily cavalry tactics. Because the question as to whether British subjects could lead Chinese troops into combat, rather than simply training them, had been settled in the affirmative, and because Brown and Lovatt were training cavalry, they were ordered to take their cadets and defend the approaches to the city, as Chong Hou's palace memorial spelled out: "When the Nian rebels threatened the Tianjin region, Polang [Brown] and Lufu [Lovatt] led the Weiyuan cavalry to inspect all the strategic passes. They made nothing of hardships and guarded against the rebels day and night."[27]

As a result of Brown's and Lovatt's actions against the Nian, Chong Hou's memorial asked the emperor to promote them again. In response, the emperor issued an edict promoting Brown to the rank of *tsungping* (regional commander) and Lovatt to the rank of *yuchi* (brigade commander). Although Lovatt's highest rank in the British army had been sergeant, and his current honorary Chinese rank was the equivalent of major, from this time forward he adopted the moniker of colonel.[28]

By the fall of 1868, when Lovatt's journal entries ceased, the Nian were no longer a threat, Lovatt's training, by all accounts exemplary, came to an end, and he returned to his tidesurveyor duties in Tianjin. While the Cooperative Policy helped to bring about a "Restoration" (*zhongxing*) of the dynasty, the efforts of Lovatt and others in the foreign-training programs during the Tongzhi period (1862–1874) failed to produce a modern, Western-trained Chinese officer corps, as the Qing made no effort to develop a truly national army. Rather, the programs were viewed as temporary expedients to quell domestic rebellion. As for Lovatt, early in 1869, he received a one-year leave of absence to travel to the United States, where his life was about to take on a new direction.[29]

NOTES

1. WNL *Journal*, October 25, 28, and 31, and November 2, 3, and 6, 1865.

2. Feng had advocated building arsenals in Shanghai and Tianjin and sending study missions abroad. For more on Feng, see Jonathan K. Ocko, *Bureaucratic Reform in Provincial China: Ting Jih-ch'ang in Restoration Kiangsu, 1867–1870* (Cambridge: Harvard University Council on East Asian Studies, 1983).

3. G. H. Fitzroy to Wilzer, November 6, 1862, in Robert Hart, *Letters, 1865–1910: Letters to Various Westerners in the Chinese Customs Service*. MS Chinese 4.1. Houghton Library, Harvard University; Richard J. Smith, "Foreign Training and China's Self-Strengthening: The Case of Feng-huang-shan, 1864–1873." *Modern Asian Studies*, 10 (2) (1976), 203, 222.

4. John King Fairbank, Richard J. Smith, and Katherine F. Bruner, *Robert Hart and China's Early Modernization: His Journals, 1863–1866* (Cambridge and London: Harvard University Council on East Asian Studies, 1991), 268–293.

5. *Yangwu yundong [The Foreign Affairs Movement]* (Shanghai: Renmin chubanshe, 1961), III, 475 (*Tongzhi* 4.4.12 [May 6, 1865]); WNL *Journal*, December 1, 1865; Fairbank, Smith, and Bruner, 511, fn. 108; Hart *Journal*, September 20 and 24, 1865.

6. Hart *Journal*, September 6, 7, and 28, 1865; see also Fairbank, Smith, and Bruner, 219–220; WNL *Journal*, October 15, 1865. H. O. Brown had been Charles Gordon's aide-de-camp before joining the Customs the year before in 1864 as Third Class clerk in Tianjin. Emphasis added.

7. *Yangwu yundong*, III, 476 (*Tongzhi* 4.7.29 [September 18, 1865]); William Mesny, *Mesny's Chinese Miscellany*. Volume Four (Shanghai: E. Lee Printing Office, 1905), 407–408.

8. Hart *Journal*, October 14, 23, 25, 29, and 30, 1865. This represented a shift in British policy since an 1864 order prohibited British subjects from serving China in a military capacity. Presumably, Wade had already cleared this with London. Smith, "Foreign-Training and China's Self Strengthening," 201.

9. Hart *Journal*, November 1–9 and 24, 1865; Smith, Fairbank, and Bruner, 330–331.

10. *Yangwu yundong*, III, 478–479 (*Tongzhi* 4.11.8 [December 25, 1865]). Subsequently, only 300 new horses were sent.

11. WNL *Journal*, November 17, and December 1 and 31, 1865, and January 10, and 31, 1866.

12. Hart *Journal*, December 22, 1865, and January 3, 6, and 7, 1866. Emphasis added.

13. WNL *Journal*, December 1, 1865, and January 31, and February 1 and 10, 1866; Smith, "Foreign Training and China's Self Strengthening," 208. Unlike at Feng-huangshan, Lovatt gave his commands in English.

14. WNL *Journal*, February 28, and March 1 and 14, 1866; Hart *Journal*, March 7, 10, and 12, 1866. Two days later, Hart left Tianjin for Shanghai and from there proceeded to Hong Kong and boarded a ship to England where he married and spent most of the summer. He left England in September to return to China. For more on Hart's personal life, see Mary Tiffen, *Friends of Sir Robert Hart: Three Generations of Carrall Women in China* (Crewkerne, UK: Tiffania Books in association with Queen's University, Belfast, 2012).

15. WNL *Journal*, March 14, April 24, May 1 and 18, and June 6 and 20, 1866; Hart *Journal*, March 23, 1866. Emphasis in the original.

16. WNL *Journal*, July 30, and September 7 and 21, 1866.

17. *Yangwu yundong*, III, 483–484 (*Tongzhi* 5:7:26 [September 4, 1866]); see also the memorial by Prince Gong on 490–491 (*Tongzhi* 5.8.28 [October 26, 1866]).

18. WNL *Journal*, September 21 and November 4, 1866. His reading included Abbe Huc, *A Journey through the Chinese Empire* [1857] and *Travels in Tartary and Tibet, 1844–1846* [1851].

19. WNL *Journal*, September 7, November 4, and December 1 and 31, 1866. Lovatt did, however, experience two occurrences that dampened his experience that year. The first occurred in June when "a thief came into my bedroom and stole my watch while I was asleep. Went to the Magistrate about it." The second and more serious was his receipt of "a letter to say that it was rumoured in Shanghai that the Com. Bank has failed. Very unfortunate, for all my money is in it." He found out in July that the rumor was true: "the bank my money is in has really failed this time—which I am sorry for. It will disappoint my dear father in my not getting home so soon. The loss of the money don't trouble me much." WNL *Journal*, May 27, June 6, and July 6, 1866.

20. WNL *Journal*, September 7, 1866.

21. WNL *Journal*, January 10, February 15, and March 1, 1867.

22. WNL *Journal*, April 3, 6, and 7, 1867; WNL to JSL, July 27, 1875. Emphasis in the original. Richard J. Smith, *Mercenaries and Mandarins: Mesny's Chinese Miscellany*, Vol. 4, 407–408; Wilson, 383; Charles O. Hucker, *A Dictionary of Official Titles in Imperial China* (Stanford: Stanford University Press, 1985), 217 (Number 2041).

23. WNL *Journal*, March 24, 1866, and April 11 and 26, 1867.

24. WNL *Journal*, May 9, 11, and 16, June 4, July n.d., and August 12, 1867.

25. WNL *Journal*, October 6, 1867, and January 18–25, 1868, but written on February 2, 1868. One of the missionaries was Joseph Edkins (1823–1905), an evangelist, linguist, translator, philologist, and expert in Chinese religions, and had been in China since 1848, mostly in Shanghai. He moved to Tianjin in 1862 and retired in 1880. He was the author of a Shanghai dialect grammar, a Mandarin grammar, *The Religious Condition of the Chinese* (1859), *Religion in China* (1878), and *Chinese Buddhism* (1880). They were able to enter the emperor's exclusive hunting ground by giving fifty copper cash to the gatekeeper, who granted it "at once. Mr. Edkins afterwards told me they were not in the habit of allowing foreigners through and was rather surprised at the ready permission we got to pass through. At the other end, the guard seemed astounded at our going through and wanted to know where we got in, but as we all kept silence, they came to the conclusion we couldn't speak Chinese."

26. WNL *Journal*, July n.d., August 12 and n.d., 1867.

27. Hart to Wilzer, May 18, 1868, in Hart *Letters*; *Chouban yiwu shimo. Tongzhi zhao [Complete Record of the Management of Barbarian Affairs. The Tongzhi Period]*, Volume Six (Taipei: Kuofeng Chubanshe, 1965), Tongzhi 7.8.4 [September 19, 1868], 1401.

28. *Chouban yiwu shimo*; S. A. Murdock to Col. and Mrs. Lovatt, April 4, 1888. The translations of the titles come from Hucker, *A Dictionary of Official Titles in Imperial China*.

29. Smith, "Foreign Training and China's Self-Strengthening," 215–223; Mary Wright, *The Last Stand of Chinese Conservatism: The T'ung-chih Restoration, 1862–1874* (New York: 1967), 201–202.

Chapter 5

Minnesota, Jiujiang, and Taiwan, 1869–1877

WEDDING BELLS

Up to this point, as a bachelor approaching thirty, Lovatt had not engaged in any affairs of the heart. But midway through his cavalry drilling in Tianjin in the summer of 1866, he had a chance meeting with a female missionary who had just arrived from Minnesota that would lead to his engagement. Although we have Lovatt's bare-bones account, a more detailed account surfaced eight decades later in a newspaper article entitled "Romance, Courage in the Story of a Tiny Red Shoe; Milwaukee Woman Writes Most Vivid Recollection; It Takes Us to Old China." In it, an elderly woman recalled a story told to her by her father when she was young about his father, Dr. Tanner, who had acquired from one of his patients a tiny red shoe once worn by a Chinese woman with bound feet. By combining the two accounts, we get a more complete picture of how Lovatt met his wife.[1]

The newspaper article begins with the meeting between Lovatt and the missionary:

> In 1866 . . . Effie Gray taught [at a] country school in Lakeland, Minn. [She] had been educated at Oberlin [College in Ohio] and was imbued with the missionary spirit. She . . . became attached to her pupils, especially one in the [senior] class, Jennie Shaw, who was very attractive and had that rare gift—appreciation of ability and the nobility in character. At the close of the school year, Effie Gray was given a photograph album with pictures of her pupils. In July [1866] she began a long journey as a missionary teacher to Chinese girls and their mothers in Canton . . . As they neared Hong Kong, pirates . . . attacked their ship, but . . . were driven off by a detail . . . under the command of Capt. [William] Nelson [Lovatt].[2]

Although Lovatt certainly did not repulse a pirate attack in Hong Kong, he was in the area in the summer of 1866 at the same time as Effie Gray. Having just completed his second training cycle in Tianjin, Lovatt had received time off and sailed to Hong Kong, arriving on July 15. In the six years since he had last passed through on the way to the siege of Beijing, the Western community in Hong Kong had swelled to about 1,000 men and 500 women. Lovatt's memories of Hong Kong's more notable features now came rushing back, such as the "narrow streets where Chinese men, women, and children swarmed" and the merciless summer heat.[3]

High on Lovatt's list of priorities in Hong Kong was attending religious services and interacting with the missionary community. His first stop was James Legge's London Mission Society chapel, where he commented favorably on Legge's sermon, sang familiar hymns, and was "glad once more to be in the house of the Lord." The two men had become acquainted in 1860, and now in 1866 Legge gave Lovatt letters he had been holding for him. At the service, another missionary invited Lovatt to tiffin, where servants brought beef, mutton, ham, potatoes, toast and butter, lichee, peaches, and pineapples. And (Charles F.) Warren of the Church Missionary Society and head of St. Paul's College offered Lovatt lodging at his school. At one of these occasions Lovatt first encountered Effie Gray.[4]

Resuming the doctor's story, "Capt. Nelson [*sic*] called [on her] . . . and inquir[ed] [about] the shock of the pirates. Effie brought [out her school] photograph album. When they came to [Jennie Shaw's] picture, Capt. Nelson exclaimed, 'Upon my word, she's pretty!' He made no secret of the attraction the picture had for him and asked Effie Gray to introduce him by letter." The smitten Lovatt sat for a photograph and enclosed it in a letter to her, then departed Hong Kong on July 21, 1866, to return to his training duties. Back in Tianjin, Lovatt kept up his correspondence with Jennie for the next seven months until, in February 1867, he popped the question: "I have served nearly seven years here and in a few months will be given a year's furlough. May I come to Lakeland, and if everything is agreeable, will you marry me?" Seven months later, in September 1867, he "received from J. L. S. her answer to my letter of the preceding February. I liked it." Jennie had accepted (figure 5.1).[5]

Jennie's parents, Joseph and Jane Ann, originally hailed from New York. Their first child, Jennie, was born August 3, 1848; a second daughter, Jessie, followed in 1851; and a son, John, was born in 1856. Following the adage of "Go West, young man," Joseph Shaw left his wife and three children in 1857 for Minnesota where he worked as a day laborer on farms and in the logging industry near St. Paul, earning between three and five dollars a day. Aspiring to be a farmer, he wrote to his wife that "if I succeed in getting a piece of land which I think I can if I have my health, I can get it ready. I think this is as fine a land as I ever saw." Two years later, he brought his family from New York

Figure 5.1 Photograph Jennie Shaw Sent to Lovatt in 1868 of Herself with the Inscription "Ever Your Friend." Courtesy: Dorothy Shaw Gillette.

to Lakeland in Washington County, purchased some land, and began to farm. Four years after moving to Minnesota, a fourth and final child—daughter Bessie—was born in 1863. The Shaws were pioneers in what was essentially a small rural community. On their farm, which they named "Plum Grove," they grew wheat and oats. The nearest towns of any size were Stillwater, 9 miles to the north, and St. Paul, 20 miles to the west.[6]

Although Lovatt learned in the fall of 1867 that Jennie would marry him, he had to wait for over a year to get a leave of absence from Hart because he was still needed to train Qing cavalry and help suppress the Nian Rebellion. When Lovatt finally arrived in Minnesota in the spring of 1869, his first visit to the United States and his first meeting with Jennie, the Shaw family saw to it that a local woman acted as their chaperone, "to watch our courtship," as Lovatt put it. Jennie was apparently quite a catch if the note to Lovatt from family friend and Washington County Register of Deeds is any indication: "Dear Sir, The man who would travel halfway around the Earth to wed an unsophisticated country maid should be rewarded as you will be with a wife such as yours will be, a jewel to please the eye and a treasure to please and be ever near your heart. Such is my Jennie Shaw." On March 8, 1869, the couple applied for a wedding license, and three weeks later, on March 29, 1869, William Nelson Lovatt, age thirty-one, was married to Jennie L. Shaw, age twenty, by the local Presbyterian minister.[7]

Following the wedding, the newlyweds left for Chicago, where they arrived on April first, and where Lovatt wrote to his mother-in-law that "I cannot give you an idea how perfectly happy I am and how truly grateful I feel to our Heavenly Father for having guided and directed me to your Northwestern home." From Chicago, they went to New York, first to Niagara Falls, then to Binghamton to meet his wife's relatives, and finally to New York City, where they sailed to England so Lovatt could introduce his bride to his father and his three siblings and to spend the summer. They returned to Minnesota in the fall of 1869 and spent the winter there. Here the doctor's story continues:

> [Jennie's] parents could not consent to her taking the long and hazardous journey to China, so they persuaded Capt. Nelson to stay in Lakeland and take over the farm. He consented to stay through his furlough. He had neither training nor experience to farm successfully in a new country, so before his furlough expired he had persuaded everyone that the best place for him to earn a living was in the British service.

Lovatt and Jennie, now pregnant with their first child, departed Minnesota in late January 1870, taking the newly completed transcontinental railroad to San Francisco where they spent eight days at the Occidental Hotel until they could board the Pacific Mail steamship to Japan.[8]

JIUJIANG, SPRING 1870–SUMMER 1874

Because Hart had assigned him to Jiujiang, the Lovatts sailed from Japan to Shanghai, where they put up at the two-dollar-per-day Astor House, the city's first Western-style hotel. Arriving with less than ten dollars in his pocket, Lovatt was able to collect three months back pay from Commissioner Thomas Dick, who had been his first commissioner in Hankou in 1863. With that money, Lovatt bought passage on the *Plymouth Rock* for the 500 mile voyage up the Yangzi River, arriving on March 14, 1870. Two months later, on June 25, 1870, the Lovatts' first child, Helen Margaret (Nellie), was born.[9]

Jiujiang was one of now fourteen treaty ports in 1870, located near where Lake Poyang meets the Yangzi River in Jiangxi Province. Hart had first visited Jiujiang in 1861, the year it had been designated as a treaty port, and established a customs office there with an annual allowance of 3000 taels (about $5,000) from the Zongli Yamen. As a treaty port, it required the appropriate infrastructure, and the American consul there, William Breck, who doubled as a clerk for Russell and Company, had secured 500 yards along the south bank of the river, where lots were leased to foreign firms. This became the Bund (*waitan*), from which wooden jetties protruded to reach the steamers that brought in opium and took out tea, silk, and porcelain from the famous nearby porcelain-producing city of Jingdezhen. Despite these advances, Jiujiang was still a backwater port by the standards of the time, with only eight British and three American firms in 1870. When William Mesny visited there, he found that "the few [25] foreign residents there were still subject to much annoyance from local thieves and passing soldiery."[10]

Edward B. Drew was the commissioner when Lovatt arrived in 1870. In 1872 Drew was transferred and replaced by Henry C. J. Kopsch, a Briton who had been a student interpreter under William MacPherson, who had succeeded Thomas Dick as commissioner at Hankou in 1863. Kopsch had joined the Customs in 1862, had attained the rank of commissioner in 1868, and would serve in Jiujiang until 1877. Lovatt's other two superiors who became lifelong friends were Kopsch's two assistants, the Briton F. Neville May and the German Paul Georg Von Möllendorff.[11]

Other foreigners in Jiujiang in the early 1870s consisted mainly of missionaries, businessmen, and diplomats. Several Protestant mission organizations were represented, including the American Methodist Episcopal Mission, the China Inland Mission, and the Woman's Foreign Missionary Society. Among those missionaries were Virgil C. Hart and his wife Adeline, Andrew Strittmatter and his wife Mary, Henry H. Hall, John Hykes, Lucy H. Hoag, Gertrude Howe, and John E. Cardwell, whose wife had delivered Nellie Lovatt. Representing Catholicism was a French bishop and four French priests, whom Lovatt referred to as the "Roman chapel." The few businessmen dealt in insurance and shipping, such as Jardine and Matheson, Russell and Company, the China Navigation Company, and R. Francis and Company. Rounding out the foreign community were two diplomats, Walter Edward King, the British vice-consul, and S. C. Rose, the American consul who had succeeded William Breck. Joining this small foreign community were temporary visitors such as tea buyers and crews from the passenger and cargo steamers and the gunboats that plied the Yangzi River.[12]

In such a small foreign community, the Lovatts felt vulnerable to anti-Western sentiment. Just four days before Nellie was born, the Tianjin Massacre of June 21, 1870, took place, during which the French consul, ten nuns, and several other foreigners were massacred by a mob incited by local gentry who accused the Catholic missionaries of kidnapping children and extracting their eyes and blood for nefarious purposes. Fear raced like wildfire throughout the treaty ports, including Jiujiang. Hart, who had just arrived in Shanghai after a tour of the Yangzi River treaty ports, including Jiujiang, wrote that "at all the ports much alarm is felt." It appeared to Hart in that summer of 1870 that war was imminent: "The seventh Prince [Yi] and all the officials are for war, Prince Kung [Gong] and two or three others are for peace . . . I fear we must have war, or at all events a very unsettled, unsafe, and unsatisfactory state of things for many months to come." In a letter to Drew in Jiujiang, Hart wrote that "the people's demeanour is certainly changed, and their faces do not look as pleasant as they did four years ago."[13]

The Tianjin Massacre was big news not only in China but also in the United States, prompting Jennie that summer to assure her parents that she was safe. After complaining of the 92-degree heat and the mosquitoes, she wrote,

> do not let this late trouble at Tientsin alarm you. Will says we are more safe now than before, for the Chinese would not dare to engage in a war with all the foreign powers as they know their strength too well for that, and says proclamations have been issued everywhere commanding the people to be peaceful and not to molest foreigners.

Indeed, by the fall of 1870, tensions had eased, Chung Hou of the Zongli Yamen led an apology mission to France, and Hart observed that "I believe we shall be quite quiet here all winter." For the moment, at least, Jiujiang was safe, and one could safely go downriver to visit Shanghai, such as the trip in November 1871 that merited a notice in the *North China Herald*: "William Lovatt, wife, and family arrived in Shanghai from Chinkeang aboard the *S. S. Tunsin*." In short, the Tianjin Massacre did not seem to frighten Lovatt into leaving China and its Customs Service (figure 5.2).[14]

Nonetheless, antiforeign sentiment was constantly on the minds of the customs personnel. Ever since the Unequal Treaties had been signed calling

Figure 5.2 The Lovatts with Helen (Nellie) and John in Juijiang, 1874. Courtesy: Kathryn Beard.

for diplomatic equality, the Chinese government had delayed the audience the West had demanded, citing the youth of the new emperor Guangxu. But when the emperor reached his majority in February 1873, the Western powers renewed their demands for an audience on the basis of equality rather than subservience and the kowtow. Hart feared the audience question might rekindle the antiforeignism that had been evident in the Tianjin Massacre, but despite his fears, the audience proceeded without incident in June 1873. Jiujiang, however, was not so lucky. In that same year, Lovatt's missionary friends in the American Methodist Episcopal Mission attempted to open a station in Ruichang, 25 miles west of Jiujiang, only to be driven out by a mob incited by three local gentry. In October of the following year, they attempted unsuccessfully to rent a building in that city, and when they returned a month later, two of the missionaries were beaten.[15]

SECRET MISSION TO TAIWAN, SUMMER–FALL 1874

While keeping a watchful eye for antiforeign flare-ups, it was an international crisis that would have a direct impact on Lovatt. In December 1871, fifty-four fishermen from Liu-ch'iu (Ryūkyū) were massacred by Botan tribesmen in eastern Taiwan. Declaring the victims to be their subjects, Japan demanded redress from China, but when negotiations bogged down in the spring of 1874, the Japanese government, convinced that the Chinese government either could not or would not punish the perpetrators, launched an expedition led by Saigō Tsugumichi against the perpetrators. When China prepared to retaliate that summer, Lovatt became caught up in the military response.

In Beijing, Hart was alive to the threat this invasion posed—"China is behindhand: the Japs have the start everywhere"—and embarked on two covert strategies to help China, one long term and the other short term, without the knowledge of the British government, which was officially neutral in its mediating role. For the long term, Hart planned to strengthen China's navy, asking his assistant in London, James D. Campbell, "to ascertain *most quietly and most confidentially* for me what it would cost to supply a most peaceable-looking steamer, to steam 15 knots, and carry one gun capable of piercing *20-inch* armor at 500 yards. Find out very quietly and telegraph answer. *I don't want any one to know that China contemplates anything of the kind.*" In doing so, Hart hoped to bring the two countries closer together: "I want to make China strong, and I want her to make England her best friend."[16]

In the short term, remembering Lovatt's military service in Dagu, Beijing, Shanghai, and Tianjin, Hart decided to reassign him temporarily and in secret to Taiwan to train and possibly lead Chinese troops against the Japanese. To avoid running afoul of the neutrality policy of the British government, Hart had Lovatt pose as an "engineer," while lamenting the need to employ this subterfuge: "if English Consuls were to give support to Englishmen [like Lovatt] in Chinese employ, we could make England and China the best of friends, and prevent China being made strong by inimical [Russian] hands." That Lovatt's assignment was military in nature was apparent when Hart asked Campbell in London to "tell Winstanley [who had trained Chinese troops at Fenghuangshan] there is a probability of his being employed."[17]

Lovatt learned of his temporary new assignment and "profession" on August 19, 1874, when Commissioner Kopsch informed him, "I am directed by the Inspector General to instruct you to proceed to Foochow at once." That it was a matter of some urgency was apparent when Kopsch added that "you will accordingly lose no time in carrying out these instructions" involving "special duty for a period of two or three months." Customs would furnish his passage to Shanghai and on to Fuzhou, the treaty port on the east coast of China that served as a jumping-off point to Taiwan. Lovatt guessed his ultimate destination was Taiwan when Kopsch told him that "as the nature of the duty in question may take you to places where no provision is made for the presence of married foreigners, you are advised to leave your family at this port [Jiujiang]." That it might involve hardship or hostilities was suggested by the fact that the Fuzhou Customs was to allot him an additional 50 taels a month. Clearly, Hart saw Lovatt's temporary duty in the context of hostilities, writing that "war is quite in the cards" and later telegraphing that "war almost certain."[18]

Despite Hart's efforts to keep Britain in the dark, British minister Thomas Wade learned about the dispatch of military advisers like Lovatt to Taiwan and alerted his consuls in the treaty ports to prevent such departures. In Jiujiang, British consul King quickly guessed the reason for Lovatt's abrupt departure and issued him a warning:

> Sir, I have reason to believe that your sudden departure hence yesterday was for the purpose of taking some part in the events resulting from the disagreement of the Chinese and Japanese Governments on the subject of the invasion of part of Formosa by the latter. I am advised by the Minister [Wade] to caution you against taking any part in operations on either side.

But Lovatt was already en route to Fuzhou and did not receive King's admonition until after he had already arrived in Taiwan.[19]

Having failed to prevent Lovatt's departure, King turned his attention to Commissioner Kopsch. Deeming that Kopsch had violated British neutrality policy by transmitting Hart's order to Lovatt, and believing he was following Wade's instructions, King placed Kopsch under arrest, causing Hart to rail: "At K'kiang, Consul King has *arrested* Commissioner Kopsch!" Furious, Hart vowed that "Consul King will 'catch it' in [this] affair (Kopsch)!" lamenting that "this is a sad reflection after twenty odd years of fairly cosmopolitan, but yet essentially Anglo-Chinese work." And if Kopsch could be arrested, so could Lovatt upon his return. While both Kopsch and Lovatt were British subjects, they were employees of the Chinese government, so the issue became whether they were subject to arrest by a British official for acts performed in the line of duty. The record is silent on the eventual disposition of the case. Presumably Hart spoke to Wade, Wade telegraphed King, Kopsch was released, Lovatt would not be arrested, and amends were made.[20]

Lovatt meanwhile had reached Fuzhou and set off for the treaty port of Taiwanfu (Tainan), arriving in the second week of September, still under cover, as a local chronicler recorded: "8–10 September 1874: Europeans lately arrived at Taiwanfoo, in or for Chinese service:—Mr. H. N. Lovatt (of Kew-kiang Customs, a British subject) [*sic*] to assist in engineering." His voyage across the Taiwan straits had been unpleasant, due to bad weather and poor Chinese seamanship. Nor did he like Taiwan, dubbing it "the land of big mosquitoes, fever, and typhoons." Regarding Taiwanfu specifically, "I have never known [mosquitoes] to be so numerous, except in the home and birthplace of their race, the city of Tai-wan-foo. In that favored city the war against mankind is carried on by day and night, no intermission. 'Forward, ever Forward' is their battle cry, and to their honor, joyously they keep up the assault." Lovatt subsequently was transferred south to Takao [Kaohsiung], another of the island's four treaty ports, of which he wrote, "I don't know of any place more likely to disgust [one] with China than Takao in Formosa."[21]

Lovatt's correspondence does not indicate what he did in Taiwan, but he clearly performed no military duties because China never engaged in hostilities against Japan. The entire affair was settled by the end of October when Japan agreed to withdraw its forces and China agreed to pay an indemnity of 500,000 taels ($750,000). Lovatt returned to Jiujiang in late 1874, with Jennie "look[ing] over the railing" as he approached their house, *Taiping Kung*, to resume his normal customs duties.[22]

DAILY LIFE IN JIUJIANG

By now, Lovatt's family numbered five. Their second child, John Edward (Jack), had been born on March 19, 1872, and on January 6, 1874, Ida Elizabeth was born. But in the summer of 1875, it was decided that Jennie and the three children should return to Minnesota because eighteen-month-old Ida was in poor health. To accompany them as far as Japan, Lovatt had to ask for a leave, which Commissioner Kopsch grudgingly granted and for a minimal amount of time, causing Lovatt to grouse about the hypocrisy: "I will not forget how stingy he was about the leave he gave me to go to Japan, and now he will take care he goes as far as he can himself. He is a thoroughly selfish man." Nonetheless, on July 1 the Lovatts, accompanied by their "boy" and their amah, departed for Shanghai, where they stayed again at the Astor House before departing for Japan, spending a day in Kobe and going on to Yokohama where Jennie and the three children boarded the mail steamer *Atlantic* for San Francisco, departing on July 17. When they arrived back in Minnesota on August 12, 1875, they moved in with Jennie's parents, and Dr. Tanner was called to treat Ida.[23]

On the same day that Jennie and the children departed Yokohama for San Francisco, Lovatt, his "boy," and the amah boarded *The Golden Age* for the trip back to Shanghai, stopping first at Kobe and then Nagasaki before departing Japan on July 23. Upon arrival in Shanghai, he checked in at the Astor House and picked up the mail that had been held for him by the manager, who invited him to dinner. He also attended services at the Union Chapel presided over by James Thomas of the London Mission Society and hired a jinricksha with two coolies to make his rounds. Naturally, customs business occupied much of Lovatt's time while he was in Shanghai. He first wrote to Kopsch to assure him that he would be back on time, and then went to the Shanghai Customs House to look in on his colleagues there, one of whom was the tide-surveyor J. S. Halsey, who "bored me with his troubles in the Custom House [as] he seems to be in troubled water with everybody." While there, Lovatt picked up the latest gossip and rumors, and as he boarded the *Nanking* on the evening of July 27 for the trip upriver, he concluded that "I am glad I do not live in Shanghai. It is an awful place for scandal and gossip."[24]

Having been compelled to rush back because the commissioner had insisted he return by the first of August, Lovatt disembarked in Jiujiang and the next morning went to the three-room Customs Office when it opened at ten and reported to Kopsch, "who seemed the same quiet, cool fellow, and took over my duty." At that time he also met for the first time his new assistant, W. J. Sayle, who was forty-six years old and had previously worked in the Hankou customs as an examiner. Initially, Lovatt said, "I rather like" him, and described him as "a good, sober, quiet, steady going old fellow, rather ugly, and very seedy looking." Soon, however, Lovatt's opinion of him changed: "Mr. Sayle is so stupid and does so many wrong things that I have thought I would have to report him." So when Sayle left for Shanghai "to take unto himself a maiden to keep his old bones warm this winter" and returned with his new wife, Lovatt felt compelled to keep his distance from the couple because of their awkward working relationship: "I . . . called on Mrs. Sayle, the first time for months, because I did not like showing any degree of friendliness to Mrs. Sayle when I did not know the day Sayle would do something so very wrong or neglectful that I might have to report him."[25]

Jiujiang, like the other treaty ports, was growing into a multinational community consisting of French, Germans, Scandinavians, Americans, and Britons, in addition to Chinese. As one customs official posted there at the same time as Lovatt noted, "all white men held together and sank their separatist tendencies. Chinese and foreigners were the two broad racial distinctions. Taken as a whole, there was very little animosity between the two." To be sure, there were some occasions for interaction and, with the exception of missionaries, Lovatt had more than most, as he could speak the language and was not averse to traveling in the interior, sleeping in teahouses, or bargaining with storekeepers. Since his quarters were, in effect, in a gated community, he saw the Chinese gatekeepers every day as he came and went: "The boy at the gate is very sick with fever. His old opium smoking father is attending to the gate himself now." And there were his Chinese servants: a cook who was paid $5 a month, a gardener, a punkah (fan) coolie, and his "boy," who announced meals with "*chih fan lai liaow* [come and get it]" and about whom Lovatt complained was getting lazy: "I wish you [Jennie] were here to stir him up, and teach him that life does not consist altogether in sleeping and eating rice."[26]

Without female companionship for the first time since his marriage six years earlier, Lovatt quite naturally had sex on his mind. Soon after seeing Jennie off in Japan, he wrote about his "dreams of soft, milky breasts," and felt guilty in doing so: "Though I feel wicked [and] there is a roguish vein come over me, I don't want to put naughty things in my letter. I must be virtuous." In yet another letter he wrote "how I have longed to have you in my arms and kissing those warm and loving breasts." Slightly embarrassed, he wrote: "Would you like a ________ letter? Have I not been very good for a long while? I am feeling I should like to be bad a little." The closest he came to an X-rated letter was after a solo hiking trip: "I proceeded to the top of the ridge and gazed southward, and while looking into the pale thin mist of futurity, I placed my hand where I felt strong feelings rise. The soft south wind gave me sensations of delight and called up days of love and happiness, when you and I stood as we beheld the same feelings rise in each other."[27]

Bachelors or married men who were alone in China did have sexual outlets available: "The night side of Chinese life [in Jiujiang] was to be had for the asking all around us," and extramarital liaisons were viewed as "a temporary measure." Hart, for example, had a long-standing relationship in Beijing with a Chinese woman, Ayaou. One affair in Jiujiang involved a Mr. Gramm, who married a twenty-two-year-old Chinese woman, and who Lovatt described as "an aged and venerable sinner, who cannot with time forget the follies of his youth, but carries them on into old age." There is no evidence that Lovatt availed himself of the opportunities: "There is hardly a man in any good position who marries a girl in China. All prefer to go home for their wives. The young girls in China who do get married are not as a rule very well settled."[28]

A typical Jiujiang workday for Lovatt began when he awoke and rang the bell for the boy to bring tea and toast. Then, "I do an hour and a half walking, *doing tiger* every morning, swing the clubs, setting up drill." Upon his return, the boy brought the water for his bath, followed by a breakfast of oatmeal, two eggs, and a cup of tea. At ten he reported to the customs house to begin his six-hour workday, five days a week. If a steamer had come in, his *ting chai* [office attendant] brought in the mail and *The North China Herald*. At noon he had bread and butter, cold beef, and a cup of tea while he studied Greek with Andrew Stritmatter. Afternoons at the office, "when I have nothing else to do," he read French with the French hulk-keeper of the *Sultan* docked in Jiujiang. Because the afternoon temperature in the summer would often go above ninety degrees, he had the punkah going, although this did not prevent the occasional heat-induced boil. Returning to his quarters at four in the afternoon, the boy would have "the usual" tea and toast ready. At 7:00 p.m., dinner, followed by two pipes of tobacco, reading or chatting with a customs colleague. He retired at 10:00 or 10:30 p.m. after a drink of cold water. In short, "very regular habits and nothing very luxurious."[29]

Given this daily routine, Lovatt looked forward to the weekend when, as in the other treaty ports, meals were a major social activity. Lunches, or tiffin, lasted well into the afternoon and were often substantial, consisting of chicken or meat provided by the skippers of visiting steamers, followed by walks or rides in the countryside. Dinners began late, around 8:00 or 8:30 p.m., dressy affairs with white linen mess jackets and duck trousers, with "metallic" fare—tinned soup, fish, meat, vegetables, and plum pudding.

Liquid refreshment consisted of sherry, claret and soda, and bottled beer, with whiskey and soda during the card or board game afterward, which most of the bachelors or those whose wives were absent engaged in, Lovatt being partial to euchre, cribbage, dominoes, California Jack, and billiards, while indulging in a Manila cigar. While meals were the major social activity, they were not the only ones. Lovatt, for example, in early 1873 organized a literary society to read the plays of Shakespeare.[30]

Weekends were also good for getting away from it all. Lovatt occasionally went hunting for snipe or duck, or went on an excursion to a local temple: "Tomorrow is Sunday and your beloved contemplates paying a visit to his old friend the priest at Kiufeng tomorrow morning and inhale the mountain air. I shall take a chair and four coolies and the boy with me—the boy rides now in the old chair, and has two coolies, so you see we go in style." Or, he could go to the customs bungalow in Lushan to enjoy "lovely views of a grand panorama of mountain, plain, and river, cool nights, and a natural bathing pool of crystal water."[31]

Weekends were also the occasion for church services both for the small foreign community and for the local Chinese population. If Lovatt was not away on a weekend excursion, he normally attended: "There are not many [who] go to church. There was just eight of us and Hykes, who read the service very well." Chinese services drew a larger crowd, and one incident caught Lovatt's attention both for what it said about Chinese superstition and for what it said about the potential for antiforeignism:

> Hykes had quite an affecting incident. While he was preaching to about one hundred people in the chapel, an old opium smoker staggered in and lay down on one of the benches and wanted a drink of water, but the chapel keeper would not give him any, and wanted to haul him out of the chapel, suspecting he might die there, and you know it is considered very bad for a man to die at your house, or opposite to it, but Hykes made the man give him some water, and when the poor fellow had a drink he lay down and died. The Chinese never said anything, fortunately. The chapel was full of people, with the doors and windows open. Still one can readily understand what a serious row might have been got up if the thing had occurred less publicly than it did. The [district] magistrate called to see the man, and then had him taken away, so the affair has ended.[32]

Weekends also provided the foreign community an opportunity to engage in lawn games such as croquet, quoits, tennis, or cricket. The cricket matches were often highly organized affairs, with customs men matched against the foreign merchants or the sailors on gunboats. Although some matches were planned well in advance and sometimes involved travel to ports like Hankou, others materialized spontaneously, and not always on the weekend:

> Yesterday after office hours I went across the creek. Presently the *Hornets* came on the ground to play so we made a match with them, and had a very amusing game, if not a very scientific one. The sailors laughed, tumbled about all over the cricket field, made jokes, and acted in their comical way. The new Captain appears to be very kind to them, and permits them to come on shore pretty often.

Nonetheless, Lovatt was mildly critical of the sailors: "they are an awful drunken lot. It is an article of their creed, and [it] looks as if they had sincere desire to live up to their faith. Still, [the] poor fellows deserve more pity than blame." He added, "I like them very much, only they unfortunately drink a great deal too much, especially the crew of the gunboat we have here now. They drink *like salt-water fishes!!!*"[33]

Lovatt's criticism of excessive drinking on the part of the gunboat crews stemmed from the fact that he had for so long prided himself on being a tee-totaler. But as time went on, he sometimes indulged in a *xiao pingzi* (a small bottle) of claret or champagne at social occasions: "[Despite the 96 degree heat] I feel remarkably well and not a single boil — which I attribute to my extreme temperance in eating, and next thing to total abstinence in drinking. In fact, I was going to say I was a total abstainer, but that would not be strictly true, though very near it."[34]

When Lovatt was not engaged in a game of cricket or other physical activity, the Bund provided a gathering place for the foreign community. In the summer, because there were few travelers, except for the occasional foreign tea buyer, the arrival of the riverboat was a major event:

> The Bund at Kiukiang on a summer's night was a fearsome experience. The whole community—some fourteen persons or so in the Club—would lie breathless in long chairs on the tennis lawn, waiting for the arrival of the up-steamer from Shanghai that brought us mails and provisions. When the faint beat of the engines could first be distinguished far down the Kiukiang Reach, we were once more alive to the outside world that in the intervals seemed so far off and remote.

Naturally, Lovatt and the others were disappointed when the steamship company announced it was reducing the number of sailings during the summer of 1875, because the foreign community knew the captains and looked forward to their visits.[35]

Of course, there were times when Lovatt could not lounge on the Bund due to the flooding of the Yangzi that sometimes occurred in the summer, when "the water lapped over the Kiukiang Bund and we had to do our visiting over planks or in sampans." When that happened, naturally it carried with it all that had been dumped into the river: "I will be glad to see the water go down for it does not smell very pleasant." Cold winter weather also dissuaded the foreign community from lounging on the Bund, but it nonetheless remained a good place to stroll, where "many fine trees, and their branches and leaves all bedizened with frozen snow made an exquisite show for foreigners and Chinese alike." Those trees occasionally served other functions than simply as scenery:

> This morning I got up earlier than usual, and went round and got the doctor out, and we went for a walk on the bund. At one of the bund gates we found the Policemen had got a Chinaman who had been trying to hang himself [from a tree] in the night. I asked him why he wanted to hang himself. He said his wife had hung herself and he did not want to live. I told him to be good, virtuous, and happy. He looked grateful for the advice. We parted, he to the city to get bambooed [caned] for not doing the thing he undertook.[36]

There were other summer annoyances in addition to the heat and flooding—mosquitoes:

> In the numerous campaigns that I have been in against these enemies of our race, I have never seen them fight with so much vigour and determination as they have done during the last three evenings, and I have never known them to be so numerous. Last night they forced me into the musquito house, and even there, there were several gallant fellows in the citadel who received the reward for their gallantry and courage.[37]

Now alone, as he would be for much of his career in China, Lovatt had established for himself a reasonably comfortable expatriate existence as an upper-level customs officer.

MISSIONARIES AND CUSTOMS PERSONNEL

Now that his family had returned to America, Lovatt had more time to observe the missionaries in his midst, and clearly there were some he admired. His Greek teacher, Andrew Stritmatter, was "the best fellow in the [Methodist] mission, true to his word, and without humbug." Gertrude Howe, another American, took in orphans:

> Poor Miss Howe is worried to death with her babies. One has been sick a fortnight and is not expected to live, and she is pretty worn down. What a noble girl she is, sends home every dollar she can, denies herself the necessaries of life by it, and wears herself completely out in trying to benefit these callous Chinese. Such a life must leave a mark, even on the most indifferent. I have a great admiration for her.

Soon thereafter, Howe adopted a sixteen-day-old girl, "to the intense disgust of all the mission. She has named her Paulina something."[38]

Two British missionaries from the China Inland Mission earned Lovatt's particular praise. One was John McCarthy, with whom Lovatt often chatted after dinner: "He is a good natured, pleasant-tempered fellow, and I like him better than the other fellows of their mission." Also from the same mission was Charles H. Judd: "I rather like Judd. He is more of a gentleman than the others."[39]

Yet another missionary Lovatt liked, despite being "full of odd notions," was David Hill of the English Wesleyan Mission, who lived only on Chinese food and refused to spend more than 80 copper cash [nine cents] per day: "Hill thinks it has a beneficial effect on the Chinese and the native church. He undoubtedly is a good fellow." Soon thereafter, Lovatt noted that Hill

> is going back [to Hankou] in a native sanpan . . . and thinks it may be his duty to travel and preach the gospel in various places, and to do this he may have to sever his connection with the Methodist society. Of course, he would do that at once, when he feels it his duty to do so. He is a real good fellow, I like him very much, and I am sure the Chinese respect him.[40]

Lovatt also gave high marks to the Catholic missionaries in Jiujiang. Lovatt encountered a new arrival "airing himself on the Bund this morning in his Chinese clothes. They seem to be flourishing, for they have a new man every year and I imagine they are getting a great many converts." Perhaps one reason for Lovatt's admiration was that they embraced Chinese culture, as did Lovatt to a certain extent:

> There is no doubt a great deal to be said for their way of conducting mission work. The best is their thoroughly identifying themselves so thoroughly with the natives. They come to China to live and die with the people, they go right into the interior and live with them. Let the men be good or bad, conduct like this must impress even a stolid Chinaman.

But not all missionaries came in for praise.[41]

Lovatt was well aware of the shortcomings of the mission enterprise, both in general terms and in specific instances, often giving chapter and verse. One criticism he had was that most of the missionaries lived lives separate from the Chinese, unlike David Hill and the Catholic missionaries, and the apparent wealth of the missions resulted in "rice Christian" congregations: "Our missionaries are always foreigners in every sense of the word, and too often the natives try to get all they can out of them. I am convinced money in a mission is the greatest enemy." Lovatt also accused many missionaries of being lying hypocrites: "What frightful lies these people do tell. Sometimes when I think of the way religious people act, it is enough to make one hate the name of it, but still there are a few good people, but I am positively afraid that amongst missionaries it is only one in a hundred." Lovatt cited one typical example in the person of A. W. Nightingale of the Wesleyan Mission, whose sermon "all the time told the usual amount of lies."[42]

Lovatt also faulted some of the missionaries for putting on airs and failing to hold their temper. For example, while he admired Charles Judd, the same could not be said for his wife, Elizabeth, who "has a devil of a temper. Many of these very pious people have. It is perhaps well for the world that they are religious, as for very shame they can't go too far." Elizabeth Judd was attending another missionary, Mary Bowyer Baller, who was giving birth to a son, and who also came in for some scorn from Lovatt. Baller "is just like the rest of that [China Inland] mission, all affectation, and absurd. I believe they must keep a mould somewhere in England in which they cast the women who are to be their missionary wives, for Mrs. Cardwell, Mrs. Judd, and Mrs. Baller are all the same size, the same canting style, and [the same] affected manner." Her husband fared little better: "Mr. [Frederick W.] Baller called, and we had a good argument. These fellows are everything but followers of our Saviour. I don't understand how they have the impertinence to call themselves religious men."[43]

Lovatt criticized other missionaries for failing to practice simple Christian charity. When one of Lovatt's fellow military trainers in Tianjin and later customs colleague in Hankou, W. Dix, died, Lovatt sent around a subscription list on behalf of his wife and collected $132,

> nearly all subscribed by Customs people, which I am very glad of. Miss Howe gave five dollars, but none of the others gave a cent. It seems strange that the gospel should be preached, and so little of its fruits shown, by men professing it. I am disgusted, and if they ever send a subscription list round I will not give a cent except to Miss Howe.[44]

Others came under fire for laziness. Charles Hale "was never able to do much, and at his best never wanted to do anything but travel round, which looks big in print, and simply means, in his case, traveling at the expense of the mission." Another was Young J. Allen in Shanghai, "who gets a capital salary from the Chinese Government and only helps in mission work occasionally on Sundays." Allen had accused Lovatt's friend Henry Hall of faking illness, and added that if he were really sick, "a few missionary graves would do China good." This flippant remark angered both Hall and Lovatt: "I don't wonder that Hall was mad. He didn't feel like doing China good in that way, and Allen was hardly the man to speak in that way."[45]

Lovatt saw John Hykes as singularly unsuited for the Chinese mission field. Noting that he was a single man who wished to marry and go home, Lovatt wrote,

> I pity the poor girl that marries the great baby. I believe if he could marry a good strong woman that could spank him soundly, he might be improved. He is an awful lout, and the greatest coward I ever met, and for a missionary to be so awfully afraid of going to heaven by a well-directed stone from a heathen hand is something comical.[46]

The missionary who came in for the most criticism, however, was the American doctor W. E. Tarbell, who suffered from a multitude of faults, including addiction to alcohol and drugs. Originally, Lovatt had been unaware that Tarbell drank at all: "Capt. Andrews told me on my way up river that the Doctor would drink, but I said no, I thought he was a teetotaller. He laughed and said, 'no more.'" Then, "[Charles] Hale told me that Dr. Tarbell was a regular drunkard, so much so that he drank the alcohol he has in the medicine chest, that he had been drinking all the way out, and was drunk in his cabin on his arrival here, so much so that [Reverend Virgil C.] Hart had to get him out of his berth." He reminded Jennie that when the two of them had encountered Tarbell, "he was sick upstairs once or twice when we called. Well, he was just in one of his drunken fits." Tarbell carried little bottles of brandy in his pocket so that he might "refresh himself" when out: "He has been *expanded* . . . better than saying, 'on the bust,' three times since his arrival. He drank pretty near all Mrs. Mason's brandy in making diarrhea medicine." To make matters worse, "when he doesn't get spirits, he takes opium."[47]

The Methodists did their best to rehabilitate Tarbell:

> The mission have had him up before them for being drunk, insolently drunk, and prayed with him, but all to no purpose, the Doctor being able to make longer and louder prayers than any of them. Mrs. Hale says he prays the longest, asks long blessings, and appears a perfect saint, and he feels injured if he is not considered so.

Two months after that "intervention," it was clear that it was not working: "The Doctor was happy and glorious at the prayer meeting not long ago. He is always religious when tight." Since the local mission was unable to sober him up, "[Reverend] Hart has written two letters to Bishop [Isaac] Wiley and requested him to recall Dr. Tarbell." The bishop and the Mission Board, however, refused to recall him, citing the money they had invested in sending him to China in the first place: "He [Hart] received a letter from the Mission Secretaries who say that no man ever had a better fit out than Dr. Tarbell, and mention[ed] a very large sum indeed." But to hear Tarbell tell it, "the Mission treated him very shabbily in New York when it was a positive fact they treated him the very reverse." Lovatt concluded that "it is perfectly awful this way some men try to get dollars and then call themselves Christians."[48]

Tarbell also had a poor bedside manner. In one instance Lovatt recounted, "I went to tiffin and listened with all the patience I could to all Dr. Tarbell's rascalities, especially in his treatment of Mrs. Hall, and feel that he is much worse than Judas Iscariot could ever have been. There certainly is a depth of wickedness in man that is awful to contemplate." And in yet another instance, "Hart came round on Saturday night and we had a long chat. He seems very dissatisfied with Tarbell, thinks he did not attend Mrs. Hart very attentively, and altogether he feels very much put out with him."[49]

The good doctor also turned out to be a thief:

> Mrs. Hart was telling me some of Dr. Tarbell's goings on, and [Reverend] Hart was also full of Tarbell's dishonesty in taking things belonging to the Mission. It appears he has taken all the valuable musical books and instruments that Hart says was purchased by the Mission in New York for him. I am sorry Tarbell has acted in this way for it will injure him a good deal in the estimation of the Bishop and people at home.[50]

Making matters even worse, after less than a year in Jiujiang, Tarbell began plotting to get himself sent back to America early at mission expense. To do this he enlisted his wife as his coconspirator by having her pretend to be gravely ill and unable even to get out of bed, a ploy met with a healthy dose of skepticism: "Hart believes that Tarbell has planned the whole scheme, even to making Mrs. Tarbell go to bed." Lovatt also had his doubts: "It is certainly a strange affair, for I thought Mrs. Tarbell about the strongest woman here, but one hardly knows what motives are underlying actions that is only seen by outsiders like myself." Citing his wife's "illness," Tarbell took her to Japan, where she could receive better medical treatment, he returning to Jiujiang alone to continue his scam: "The *Hirado* came in last night and by her came Dr. Tarbell from Japan. He has returned to Kiukiang to obtain the sanction of the Mission to their returning home on the ground of Mrs. Tarbell's health, and of course to obtain funds for that purpose." Upon arriving, Tarbell went to see Reverend Hart to ask for the funds, and Lovatt was a witness to Hart's reaction: "I stepped into Stritmatter's room and there Hart and his wife soon joined us, and of course the conversation turned upon the Tarbells. I never saw Hart so mad. He says it was their determination to go home when they left here for Japan and I think he disbelieves the whole of Tarbell's story." Lovatt added that "when [the Tarbells] left for Japan, [Hart] thinks they had determined to never return to Kuikiang."[51]

Unfortunately for Lovatt, both sides attempted to enlist him as ally, placing him uncomfortably in the middle. On one side was the doctor, with whom Lovatt had occasionally gone duck hunting: "This afternoon Tarbell has been in my office and is feeling very much annoyed with Hart for not trying to get the money." On the other side, Tarbell's accusers bent Lovatt's ear:

> I am quite sick of hearing [the Halls] complain of Mrs. Tarbell and the Doctor. It is just about the most disagreeable thing to have to do with dissatisfied people in the world. They lack even the decency to keep their troubles to themselves, knowing that other people have their own to bear, but are constantly begging for sympathy. I am really tired of hearing them complain.

To avoid being placed in the middle, Lovatt was prepared to forego one of his singular pleasures: "[The Halls] intend to go to the Bungalow next week, and want me to go out for the day, but I don't know about it. If it is to be Saint Hall versus Sinner Tarbell all day, I doubt if I should care much about it."[52]

One would think that Tarbell would be on his best behavior upon his return to Jiujiang to convince Hart and the Mission to pay for his trip back to the United States. But Tarbell could not even manage to stay sober for the two weeks he was there:

> I was round at Mr. Hart's house yesterday afternoon, and find Hart has found Tarbell out completely. Ever since Tarbell's return he has positively been drinking like a whale or some other large fish. That is, he is drinking whiskey all the time. It does seem strange that he could not keep decent for the few days he remained here and now Hart intends to complain of him to Bishop Wiley, and I think Tarbell can hardly expect anything else.

While constant inebriation was a contributing factor, it was Mrs. Tarbell's "illness" that made the outcome a foregone conclusion. In fact, Hart had already made up his mind on the very day Tarbell returned from Japan: "Hart told me he would not be responsible for the money if the meeting decided to send him home." After Tarbell made his appeal for passage money, Lovatt revealed, "Hart does not know what to do about Tarbell. I think his idea is now to let Tarbell wait in Japan until they get money from home for him." As a result, Tarbell returned empty-handed to his wife in Japan to wait there in hopes of getting money from America. After Tarbell left the second time, Lovatt reflected on the episode: "I have heard nothing from Dr. Tarbell since he left here. I am afraid he will kill himself with drink. I think Tarbell is one of the hardest cases I have ever known." Soon thereafter, word arrived that "Tarbell had telegraphed from Yokohama [that] Mrs. Tarbell must go home. Hart and his wife believe it was all made up on their part. I don't think Mrs. Tarbell was real sick when she left here, whatever was the matter with her."[53]

The entire episode left Lovatt shaking his head: "Of course it is none of my business, but I am sorry to see my friends and acquaintances go home in the way they do. It must hurt the missionary cause very much. I certainly sympathise with Hart. I think it well for Tarbell to go home. Providence certainly never intended him for a missionary." Sarcastically, Lovatt added, "it will be comforting to the people who subscribe to know that he [Tarbell] has cost the society something like five thousand dollars for this visit to China, and a twelve month observation of this particular people." And in a further dig on missionaries, he asked rhetorically, "Did you ever drink any holy water? No? Well, it tastes just the same as any other water."[54]

Lovatt contrasted the ineffectiveness of the religious community to reform one of its members overly fond of drink with Robert Hart's more stringent Customs methods. When J. Edwards, an assistant examiner in Shanghai, got drunk and fell out of a ricksha, breaking his thumb, Lovatt related that "Edwards has got into a serious scrape. I think it will go hard with him at Peking. If he is not dismissed, he will certainly be reduced in rank and pay, and that will at once take away the twenty five taels rent allowance. It would serve him right to turn him out, the good for nothing fellow." When Edwards was, in fact, later suspended from duty, Lovatt wrote,

> I am very sorry for his family, but he cannot have expected anything else. He has been warned repeatedly in Shanghai. I should not be surprised if the Inspector General reduces him to second or third class Tidewaiter, and sends him on probation to another port. It will be a very serious loss to them from Taels 115 per month to fifty or sixty, and I doubt if he is ever likely to attain his old position in the service.[55]

In desperation, Edwards decided to head north to plead his case in person:

> Yesterday I had Capt. Lisdale of the *Leepun*(?) to breakfast and he told me that he took Mr. Edwards to Tientsin to see the Inspector General, but Mr. Hart would not see him, and sent him word that the only way he could take his case into consideration would be through the Commissioner of Customs [Drew] writing on his behalf, so Edwards has returned to Shanghai. It is truly very sad to think of the misery he has brought on himself and family through his drinking habits.

Apparently, Drew intervened on Edwards' behalf:

> I received a letter from [illegible] yesterday in which he tells me Mr. Hart has restored Mr. Edwards to his former position in the service, but to be placed at the bottom of the list of his rank. This is a most fortunate thing for him, and should he get into any more scrapes, it is to be hoped he will take it into his head

to leave for the happy hunting grounds, where beer, brandy, and soda spring from fountains or run past in streams.

And the Shanghai customs was not the only post where this occurred, as a similar situation arose in Jiujiang.[56]

One of Lovatt's subordinates also had a drinking problem: "I think [W.] Brandon will not be long here. I have had him up [on report] twice. He is a regular New York rowdy and sly tippler, takes brandy as if it was his mamma's mild, and worse than all, he is a lazy useless fellow." Sure enough, within a month, Brandon was "glorious" on one of the steamers, and Commissioner Kopsch wanted to report him to Hart, which would have almost certainly led to his demotion, as Edwards in Shanghai experienced, or even dismissal. Knowing he was in trouble, Brandon asked Lovatt to intervene on his behalf:

Kopsch was much opposed to letting him off, but I urged very strongly to give him one more chance and he did. I told Brandon when he wanted to get beastly drunk to come to me, and I would be most happy to give him a day's leave, and then he could drink by the bucket. He promised to keep all right. I hope he will.

With a self-satisfied tone, he concluded: "Now look at my efforts to reform a man. I can just do the proper thing. In the Customs we manage things better than missionaries." At the same time, he feared his method might not work even for Brandon: "I believe my pupil in learning sober ways has not been right for over three days to brandy." In fact, Lovatt's prediction that Brandon would probably get into trouble again soon came true: "Brandon came in to tell me his troubles. It appears when in Shanghai and hard up, he gave his note of hand for $140 in payment of his expenses and now Adams has got hold of it cheap and is putting the screw on him."[57]

Like Tarbell, Brandon was unable to resist the blandishments of alcohol, despite Lovatt's best efforts:

On going into the Customs Office Mr. Sayle told me W. Brandon had drank not wisely but deeply, and was positively incapable of performing his duties. I called to see him, and found it but too true. He had worshipped but too devoutly at the shrine of Bacchus, consequently his interview with the [new] Commissioner [Moorhead] will not be of the most pleasing kind. After seeing him, I told him to . . . take his rest. . . . I am truly very sorry for Brandon. I like him very much, but I can see nothing for men of his stamp but total abstinence. It is a choice of two evils, whiskey or ice water, and I think he had better select the latter. I hope he will turn over a new leaf and behave himself . . . Yesterday, I saw Mr. Moorhead and found he would settle Brandon's affair by fining him and making him promise to keep sober in future, and as this is Brandon's second offense, I think he must be satisfied to get off in that manner.[58]

Lovatt was able to delve deeply into the local scene involving missionaries and customs personnel. At the same time, he was well aware that international events could bring serious repercussions that might impinge on his career and even his life in China. Just as China and France appeared to be on the brink of war five years earlier over the Tianjin Massacre, now China and Britain appeared to be moving toward a war that could potentially affect Lovatt and every foreigner in Jiujiang.

THE MARGARY INCIDENT, 1875–1877

Augustus Raymond Margary, a twenty-eight-year-old member of the British consular service, was murdered in Yunnan Province on February 21, 1875, near the border with Burma. He had been traveling with the explicit permission of the Zongli Yamen on an official mission to open a trade route to Burma, and had passed through Jiujiang. Although it was unclear who had committed the murder, responsibility for the matter fell to the provincial governor. Thomas Wade demanded a full investigation, punishment of those responsible, compensation for Margary's family, and the opening of a trade route through western China to Burma and India. But the Chinese government temporized, prompting Wade to contemplate the withdrawal of the British embassy, a sure sign of hostilities. Rumors to that effect soon reached Lovatt's ears: "It is true that Mr. Wade intends to haul his flag down on the 28th of September if his demands are not complied with, the Persian Minister says he will do the same, so also, I think, will the French. You know the latter still owe the Chinese something for that Tientsin massacre."[59]

Determining the accuracy of the rumors was not easy. Newspapers and mail from other parts of China arrived days or weeks late on the river steamers, and the rumors carried by their crews were not always reliable, resulting in a situation where "things appear to be in a strange unsettled state here in China. No one appears to know what may turn up at any moment." One rumor that circulated in Jiujiang, for example, fixed the blame for Margary's murder on the King of Burma, "who is afraid of losing more territory to the British and wants to prevent the opening of a trade route to China. The King was acting in concert with Chinese authorities who have promised to help him in case of a war with England." Another rumor was that

> the Governor of Yunnan has removed every official who was likely to be mixed up in the Margary case to distant parts of his province. And that on the arrival of the [investigating commission], the Governor would have all the criminals of the province there, whom he was going to behead anyways, and make the commission believe that these were the men who killed poor Margary.[60]

Lovatt downplayed reports of an imminent conflagration:

> With all such warlike rumours, it is all smoke. The Chinese will give in. They have everything to lose and nothing to gain. Think of all their fine new steamers seized and their arsenals reduced to ashes within three days after the declaration of war by the British fleet. The Chinese will argue as long as they can and will then give in. I feel sure peace will predominate.

And that was the outcome he preferred: "I should like peace, if it would benefit China. I should be sorry to see war, for it will leave a bad feeling, and that feeling will grow. It is not pleasant to think of so many millions of people hating us."[61]

In fact, rumors alleging Western assaults on Chinese children and the cutting off of *bianzi* (queues) were circulating, creating fear among the Westerners: "Miss Combs says in a letter to Mr. Stritmatter that the foreigners always go about armed in Pekin, and that a lady dare not go out alone." But Lovatt concluded that these reports of antiforeign activity are "not worth much. It is rumour, and nothing more." Moreover, the sheer volume tended to cancel them out: "There are any number of rumours which find their way even to Kiukiang. I should think anyone of a highly nervous temperament living in the interior cities of China would be feeling very unhappy at the many rumours that are spread about, but perhaps their number and conflicting statements may have the effect of rendering them harmless."[62]

Knowing that his wife back in Minnesota must be worried, he reminded her that God had protected him in battle, and that the foreign community had several layers of protection if the rumors turned out to be true. For one thing, the number of gunboats in the area had been increased to three, including the *Mosquito* and the *Swinger*. In addition to gunboats, were "the fine steamers going daily and gayly down the river, with plenty of good bottled beer, stout, claret, champagne, and all that is good for the soul of man, and to fill him with courage (Dutch), and make him valiant, as we advance down the river in safety to the place of security—Shanghai." Lovatt concluded, "let not your heart be troubled." Lovatt admitted, however, that "I suppose when everything is settled, we shall fall back on the usual number [of gunboats]."[63]

After reassuring his wife that he was safe, that the rumors were overblown, and that he desired a peaceful outcome, it was clear that Lovatt was of two minds regarding another Sino-Western conflict. He was skeptical the Chinese would cooperate with Wade's demand for an inquiry into Margary's murder, cynically remarking that "the Chinese are supposed to send a commission of high officials along with British officials as an official inquiry to the Margary murder, but the Chinese officials 'immediately fell sick,' so the mission has not gone." While Lovatt was confident that the Chinese "can't hoodwink Mr.

Wade [who] I hope will put the Chinese through [the ringer] this time," he feared that Wade might not be aggressive enough. The British minister "is a good old fellow, only a little too much in favor of the Chinese." And the fact that the Chinese government was stonewalling led him to conclude that "things are certainly in a critical state in China. The British fleet is being collected at Nagasaki, so that a telegram would reach them at once from Shanghai."[64]

Despite what he had first written about his desire for a peaceful outcome, Lovatt now hoped and expected that the British fleet would be ordered into action. Several factors guided his thoughts, first and foremost being Britain's imperial responsibility: "We must fulfill our destiny. War is the only real thing that will make the Chinese officials move, and would be an undoubted good to the country to bring this conceited nation to their senses." He added that it would be "a good thing for China if England will only pound a little sense into her." A war would be "a blessing to ignorant, vain oriental nations, and in it is the only hope of breaking down within a reasonable time the blind prejudices of the Chinese, so that out of great evil may arise great good." If England failed to act decisively, "the Chinese will remain rooted in their prejudices, and Great Britain will, I am afraid, look back like some fond parent on the erring child he has forgiven, when he ought to have punished, and feel if I had only done my duty on that occasion I should not have troubles now." And it was certainly better to have England take the lead, otherwise China "may fall into the hands of Russia, France, or any other nation who will not deal with them in that motherly way England would, and they will learn the difference between the birch-rod of England and the knout of Russia." Indeed, the Chinese should be grateful to England, since "the Taipings were stamped out for them" by him and Charles Gordon. Clearly, Lovatt's regard for the people of China did not extend to China's high officials, who he viewed with disdain.[65]

Second, China had never fully adhered to the treaties signed after the Opium Wars. This worked to the detriment of British trade: "They have said that 'we don't like you, we would like to limit you to the coast, and only then allow you to put cargo into Chinese junks, and prevent you all from landing on Chinese soil.' I hope the present imbroglio will not be allowed to drop without achieving some good in the way of opening up trade." Moreover, a conflict would force the Chinese to adhere to Western concepts of diplomatic relations: "A war with England would [make] the Chinese feel, to be safe and happy, they must form one of the happy family of nations in sincerity."[66]

Finally, a war would enjoy widespread support among the foreign nationals in China: "all classes of foreigners in China would hail a declaration of war, with that stern pleasure that one is apt to feel in the performance of a very disagreeable duty." Moreover, "the missionaries to a man look to a war with that silent joy religious people often feel, for the Chinese government has placed every obstacle in their way."[67]

Lovatt's militaristic tone may have stemmed in part from the legacy of Admiral Lord Nelson, after whom he was named: "My distinguished ancestors [have produced] numerous warlike sons [whose] deeds of valour were unfortunately not always encompassed by peaceful means." Referring to his own career in the Royal Artillery, he reflected that "I also felt the same impulse [as] the true spirit of my heroic ancestors." He also hoped that his son John would follow a military career and "continue the same interest with unflagging zeal until the last of the Lovatts shall stand on some mountain peak and, in the words of Campbell's last man, hurl defiance at the sun."[68]

Given these pro-war sentiments, Lovatt was pleased when conflict appeared imminent: "I felt very bad until I read the newspapers and saw that there was every prospect of a fight. It put me in better humour." When it later appeared that hostilities might be averted, he was disappointed: "The Str. *Shanghai* was up early yesterday and I see by the paper [that] unfortunately there is not likely to be any truth in [rumors of war]." Subsequent steamers visits confirmed that peace had gained the upper hand: "The up steamer last night brought word that the rumours about war being declared is all nonsense. So the good time [war] is still to come." Finally, when by October the affair had been settled, he groused that "there is going to be no row after all. I and everybody else who take any interest in [China] must feel convinced that a great opportunity has been allowed to pass by England." Wade, who was "satisfied" with the assurances of the Chinese government, "has failed to do [England's] duty." Still, Lovatt recognized that his wife would be relieved: "I think you may feel easy about there being no prospect of a fight. All is quiet at Peking—and bad luck to all—there will be no chance of thrashing the Chinese—they have conceded everything." In September 1876, the Chefoo Convention was concluded in which the Chinese government paid an indemnity of 200,000 taels to the Margary family, dispatched an apology mission to England, and agreed to open more treaty ports.[69]

As the threat of war receded, Lovatt turned inward to reflect on his own physical and social attributes in a letter to his wife. Only thirty-eight years old, he complained that his hair was turning prematurely gray, which he blamed half-jokingly on "a peculiar climate and my early marriage." Even the local Chinese thought he was older than he really was:

> I came to the village [and] while there the Chinese gathered round, a very good humoured crowd, and began to inspect me. First, they put me down at sixty years of age, so you see that your absence is having a very terrible effect on me, and making me very old looking. In fact, my hair will not be gray when I come home, but positively white.

Physically, while he weighed in at 211 pounds, he assured his wife that he carried his weight "without any prominence, which I attribute to the vast amount of hard walking I do. I feel like iron." And he still seemed to enjoy his Chinese surroundings: "They [the villagers] came to the conclusion that I was a pretty good fellow, [and] spoke their language like a native, [due to] my long residence with them."[70]

Lovatt also turned his attention to his own future in the Customs. Fall was normally when transfers and promotions were announced, and Lovatt thought it possible he might be in line for one in the fall of 1875: "I think it is just possible I may get a change this October. Mr. Hart may transfer me to some other port, tho I would much prefer an increase and remain here. I like Kiu-kiang, and somehow feel I should not like to leave it, for . . . there is positively a vast amount of comfort." If he were transferred, one posting he would not mind was Tianjin, where he had trained Chinese troops ten years earlier: "Mr. Reeks returned from Tientsin, and by his report, and the many kind messages he brought me, I don't seem to be forgotten." But Lovatt was not promoted or transferred, so he pinned his hopes on a raise: "I have heard that Mr. Hart has been allowed an extra 350,000 [pounds] to work the Customs, so perhaps in the Spring . . . Bob may give a general increase of pay—I hope so." But Lovatt did not get a raise either, so his third option was to apply for a leave: "I must see by the departures of others what my chances are. Perhaps Robert Hart will do something yet. I don't despair. You know I draw from *Hope* like from a bank." But his application for a leave was not granted either, so he settled in for yet another year in Jiujiang.[71]

The winter of 1876–1877 saw "plenty of snow on the ground, about four inches, the thermometer standing at the freezing point in the shade, but thawing in the road." As he wrote to his wife, "There is this difference, however. You have fine, bright, clear days [in Minnesota] whereas we have dull, gloomy skies, with soft slushy snow." Lovatt made the best of the holiday season, visiting a temple and spending Christmas at the Poyang Lake customs bungalow. But before the winter had run its course, Lovatt learned at the end of January 1877 that, after nearly seven years in Jiujiang, he had been transferred to Wuhu.[72]

NOTES

1. *Milwaukee Journal*, June 17, 1942. WNL to JSL, September 23, 1880.

2. *Milwaukee Journal*, June 17, 1942. There are some inaccuracies due to the passage of time, making it unclear if Effie Gray is the correct name, as I cannot find any record of a missionary with that name. The article continued: "Effie's first letter home told of this attack; of waiting for a pilot to take them upriver to Canton; and

of the teeming boat life on the Pearl River. She made vivid her horror at seeing dead Chinese girl babies floating on the tide. Effie Gray was warmly welcomed by the missionaries and soon became settled in her work."

3. WNL to Dear Folks at Home, July 16 and 20, 1866. Lovatt would himself die of sunstroke.

4. WNL to Dear Folks at Home, July 16 and 20, 1866. James Legge (1815–1897) first went to Hong Kong in 1844, spent thirty years there, and is noted for translations of several of the Chinese classics. Warren returned to England in 1867.

5. *Milwaukee Journal*, June 17, 1942; WNL to Dear Folks at Home, July 16 and 20, 1866; *WNL Journal*, October 6, 1867 and February 2, 1868; Michael Lovatt (Lovatt's grandson) to the Author, July 3, 1999, based on recollections of conversations with his father, William Harold Lovatt. Lovatt appreciated Chinese handicrafts: "Some of the Chinese curiosities are very pretty. I bought a paper knife which had a beautifully carved handle and because I could get it for a quarter. The carving is exquisitely done."

6. Joseph Shaw was born in Ithaca in 1818 and in 1847 married Jane Ann Mitchell, born in 1826 in Lisle. In 1865, Lakeland had 386 residents, 189 men and 197 women. 1865 Census. *Minnesota State Census Records: Washington County*, Roll 17; Joseph Shaw to Jane Ann Shaw, May 16, 1857, in the *Joseph Shaw Papers, 1857–1889*, Minnesota State Historical Society Research Center, Folder P710; Willard E. Rosenfelt, ed., *Washington: A History of the Minnesota County: Fifty-Six Vignettes of the Past* (Stillwater: The Croixside Press, 1977), 315; Edward D. Neill, *History of Washington County and the St. Croix Valley* (Minneapolis: North Star Publishing Company, 1881), 423; *Minnesota Genealogist*, 12 (1), 15.

7. *Milwaukee Journal*, June 17, 1942; WNL to JSL, October 17, 1876; Mitchell Y. Jackson, Register of Deeds, Washington County, Stillwater, MN, to William Nelson Lovatt, March 26, 1869; *Washington County Marriage Records*, Record A500, 49; *Minnesota Genealogical Journal*, 6, 593. Although the service was conducted by a Presbyterian minister, the Shaws were Methodists. When Lovatt met their friends, he disapprovingly noted that among those was a Mr. Hamilton, "who drank, not wisely, but deeply." Another was a Mr. Staples, a "son of Bacchus," who "still worships at the jolly god's shrine."

8. WNL to Mother, April 1, 1869; Jennie Shaw Lovatt to Mother, July 4, 7, and 9, 1869; *Milwaukee Journal*, June 17, 1942. Lovatt's trip to England with his new bride would be the last time he would see his father, who passed away two years later in 1871. The February 1, 1870, bill from the Occidental Hotel in San Francisco was for $75.25 for seven nights at nine dollars per day, one day at six dollars, a baggage charge of $1.25, coach at $2, bath at 50 cents, and wine at $2.50.

9. "Nellie" to "Grandma" Shaw, July 7, 1870; Jennie Shaw Lovatt to Mother and Father, July 17, 1870; WNL to JSL, June 5 and September 14, 1877, and January 20 and May 30, 1880; Elijah Burghardt Woodworth, *Descendants of William Woodworth of Scituate, Mass* (Boston: Elijah B. Woodworth, 1901), 37–38. Upon her arrival, Jennie reportedly kept a diary entitled *Far East Journal*, but this has not been located. Lovatt had originally planned to take Jennie 137 miles upstream so she could give birth in Hankou where there was a larger foreign community, and where Lovatt

had previously been posted, but Nellie was born prematurely, so Mrs. Cardwell in Jiujiang made the delivery.

10. Hart *Journal*, July 20, 1865; Fairbank, Smith, and Bruner, 222–223; Hart to Drew, January 19, 1869, in Hart *Letters*, Houghton Library, Harvard University, bMS Chinese 4; William Mesny, *Mesny's Chinese Miscellany*, Vol. One, 463.

11. *The China Directory for 1874* (Hong Kong: China Mail, 1874; Reprinted Taipei: Ch'eng-Wen Publishing Company, 1971); Hart to Drew, January 19, 1869, in Hart *Letters*; Rosalie Möllendorff, *P. G. von Möllendorff: Ein Lebensbild* (Leipzig: Otto Harrassowitz, 1930), 22. Below Lovatt in the thirteen-member Jiujiang customs office were three examiners—J. C. Porter, C. F. Moore, and G. Ballantine—and six tidewaiters—W. G. Harrison, A. Wilgaard, R. Brown, A. Castro, G. Swainson, and A. J. Reeks. After graduating from Harvard in 1864, Drew joined the Customs Service in 1865, and in 1869 was appointed to Jiujiang at a salary of 300 *taels* per month.

12. Alfred J. Broomhall, *Hudson Taylor and China's Open Century. Book Five: Refiner's Fire* (London: Hodder and Stoughton and the Overseas Missionary Fellowship, 1985), Appendix Five, 452; WNL to JSL, August 22, 1875; *The China Directory for 1874.*

13. Hart to Campbell, July 1 and September 1, 1870; Hart to Drew, September 28, 1870.

14. Jennie Shaw Lovatt to Mother, August 6, 1870; Hart to Campbell, October 4, 1870; *North China Herald*, November 29, 1871, 911.

15. Broomhall, *Book Five*, 425–426.

16. Hart to Campbell, August 29, 1874; Hart to Campbell (telegrams), September 1 and October 19, 1874. *Archives of China's Imperial Maritime Customs*. Emphasis in the original. Campbell (1833–1907) was the director of the Custom's Service London Office. Saigō Tsugumichi was the younger brother of Saigō Takamori.

17. Hart to Campbell, August 29, 1874; *The China Directory for 1874.*

18. Kopsch to Lovatt, August 19, 1874; Hart to Campbell, September 30 and October 2, 1874; Hart to Campbell (telegram), October 19, 1874. Kopsch initially gave Lovatt his instructions orally and only later in writing in a letter that he did not receive until September 27 when he was already in Taiwan.

19. British vice-consul Walter Edward King to Lovatt, August 20, 1874.

20. *Archives of China's Imperial Maritime Customs*, Hart to Campbell, August 29, 1874, note 6; Hart to Campbell, September 11, 1874. Emphasis in the original.

21. Unidentified to Lovatt, February 10, 1875; WNL to JSL, March 23, May 22, and August 16, 1876, October 6, 1877, and December 18, 1890; William Gregory's "official record" of Japanese expedition, part 4, included in Gregory's September 11, 1874, dispatch to Wade, in Robert L. Jarman, ed., *Taiwan: Political and Economic Reports, 1861–1960*. Volume One (Slough: Archive Editions, 1997), 490. The same report said that "Monsieur Berthault, civil engineer, three or four other Frenchmen, including one Mr. Dubois, to instruct troops; – Mr. Segonzae still here; Mr. [Prosper] Giquel still absent." The other two treaty ports on Taiwan were Tamsuy and Keelung. I am indebted to Douglas Fix for alerting me to this source.

22. Unidentified to Lovatt, February 10, 1875; WNL to JSL, March 23, May 22, and August 16, 1876, and May 8, 1880. See also Robert Eskildsen, "Of Civilization

and Savages: The Memetic Imperialism of Japan's 1874 Expedition to Taiwan." *American Historical Review*, April 2002, 397–398.

23. WNL to JSL, July 19 and December 30, 1875, March 19, 1876, and February 6, 1878. The *North China Herald* of July 10, 1875, 29, identifies the ship as the *Nevada*. Because she was traveling without her husband, the captain promised to arrange for someone on board to help her with child care.

Dr. Tanner's story concludes:

> Many women of China were oppressed, including the high born lady with her deformed feet [from whom Jennie got the red shoe] as well as the little girls of the mission school, many of whom had been rescued from the fate of drowning of unwanted girl babies. As the small shoes had never ceased to be a marvel to Jennie, she brought home a pair because they told so much. Your mother went with me when I treated Ida many times. Jennie gave her the little red satin shoe. Sixty years have passed since my father told me this story. I still have the tiny red satin shoe, but because it has become fragile, I have put it away with other treasures. It is a far cry from the high born ladies hobbling about on deformed feet and the unwanted girl babies of old China to Mme. Chiang Kai-shek, exponent of the new China and wife of the Chinese leader. *Milwaukee Journal*, June 17, 1942

Jennie's father, now fifty-seven, had purchased twenty-five additional acres, making him one of the largest landowners in Lakeland. Of that land, he allotted eleven acres to his son John, who was now eighteen, and two and a half acres to Lovatt and Jennie, should they decide to return. Jennie's mother was now forty-eight, her youngest sister Bessie was twelve, and her other sister Jessie was twenty-three. Jessie was in poor health but went ahead with her marriage to Clinton Fiske in January 1876 and died six days later. *Plat Book of Washington County, Minnesota* (Minneapolis: Northwest Publishing Company, 1901), 26; *Minnesota State Census Records: Washington County, 1895*, Roll 103; Woodworth, *Descendants of William Woodworth of Scituate, Mass.*

24. WNL to JSL, July 19, 22, 23, 26, and 27, August 7 and 25, September 30, and October 5, 1875. Emphasis in the original. The jinricksha had just recently been invented in Japan.

25. WNL to JSL, August 1 and 15, October 14, and November 22, 1875, and July 24, 1876.

26. WNL to JSL, August 1, 1875, and July 7 and August 19, 1876; King, 22, 29, 50–51. King arrived in Jiujiang as Senior Assistant in December of 1878, and departed eight months later in September 1879 for Yantai. Lovatt had departed in 1877. King returned to Jiujiang from September 1885 to February 1887. A punkah was a fan consisting of a canvas-covered frame suspended from the ceiling and operated by a cord.

Lovatt's "boy" was actually a grown man with a fixed salary, and the term "boy" was the common, condescending term used for a Chinese servant by Westerners in China at the time.

27. WNL to JSL, November 22, 1875, and March 21 and 24, April 13, and July 3, 1876, and May 13 and June 18, 1877.

28. King, 22 and 29; WNL to JSL, July 24, 1876 and August 19, n.d.

29. WNL to JSL, August 1, 6, 9, 10, 15, and 25, and October 5, 10, 20, and 24, 1875, June 9, July 1, August 9, and October 11, 1876. Emphasis in the original.

30. WNL to JSL, August 25, 1875; King, 22, 32–33; Susan Tropeano [Mrs. John N. Lovatt] of Danvers, Massachusetts, to the Author, June 10, 1999. The inaugural meeting of the literary society, at which they read *The Tempest*, took place at the Lovatts' house on January 10th, 1873, and present, in addition to the Lovatts, were the three missionaries Lucy H. Hoag, Gertrude Howe, and Virgil C. Hart. They later decided to include Rev. and Mrs. J. E. Cardwell, Rev. Henry H. Hall, and Paul Georg Von Möllendorff.

31. WNL to JSL, July 1, 1876; King, 33, 49.

32. WNL to JSL, October 15 and September 26, 1876.

33. WNL to JSL, March 22 and April 2, 1876. Emphasis in the original.

34. WNL to JSL, May 22, 1876.

35. WNL to JSL, August 10, 1876.

36. WNL to JSL, August 8 and 9, 1875, and May 1, 1876; King, 49.

37. WNL to JSL, August 16, 1876.

38. WNL to JSL, August 7, 1875 and September 23, 1876. Gertrude Howe adopted several Chinese girls, two of whom deserve mention. One was Kang Cheng (Ida Kahn, died 1931) and the other was Shi Meiyu (Mary Stone, died 1954). Adopting these two girls prevented her from taking the usual furloughs in the 1880s. They were brought to the United States by Howe who enrolled them at the University of Michigan in the 1890s where they trained as Christian missionary physicians, following a plan that Howe and Shi Ceyu (Shi Meiyu's Christian pastor father) had formulated to educate and liberate the girls, involve them in humanitarian service, and challenge American and Chinese racial prejudices along the way. They worked as doctors and as Methodist missionaries with the Women's Foreign Mission Society (WFMS). After the Boxer Rebellion, Kang, Shi, and Howe returned to China. Shi opened a mission hospital and nursing school in Jiujians, training young Chinese women for medical careers. In the 1920s, Shi left the mission hospital because the WFMS continued to discriminate against Chinese Christian "native workers" in pay and reserved leadership positions for Western missionaries. But in the Chinese-run Bethel Mission that Shi founded and operated until the Sino-Japanese War began in 1937, Shi maintained her belief that Christianity could "save" China.

Kang Cheng worked in Nanchang after she returned to China where she opened a dispensary and hospital for Chinese women. Kang promoted Christianity among her patients and students and pushed to overcome local resistance to Western medicine by cultivating the moral and financial support of Nanchang's gentry, but, when necessary, she returned to the United States to fundraise. After the 1911 Revolution, she published a popular short story that gained Liang Qichao's praise, "An Amazon in Cathay," promoting her view that women should serve the nation through medical and service professions rather than fighting alongside men on the revolutionary frontlines. See Jane Hunter, *The Gospel of Gentility: American Women Missionaries in Turn-of-the-Century China* (New Haven: Yale University Press, 1989), and Connie A. Shemo, *The Chinese Medical Ministries of Kang Cheng and Shi Meiyu, 1872–1937: On a Cross-Cultural Frontier of Gender, Race, and Nation* (Bethlehem: Lehigh University Press, 2011).

39. WNL to JSL, August 31 and October 24, 1875.

40. WNL to JSL, March 21 and June 13, 1876.

41. WNL to JSL, September 15, 1876. Although their order was not identified by Lovatt, more than likely they were Jesuits.

42. WNL to JSL, September 28, 1875, and September 11 and 15, 1876.

43. WNL to JSL, August 22 and 25, and October 1 and 17, 1875.

44. WNL to JSL, August 7, 1875.

45. WNL to JSL, July 1 and October 15, 1876. Lovatt learned of Allen's comment second hand from Rev. Virgil C. Hart.

46. WNL to JSL, November 11 and December 31, 1875, and June 23, 1876.

47. WNL to JSL, August 4, 1875. Emphasis in the original.

48. WNL to JSL, August 4 and September 27, 1875, and July 3, 1876. Issac William Wiley first came to China as a medical missionary (1850–1854), and later became a bishop in the Methodist Episcopal Church.

49. WNL to JSL, August 28, 1875 and July 3, 1876. Henry H. Hall and his wife had been in Jiujiang since 1870.

50. WNL to JSL, July 27, 1876.

51. WNL to JSL, July 19 and 24, 1876.

52. WNL to JSL, August 30, October 1, and December 26, 1875, and July 19, 1876.

53. WNL to JSL, July 19 and 24, and August 6, 13, and 16, 1876.

54. WNL to JSL, August 30, October 1, and December 26, 1875, and July 19, 1876.

55. WNL to JSL, August 29, 1875 and March 14, 1876.

56. WNL to JSL, May 31 and June 23, 1876.

57. WNL to JSL, August 29, September 27, and October 1, 1875, and August 9, 1876.

58. WNL to JSL, October 2, 1876.

59. WNL to JSL, October 3, 1875.

60. WNL to JSL, August 15 and 23, 1875; Broomhall, *Book Five*, 431–439.

61. WNL to JSL, August 23 and 28, 1875.

62. Alfred J. Broomhall, *Hudson Taylor and China's Open Century. Book Six: Assault on the Nine* (London: Hodder and Stoughton and the Overseas Missionary Fellowship, 1988), 27; WNL to JSL, August 23 and 28, 1875. Lovatt contributed a piece on antiforeignism in Jiujiang to a newspaper: "Hykes told me that letter I wrote to the [*Shanghai Courier and China Gazette(?)*] about the destruction of the Mission Chapel has been copied into their church papers." I have been unable to locate that letter.

63. WNL to JSL, August 29 and October 2, 1875.

64. WNL to JSL, August 28 and 29, 1875. The cable to Shanghai had been laid in 1870.

65. WNL to JSL, August 23 and 28, September 3 and 29, and October 6, 1875.

66. *Ibid.*

67. *Ibid.*

68. WNL to JSL, August 2, 1876. Later, Lovatt would contemplate sending his son John to West Point.

69. WNL to JSL, August 31, September 3, 28, and 29, and October 5, 6, 7, and 20, 1875. Immanuel Hsu, *China's Entrance into the Family of Nations: The Diplomatic Phase, 1858–1880*. (Cambridge: Harvard University Press, 1960), 176–179.

70. WNL to JSL, August 10 and October 1, 1875, and January 6 and September 19, 1876.

71. Wright, *Hart and the Chinese Customs*, appendix; WNL to JSL, July 27, August 28, October 5, and December 30, 1875, and October 3, 1877. In 1875, Britain controlled two-thirds of China's foreign trade, and British subjects made up a similar proportion of the customs service. Of the 121 foreigners in the customs service, 71 were British, followed in order by French, Americans, and then Germans, in addition to the approximately 1,000 Chinese employees. The number of foreign employees would increase to 480 in 1885 and to 750 in 1895.

72. WNL to JSL, January 28, 1877.

Chapter 6

A Year in Wuhu, 1877–1878

ESTABLISHING A NEW CUSTOMS STATION

Lovatt arrived at his new posting in Wuhu in Anhui Province, 200 miles east of Jiujiang down the Yangzi River, in "frightful weather a la Minnesota—snow, wind, and rain continually" on February 22, 1877. Upon his arrival, he reported to his new commissioner, F. E. Woodruff, whom he had met briefly in 1870 when they had been passengers together on the *Plymouth Rock*. Woodruff, a Yale University graduate from New Jersey, was, according to Lovatt, "warm-hearted" and "an exceedingly nice man" who "at once" invited him to dinner, placed his houseboat at Lovatt's disposal, and joined him in pheasant hunting.[1]

Despite finding Wuhu much colder than Jiujiang, Lovatt's initial impression was favorable, in part because he saw it becoming "a very important port," trading in wood, rice, and tea. Living temporarily in the commissioner's houseboat, Lovatt walked to the west gate of the city wall, along "one of the finest Chinese streets I have seen in China, about two miles long, with very wealthy firms in it." Inside the walls, he found Wuhu's main street to be "much larger and the shops better [than in Jiujiang]. There is a great deal more of the active bustle of life and a much larger business." Exiting through the east gate, he found "one of the richest [rice] plains in China." He was also impressed with the people, who appeared "strong and healthy looking, besides being very civil. Whenever we go into the main street we are followed everywhere by a lot of people [who] are quiet [and] not an unfriendly word [was] uttered, except [by] a few rude little boys. The people here appear to like foreigners to come, which will make it very pleasant."[2]

Since Wuhu was about to be opened in about a month (April 1877) as a treaty port, it lacked infrastructure. For one, there was no customs house, so Woodruff and Lovatt began surveying potential sites not only for that but also for customs residences. And regular steamer service was not scheduled to begin for another two months. With little to do until the customs opened, he and Woodruff walked almost every afternoon for three hours. Lovatt did not complain about the lack of infrastructure because

> taking all things into consideration and rough and all as it is, I would sooner have it if it will finally lead to promotion. Mr. Woodruff told me the Inspector General fully intended it as a compliment in selecting me for the opening of a new port, and thinks that after it is established and in good working order we would both be removed to a better and higher port. I have always been willing to give up ease or comfort for the chance of honor or promotion, and I feel happy to think that my present efforts may yet put me in a position to bring with it the increase of pay.[3]

Gradually the infrastructure took shape: "We are getting on fast with our buildings and will have all the alterations made by the end of this month, when I hope to have my staff and be a little more lively." A temporary customs house had been established on the riverbank as well as "a few thatched cottages for boatsmen and Chinese weighers and where I may have an office for myself." Lovatt's housing situation also improved from the houseboat, to a room "which is cold but anyway better than living in the boat," and then to a house. In that respect, Lovatt felt himself to be much better off than those who had been assigned to the newly opened treaty port of Yichang upriver, where "their whole staff will have to live in boats for a year, as they cannot get anything of a house to live in. We are a thousand times better off here, and are on the whole pretty comfortable."[4]

Just as the Customs infrastructure was being established, the transformation of Wuhu into a full-fledged treaty port continued apace. The first ship, the *George Washington*, a steamer belonging to Russell and Company's Shanghai Steam Navigation Company, an American firm, had arrived, as had the British gunboat *Frolic*. Officials such as the *daotai* from Nanking took up residence, and the American and British consuls were expected shortly. Lovatt decided to have a look at the "palatial residence" selected for the British consulate,

> built by a high Mandarin for a maiden sister. The houses or detached rooms of which it is composed are small—badly lighted and stuffy looking places—but the garden is just splendid, a fine large rockery and ornamental pond with gold fish in it, besides a very handsome and ornamental pagoda, also two nice summer houses with suitable tables, and chairs. There is in addition a large kitchen garden and several courtyards.[5]

Lovatt also made his new residence comfortable. His furniture and books had arrived from Jiujiang, allowing him to set up a sitting room, and his garden began to produce radishes, lettuce, cabbage, cauliflower, tomatoes, onions, and "quite a lot of flowers." Moreover, "my old friend Goldspink" sent him beef, cabbage, and cheese, with his meals prepared by a cook, who makes "pretty good" bread, and who had a penchant for getting into trouble: "My cook got into a row with some Chinese in buying a catty of lard, so I have told him I will *discharge him on the spot* if he gets into anymore rows." For companionship, his cat Tim "is very fond of me and always wants me to play with him. I don't care much about cats, but this one lays before the fire and is always pleased to see me, so that we are very good friends."[6]

After three months in his new posting, Lovatt had settled into a routine. Every morning he gathered his tidewaiters to go over the "easy" day's work of inspecting cargo, clearing customs, and filling out the necessary paperwork. When not working, "the sport [hunting snipe, which was then prepared by his cook] is good." Other sports included "lawn tennis every evening" and "shuttle-cock during the holiday, quoits, and tossing up the cricketball," made all the more enjoyable because "I don't think Wuhu is near so hot as Kiukiang."[7]

Additional customs staff also began arriving, not all of whom were to Lovatt's liking. One slated to arrive was his former assistant in Jiujiang, W. J. Sayle, the examiner Lovatt described as "a positively stupid bad tempered old fellow" with whom he had "put up for so long without complaining." Saying that "I am determined not to have him here if I can help it," Lovatt persuaded Woodruff to write Hart to cancel the appointment, as "it will be doing him a favor at the same time, altho he would not see it." Despite his efforts, Sayle and his wife arrived in April, and she was little better than her husband—a constant complainer about her housing, when Lovatt felt she had no reason to complain:

> I never was with such a grumbling lot. Mrs. Sayle is worse than anybody. I never meet or see her but she at once commences abusing the house and the place. They have a double portion of the house, the house is well covered with mats, and is very cool on a hot day, and this summer we have hardly any hot days. I intend avoiding her as much as possible, but isn't it miserable to live with a lot of grumbling dissatisfied people, especially when they are better off now than they ever were in their lives before?

By contrast, when a clerk and a tidewaiter arrived three months later to augment the customs staff, Lovatt made no complaint.[8]

Part of Lovatt's duties required that he deal with dissatisfied customers:

> The day before yesterday I boarded a steamer and, while waiting for the passengers to embark, I noticed a Chinaman trying to ship two large bales of straw

hats, which I quietly took possession of and brought to the Custom house. The Commissioner decided to let him pay the duty and go, instead of fining him, for which he was very thankful.

But that was not the end of the story: "Today he comes back and wants to know if the duty he paid will clear his goods to their destination." Lovatt told him he could ship the hats from Wuhu to Jiujiang, but the Chinese authorities would determine anything further, referring to the *likin* (*lijin*), or domestic, tax. The customer was

> thoroughly disgusted and thinks we have been squeezing him and vows he will never again have anything to do with the foreign Customs. He took up his permit and held it out, saying that might do for the foreigners, but what was the use of it to him? We all tried to explain matters to the fellow in turn, but I am afraid with little success. He went away grumbling and feeling we had done him.[9]

Lovatt's duties also took him on occasion to the local *yamen*. When three of his boatmen got hurt in a scuffle with some "raft people, I had to be present at the trial of the one unfortunate fellow who was caught." Lovatt then described the "very amusing dramatic airs" of the "old mandarin" who tried the case:

> He would talk to the offender in a loud and commanding tone, and give utterance to some time-honored old sentiment, such as "Hospitality is to be shown to strangers" and looking all round, he would finally look at the culprit and say, "Do you hear *that*?," as if the old sinner had never sinned himself. Then he would laugh, talk to Mr. Woodruff, smoke, drink tea, and bellow out some other sententious phrase, and in that way continued until I began to get tired of the thing, and wanted my dinner, which I did not get until about 8:30 p.m.[10]

As always, Lovatt and the growing number of customs personnel attracted inordinate attention from the local population:

> We few foreigners here are still on exhibition. That is, the Chinese come to the temporary Custom House daily and gaze upon the rude barbarians from the West, but are always very civil and polite. Our doorway is regularly blocked with them, but they are always ready to open out and allow us to pass. In fact, it is looked upon as a favor on our part going out, for then they get and view the man all over.

Even when Lovatt went hunting with Woodruff, they were followed:

> Lots of little boys surrounded me and begged for the empty cartridge cases which I gave them to their great delight. Many of them [are] very nice boys, and

> how proud and pleased they were to find I let them follow me, and laughed and chatted with them. I believe I enjoyed their company as much as they did mine, altho it spoiled all my [snipe] shooting.[11]

Creating a modicum of a social life at a new treaty port was difficult at first, as there were no merchants there yet, so in addition to his customs colleagues, Lovatt befriended the British consular officials, playing lawn tennis with Consul C. F. R. Allen, his wife, and the other staffers, dining frequently with them, and accompanying them on excursions. For his first excursion, Lovatt borrowed Woodruff's boat, and set out with Holland, a member of the British Consular service, on two days leave. "I believe I will enjoy the trip as I have not been out of this since my arrival and think the excursion will do me good."[12]

In addition to the few diplomats and customs personnel, missionaries rounded out the local social scene. Lovatt viewed them with his usual critical eye, and found several wanting. One missionary couple, the Thomases, decided to leave Wuhu soon after arriving, saying that there was insufficient proof of God blessing their work, leading Lovatt to remark caustically that "I don't see that was any business of his. I think he ought to have gone on doing his duty and leave the Almighty to do His own Holy will. I don't believe in anybody constituting themselves judges and saying what they think the Almighty ought to do."[13]

The missionaries had other faults as well. Some aired their dirty laundry in public, which Lovatt found in poor taste, such as one missionary named Scarborough who returned to England and

> has been abusing the foreign residents in China for their loose and immoral way of living. There is no doubt but it is bad, yet I feel that all they do by throwing dirt in public is to make themselves disliked more. It is strange the best and most devoted missionaries never do it. It is generally men who are unpopular and disliked in a community that take the opportunity of abusing their countrymen when at home.

Another shortcoming was insularity: "our missionary friends keep a good deal to themselves, so it is easy to account for their dullness." Yet another was the tendency to belabor the obvious: "[they] like us to sit in stuffy churches and listen to their old harangues about sin and all manner of wickedness, as if we did not see enough of it during the week without having to listen to more on our holy day."[14]

Lovatt also criticized an overemphasis on pomp and ceremony. When an Episcopalian missionary couple was transferred out, Lovatt remarked that they were probably "not very much displeased to change dirty China for clean Japan." This led him to comment on the suitability of that mission in China:

> Episcopalianism is not the Church to send out missionaries. They are too fond of the order and elegancies of civilized life, and in fact the church is for the heathen too elaborate a ceremonial to take part in which you want a congregation of ladies in black silk and nice bonnets and gentlemen in fine black cloth, so that they may kneel with grace and stand up with elegance, then the service is charming. Just imagine for one moment a naked savage kneeling. It is too horrible.[15]

Instead of preachers, Lovatt thought missionary doctors would have a greater impact: "There is no doubt [that] a man with work in him and a love of his [medical] profession would do more good amongst the Chinese than all the preachers put together, for attending them in sickness and want really appeals to their best feelings, and they are grateful for one's efforts." Lovatt, in short, preferred the social gospel approach to mission work.[16]

A major conference in Shanghai involving all the Protestant missionaries that spring of 1877 gave Lovatt additional ammunition, and since Wuhu served as a transit point for missionaries coming from the upriver ports, he was strategically placed to hear about the issues they grappled with. One was how "God" should be rendered in Chinese, a controversy Lovatt saw as meaningless:

> The term question has been found impossible to settle, those standing stoutly by "*Shang ti*" [Emperor on High], and others by "*Chu Shing*" [probably *Chu Shen*, Lord God]. The fact is, the Chinese have so many gods, great and small, that among the great gods, each is supreme in his own special kingdom, and no single one supreme over the other. Therefore, it is impossible to select the title of a heathen god and give it to the Almighty. Make the Chinese Christians and then there is no difficulty whatever, and to heathen it does not matter.[17]

The other major issue facing the Shanghai conclave was whether Chinese should be given secular higher education, a policy Lovatt supported: "The three most highly educated men in the conference argued in its favor, Edkins, Martin, and Wylie—men of note throughout the world—while the herd of professionals objected. The manifestation of intolerance by so called Christians somewhat annoyed me." Summing up, Lovatt observed that

> the missionary conference goes on much more amiably than most people expected. I hardly see what permanent good will come from it. Protestant divisions are not easily reconciled and they all keep up separate organizations. Anyway, it is a holiday and recreation for the milder sort and an opportunity for the gladiators to glare upon each other, and renew the wordy war.[18]

Of course, not all missionaries came in for criticism. One group that made a good impression on Lovatt was the Jesuits, who had arrived before he had:

> I was called upon soon after my arrival by Father Sekongiur, a Frenchman, and find him a good kindhearted man and a zealous missionary. He seemed to treasure up the remembrance of some kindness I had shown to some of his brethren when in Chinkiang [that] I had forgotten all about. I like the old fellow, and think him a goodhearted Christian.

A few days later, another Jesuit arrived in charge of building churches "who does not speak a word of English so I have to practice my French with him." Finally, "we called at the Roman Catholic mission on Saturday and were very agreeably entertained. These Jesuits are certainly most agreeable men."[19]

But most of the missionaries were Protestants, and Lovatt maintained contact with those he liked, including his old friends from Jiujiang who occasionally transited Wuhu. One of them, Andrew Stritmatter, had recently married, and when the newlyweds passed through Wuhu on the way to Shanghai, Lovatt got to meet the bride "*nee* Miss Combes M.D. Short, stout, very stout, and pleasant, an amiable and pleasant manner. Voice a little hard and rough, but a person I think I should like very much, and one I think not in any way narrow minded." Soon thereafter, Lovatt was able to report that "our friend Stritmatter seems to be settling down quietly to married life in [Shanghai]." Other Methodists were praiseworthy, although sometimes for reasons other than religious. When he heard from Stritmatter that Reverend Benton of Cincinnati was expected in Jiujiang the following month, Lovatt remarked that he "is a fine fellow and a splendid shot. I do really think the Methodist parsons of America are a fine set of fellows." Soon thereafter, Lovatt received a letter from Benton and "I expect him to come down that we may have a shooting trip together at the Chinese new year."[20]

CHINESE RESISTANCE

Meanwhile, Chinese nationalism was taking on several forms in the late nineteenth century. For some, it came in the form of anti-Western, anti-Christian agitation and rioting which Lovatt Would chronicle extensively in the early 1890s and which reached an apogee in the 1900 Boxer Rebellion. For some it took the form of anti-Manchu sentiment which erupted in the 1911 Revolution. But for others like Li Hongzhang and the Self-Strengtheners, it came as an attempt to beat the West at its own game. This included not only the use of Western armaments and tactics, but also shipping. Given the importance of shipping to the customs enterprise, Lovatt and others became increasingly concerned that the Chinese were taking over what had until then been a Western monopoly. Russell and Company had founded the Shanghai Steam

Navigation Company (SSNC) in 1862, and by 1874 it had seventeen steamers plying the Yangzi. This was followed by Butterfield and Swire's China Navigation Company in 1872, and one year later by Jardine, Matheson's China Coast Steam Navigation Company. To compete with these British and American companies, Li Hongzhang founded the China Merchants Steam Navigation Company in 1872, and five years later, in 1877, bought out the SSNC. Lovatt noted that "the opposition on the river now is very severe. Since the Chinese purchased the S. S. N. Co.'s Steamers, they are trying to run the English company off the river altogether." When the *George Washington*, formerly an SSNC steamer, sailed into Wuhu in April 1877, Lovatt used the occasion to rail against the sale: "The poor old *George W.*—to end his days an old Chinese hulk. It is too bad. It takes all the poetry out of the thing to have such a name on a hulk. I think Messrs Russell & Co. ought to be brought to account for handing the name over to the Chinese."[21]

Lovatt acknowledged that the Chinese had an advantage at the smaller ports: "There is a general complaint amongst the foreigners that trade is getting more and more into the hands of Chinese, and this is probably true of many small branches of trade which requires great economy to make profitable, and these the Chinese naturally obtain." Nonetheless, the attempt to supplant the Westerners was irksome: "Foreigners are very dissatisfied. The Chinese are just ousting them out of everything." He added that "all these river ports are going down as far as foreigners are concerned. The Chinese are getting it all into their own hands, and don't want any assistance from the barbarians."[22]

Another tactic the Chinese used to reduce the Western footprint was to put obstacles in place when new treaty ports were opened as a result of the Chefoo Agreement of 1876 signed in the aftermath of the Margary Incident: "Everybody is grumbling at the restrictions the Chinese authorities are placing on trade at the six new ports of call." Lovatt was referring to the requirement that land would now have to be rented from Chinese owners rather than from a Western "concession," leaving would-be Western renters vulnerable to the whims of a Chinese landlord. Lovatt laid much of the blame on Western diplomats:

> It really is amusing to see how the Chinese mandarins fool our ambassadors. First, the British minister [Wade] had to get a fleet to back up his demands, and when he was almost on the point of declaring war the Chinese officials concede everything, and now they make that concession worthless. It is highly ludicrous the way the political game is played in China, a regular old see-saw method—now your [*sic*] up, and now your [*sic*] down.[23]

So it was with some satisfaction that Lovatt could report that supplanting Westerners was not going to be easy. For one, Chinese inexperience meant that they had bitten off more than they could chew, "feeling the burden of their big company weighing heavily upon them." Two major shipwrecks also took a heavy toll. They lost the *Howsang*, a steamer purchased from England, near Amoy, and the *Kiang Chang*, the last new steamer Russell & Co. had built. The Chinese blamed the accidents on the Western captains:

> Capt. Friend was in command [of the *Kiang Chang*]. The steamer run on a rock between Kiukiang and Hankow about five o'clock in the morning, and tore the bottom completely out of her, so that in fifteen minutes she sunk. The Chinese are already saying, "Ah! Those bad foreigners, no have that company just now, must want to lose that steamer because he belong Chinaman." Well, the ignorant of our own lands would say the same.[24]

The cargo in these ships included opium, which had been legalized as a result of the Unequal Treaties. Lovatt and most other foreigners in China disapproved of the trade:

> The opium question, I am glad to say, fails to arouse even enough opposition to make a fight at all interesting, a positive that no decent, respectable man will argue in its favour. I think that it will soon collapse, public opinion is dead against it in England, and even in China. I shall rejoice when the vile trade has been stopped. It is the ruin of China, just as much as *gin* is the ruin of the miserable poor of London.[25]

In addition to competition on the Yangzi and the opium trade, a third issue involving shipping and infrastructure, at least indirectly, was the drought and resulting famine currently raging in north China that "is very severe. The Chinese government is doing all they can for the poor people, but I am afraid thousands will die this winter." In fact, by the time the famine ended two years later in 1879, between 9 and 13 million people would die. Lovatt blamed the lack of infrastructure in part for the death toll: "The steamers are carrying rice up for the people from all the southern provinces to Tientsin, but there the difficulty begins. The transporting of so much rice into the interior is next to impossible, and I doubt if it will ever get there, having to run the risk of bad roads and robbers." To make matters worse,

> news has just come of an awful calamity having occurred in Tientsin. The famine is so terrible in the north that all the poor people are flocking into the large cities, and in some of the cities large mat sheds are erected for the accommodation of these homeless wanderers. One of these large mat camps in the suburbs of Tientsin caught fire and some two thousand of the poor inhabitants were burnt to death.[26]

Lovatt assigned part of the blame for the famine on the unwillingness to embrace modern infrastructure:

Just think of this state of affairs [the difficulties in transporting rice from south to north] and the railroad from Shanghai to Woosung being pulled up by order of one of the most intelligent men of the empire. It is simply marvelous how the empire hangs together. There is wisdom in the action of these stupid mandarins. They see clearly their day is going if they don't present a bold front to western civilization.

As for the railroad, "the Viceroy at Nanking [Chen Baoshen] said it was forced upon them, and when China wanted railways she would introduce them herself. They have done this I believe simply out of spite to foreigners in general, but in particular to annoy Sir Thomas Wade and the British government for making them swallow the Chefoo Convention."[27]

The famine gave Lovatt an opportunity to paint Christian missionary work in a positive light: "Today thousands of Chinese owe their life and everything to the missionaries who exerted themselves to raise funds for the famine-struck district of Shantung, and who willingly undertook the very arduous labor of distributing rice and money amidst disease, suffering, and death." Clearly, Lovatt was referring to the efforts of men like Timothy Richard of the British Baptist Missionary Society who organized relief efforts in that province. As for other missionaries,

Individuals there are utter failures, but as a body they more than compare favorably with any other body or class of foreigners in China. I know them, and I know their faults, and I am sometimes inclined to judge them severely when I see them going out of their way to do some excessively stupid thing, and the fellows of [Hudson] Taylor's [China Inland] Mission seemed to be gifted in that way.[28]

But not all Chinese were as grateful to the missionaries as Lovatt thought they should be. One, Wong Chin-foo, who had been baptized by American Baptist missionaries, worked for a short time in the Customs service, during which he conspired to import arms in an attempt to overthrow the Qing government. As a result, he had to flee to the United States where he started a newspaper, the *Chinese American*, and criticized American missionaries in China, later writing an article entitled "Why Am I a Heathen?" Lovatt had little use for him:

Wong Chin foo is a great rascal and is trying to pick up a living in the States, for he knows very well the Chinese authorities would very soon have his head if he put foot on celestial soil. He is evidently a bad fellow to turn and abuse missionaries who had been his best friends, and raised him from being a coolie to a position of decency and respectability.[29]

Lovatt's critique of officials who eschewed infrastructure improvement was based in part that they were set in their ways:

> the Chinese never bring out new pieces founded on the topics, manners, and customs of the day. They go on playing the same plays, singing the same songs, and playing the same tunes that amused their very ancient ancestors. Imagine the whole English speaking people throughout the world always attending the historical plays of Shakespeare? Even in the case of the divine William, it is painful to contemplate night after night of him.[30]

While Lovatt criticized elite attitudes and behavior, he did not spare those at ground level, attributing to them a propensity to quarrel:

> Our boy [Sin fah] when in Kiukiang negotiated with a sailor on board the *Sultan* for a wife, the lady being a widow, and since the death of her husband a member of her former family household, where mouths were numerous and rice not too plentiful. The seaman told the boy he might have the lady cheap, [the family] were numerous and poor, the lady amiable, strong, and healthy, and certainly worth $26. Sin fah thought so, concluded the bargain, and secured a wife for himself. Then, it appears he met a fellow in Wuhu whom he made his friend and like a Chinaman told this friend all his affairs, how he got his wife, how cheap she was, and so on. Well, this fellow finding that Sin fah was going back to Kiukiang, suggested to him that he should pay him $10 to make him hold his tongue about Sin fah's affairs. For, said the fellow, 'you have a woman, a widow without any document saying so, and I can give you plenty of bitter things to eat (trouble) [*zhigu*], so pay me $10.' Well, this fellow made a frightful row at the Custom house and charged Sin fah with beating him. I got him pacified and sent him away with the Commissioner's card to a Mandarin, where he began to deny everything, but the old Mandarin said I will send you into the city and [the *daotai*] will get it out you. So the thing is not settled yet, but I am afraid it reveals a depth of wickedness not easy for foreigners to understand.[31]

ANGLING FOR A LEAVE

From the time Lovatt arrived in Wuhu in early 1877, Jennie had suggested that she and the children join him there. But Lovatt poured cold water on that idea: "I never had the remotest intention of bringing you here . . . , it is miserable enough for me." One reason he demurred was his poor living accommodations. Remembering their house in Jiujiang, "I should get lost in Taiping [Kung] now, after living [here] in such a small and peculiarly built house, [otherwise] I would be very happy here if I had you and a decent kind of house for you to live in." Emblematic of his substandard quarters was that only a thin wall separated him from his obnoxious neighbors: "My next room neighbour Mrs. Sayle has a very nice little girl just twelve months [old who] cries a great deal more than a properly cared for baby should." His abode was also shoddily constructed: "[last] night [the rain] came through the roof on to my bed, so I had to get up twice and get the nightwatchman help me move my bed. This house is truly abominable, hot in summer and cold in winter." If he had to spend another year in Wuhu, "I certainly should try and get another house."[32]

A second reason for dissuading his family from joining him was that Wuhu compared unfavorably with their previous posting: "if Kiukiang was dull, Wuhu is much more so." Jennie must have wondered about that characterization since Lovatt had at first praised Wuhu as having "a certain charm. The place is rather pretty, the people very civil indeed, everything reasonable in price, and a very excellent place to wear out all my old clothes. I like the place very much." To Jennie, it must have sounded like a flimsy excuse.[33]

Finally, a third reason he gave for not wanting his family to join him was that he felt their children were better off growing up in America: "Now they are learning an amount of self reliance and independence that they could not have obtained amidst a lot of servants of heathen Chinese." Moreover, "the evils, vices, and wickedness [that they would be] learning from the Chinese that would surround them [would leave] a taint in their morals that might never [be] eradicated." Extending that reasoning to the anti-Chinese agitation currently raging in California, he appeared to sympathize with the likes of the demagogue Denis Kearney: "it is there where I think the injury may be done to our race in San Francisco, not in the cry of the low class of that city of being ruined by cheap labour, but in the moral contamination of such a people." Lovatt still obviously carried some prejudice.[34]

Rather than inviting his family to China, Lovatt decided instead to reapply for leave, beginning an eight-month roller coaster of optimism and pessimism that also led him to consider for the first time whether he should stay in China or resign if he did not get it. Having unsuccessfully applied for leave the previous year when he was in Jiujiang, he now drew up a three-pronged strategy: first, butter Hart up, second, enlist the commissioner, and, third, get a doctor's note. The opportunity to implement the first part of his plan soon presented itself, as the IG was expected to arrive in Wuhu in August en route from Shanghai to Yichang, at which time "perhaps *His Majesty* will tell me what I may do in the way of leave. Perhaps Bobus will do something generous in his own good time. I must call him *Bobus* until he either promotes me or gives me leave."[35]

While awaiting Hart's arrival, Lovatt prepared Jennie for the possibility that he would be turned down again: "I am afraid all your imaginary wishes of my sudden arrival home are doomed to disappointment. Robert is not giving too much feeling after having once made up his mind." Knowing that she would castigate Hart if he were again denied leave, Lovatt found himself in the odd position of defending him, calling him "a very considerate and thoughtful man. I am obliged to stand up somewhat in his defense, for I am afraid you are too hard upon him." So, when Hart finally arrived in Wuhu, Lovatt clearly had his wife in mind during their encounter:

> Yesterday morning I boarded the Chinese Steamer *Kiang yung* and saw Bob—our Bob—our friend Bob on the deck. I went on board and walking up to him I said mentally, "You confounded old sinner, why don't you promote me, give me leave, and let me go home? [Jennie] prays nightly to the Lord to open your eyes to the distinguished ability, the long and honorable service, of her husband."

Squelching his inner voice, Lovatt stuck to his game plan: "I took him ashore and brought him back to the steamer. When in the boat [we conversed and] I agreed with him. He was very pleasant and amiable and chatted about all kinds of things, and indirectly complimented me about several things until we reached the steamer where we bowed and parted."[36]

Lovatt would have a second opportunity to butter Hart up a few weeks later when the IG was due to stop in Wuhu on his return trip from Yichang. Word of his imminent arrival came as he was on his way to the British consulate to play tennis: "Just as I was going, a boatman called to say the Inspector General's steamer was coming down, so I lost my game, and went on board, but did not see His Imperial Majesty, the Emperor of the Customs and Autocrat of all the foreigners in that Service" because he remained on board with a headache. But since Hart was scheduled to be escorted ashore the following day by Woodruff, Lovatt began the second part of his plan by asking the commissioner, "if you can manage to ask incidentally about my leave, without it appearing to be official, I will be very much obliged, for it will give great satisfaction to my wife." Woodruff said he would, but cautioned that "I am afraid there is not much probability of its being granted." Lovatt responded that he would apply anyway "if he even now said *no*."[37]

That evening Lovatt dined with Hart, Woodruff, Hart's secretary E. Ohlmer, Edmund Grimani, and Captain John Farrow of the *Ling Feng*, giving Lovatt another opportunity to curry favor: "Robert . . . was very kind and talked away in a very happy pleasing kind of way during dinner." Continuing to butter him up, Lovatt went out of his way to laugh at his jokes: "[Hart] seemed to be very fond of making puns. I can hardly tell you how bad they were but of course we laughed at the horrid things. When a fellow is Inspector General, or in fact any kind of a boss, all understrappers are bound to laugh, if only to show their intelligence that they do possess brains enough to see the joke." Lovatt thought the evening with the IG, who left the next morning for Shanghai, had gone well: "The dinner was good and abundant, and was what you would call a friendly chatty sort of a dinner, with a cigar after it, and when we left the dining room for the sitting room, the talk continued about all sorts of things until nearly eleven o'clock."[38]

During Hart's brief stopover in Wuhu, Lovatt had not learned how he had responded when the commissioner broached the issue of his leave. But a few days later, Woodruff told him that Hart had not rejected it out of hand, leading Lovatt to feel "pretty confident. If he decidedly objected to my going he would very likely have refused point blank when Mr. Woodruff asked him." Consequently, he wrote to his wife that "if the I. G. will only say I may go next April, I will try and drag along an existence until then."[39]

Although Hart had not said no, he had also not said yes, so Lovatt now embarked on the third and final part of his strategy—getting a doctor to certify that he needed a medical leave. Although the nearest doctor was in Jiujiang, Lovatt rejected that as too obvious: "to go to Kiukiang would be a mistake. It is true I would see the doctor, but I could not come right back with a certificate and immediately apply for leave, the thing would look too barefaced." Instead, Lovatt decided to go in the other direction: "I had far better go to Shanghai [where] Jardine is sure to give me the certificate, altho I am thoroughly ashamed to go up to ask for it, but what is a poor Christian to do amongst such a lot of wretches who get medical certificates without a twinge [of guilt]? I told Woodruff I wanted to go to Shanghai [and] he agreed." Lovatt spent ten days in Shanghai where he got a "first rate medical certificate" and returned to Wuhu.[40]

When Lovatt arrived back in Wuhu on the *Shanghai* at the beginning of October, all the pieces seemed in place: "I saw the Commissioner at ten o'clock and had a good long talk with him about my leave, and he thought I ought to get it, so I will write out the application today and send it in." Woodruff added that he would be sorry to see him go, but that I "deserved my leave and he hoped I would get it."[41]

It was not until the end of November that Lovatt received

> Good news. I am just too happy to tell you that a dispatch [came] from Peking last night, and Mr. Woodruff sent me word this morning that my eighteen months leave of absence [at half salary] was granted from the 1st April 1878, so I trust the pleasant month of May will find me by your side [in] the happy land of America.

And in another piece of "good news" three weeks later, Hart designated Lovatt's friend Neville May to replace him on the first of March, which would allow Lovatt to depart even earlier. In appreciation, "I have just written to thank Robert, he is no longer Bobus, for granting me the leave. [H]e really is a kindhearted, modest, unassuming man, placed in a position requiring ability of no mean order, and tact and judgment that even few men of talent possess."[42]

Having been granted leave, Lovatt now had to reassure his wife. First, he wanted to leave no doubt in her mind that he was coming home. Woodruff had cautioned him that "one is never sure of one's leave until one has left, and you know it might be countermanded." But Lovatt told the commissioner that he would not even mention that possibility: "I will not tax my wife's patience any longer. She has had enough in the disappointment of last year." Second, he had to convince Jennie that he was not really sick: "You imply a doubt about my health when in Shanghai which was, and is, first rate. But, my dear, one must be sick sometimes or one would never get leave. But I was all right, only sick of Wuhu and wanting a change."[43]

Now that Lovatt had secured a long leave of absence, and resignation was off the table, he began to focus on the long term. For one, he decided to invest in real estate, telling Jennie to buy one hundred acres of land in southwestern Minnesota. And he floated some possible locations where they might eventually retire in the United States. Finally, while he was unsure of where they might end up, there was one thing he was sure about: "We may as well give over all thoughts of farming. I simply know nothing about it, and don't believe I would ever stick to it. Therefore we will just throw farming overboard."[44]

FINAL DAYS IN WUHU

While preoccupied with obtaining his leave, customs news, often negative, occasionally intruded. Alcoholism was the usual culprit. One instance involved J. Edwards, whose bad behavior Lovatt had previously noted: "I saw Edwards in Shanghai, but only nodded to him. He is in very bad odour, and I believe the I. G. when he pays him his retiring allowance will tell him to go home." Another involved Brandon, who still "gets tight occasionally but manages to pull through." A third was Brown, who had recently been demoted by Kopsch to second-class tidewaiter for being drunk on duty. But when Brown "immediately after got drunk again, Mr. Kopsch reported him to Pekin, so he is almost sure to be dismissed. It is sad, but it serves Brown right. He was often drunk under me, but I did not like reporting him on a/c of his wife and family, but I hear he has gone awfully since I left, and is now almost constantly drunk."[45]

Others, like Halsey, were simply obnoxious. When Lovatt's friend Reeks in Yichang mentioned that he did not get along with Halsey, Lovatt concurred that "Halsey [is] very unpopular with both the indoor and the outdoor staff.

He is so confoundedly lazy, puts on so many airs, and thinks every poor beggar of a tidewaiter so far beneath him that he renders himself odious to the staff and unpopular with everybody." Lovatt then learned of another incident:

> Halsey had a terrible row with one of his Examiners in Hankow, a Mr. Mesney, who he reported to the Commissioner for insubordination, and when the Commissioner suggested to Mr. Mesney the advisability of apologizing to Mr. Halsey, he declined to do so on the ground that he was not insubordinate. So the Commissioner has suspended Mr. Mesney and referred the matter to Peking. What complicates the affair is that all the Examiners have signed a paper certifying that Mr. Mesney was not insolent to Mr. Halsey. It is unfortunate that Halsey should make himself so very unpopular, and manage to fall out with the quietest and one of the most decent members of his staff.

Lovatt would soon experience for himself firsthand how obnoxious Halsey could be.[46]

Other customs officers were disgruntled, feeling they had been unfairly treated by the IG. C. F. Moore sent in his resignation while Lovatt was in Shanghai because "he thinks Mr. Hart has not treated him well." Another disgruntled employee was his friend Neville May, who was about to replace him in Wuhu but who was not promoted: "Poor May is again passed over and is feeling completely disgusted at not getting the vacancy."[47]

However, some customs officials won Lovatt's grudging admiration. Edward Drew had come in for criticism because he "acts like too much of the school master in his intercourse with men to make him very popular, besides being a trifle stingy, and you know that is unpardonable in society in China." Nonetheless, Lovatt stuck up for him: "I like him, and always found [him] a fair, straightforward upright fellow. And he treated us well. Now [that] he is Commissioner at Ningpo he is much more comfortable, the people there being milder and not such heavy swells as the Foochow community think they are."[48]

And there was the usual gossip involving women. One involved the widow of W. Dix, for whom Lovatt had taken up a collection after her husband had died, who had remarried a fellow steamer passenger more quickly than some deemed proper. Lovatt was appalled at "the abuse that poor Mrs. Dix is receiving. I am sure I don't blame her, for what was the poor woman to do? She had a large family and could only expect to work very hard to give them even bread in England." He added that "I think Mrs. Dix has acted wisely. Of course, if she could have managed to wait a little longer it would have looked more decent, but under the circumstances I think she is not to be blamed." And the man who had been expecting to marry her—a hulk-keeper in Hankou—upon learning that she had married someone else, went off to

Jiujiang and "at once proposed to Mrs. King's maid (no, she is not a maid) and was immediately accepted."[49]

Lovatt was not the only one departing Wuhu in that spring of 1878. Edmund Grimani was transferred to Zhenjiang, and Woodruff had been granted leave, "so one half of our small community is likely to be changed in the month of March." As for the "nice people" in the British consular staff, Holland was leaving for Taiwanfu and Allen was leaving to become consul in Zhenjiang. And now that Lovatt was about to depart, he sang Wuhu's praises. When Stritmatter's wife pronounced Jiujiang "awful dull, just as bad as Wuhu," Lovatt countered that

> in fact I have much more enjoyment in Wuhu than I had in Kiukiang. Our friends there did not seem to have energy enough to go in for anything, and here shooting and lawn-tennis with frequent pleasant evenings at the British consulate make the place very tolerable, and it certainly is nice, meeting nice, polite people, who do not feel they have any other mission but to be polite and amiable.[50]

And so in early 1878, at the age of forty, and after just over one year in Wuhu, Lovatt prepared to return home to Minnesota after an eight-year absence. Since he knew that he had "not a ghost of a chance," for a raise from Hart, a 350 tael refund from a life insurance policy gave him a welcome cash infusion that "will take me home very comfortably." Of course, he could not leave until his replacement, Neville May, arrived and was brought up to speed. May arrived in early March, and since it took only "a few days [to] put such an old hand into the way of doing things," Lovatt was able to leave for home two weeks early.[51]

Lovatt departed Wuhu in mid-March aboard the *Kiang-yuen* for Shanghai, where he handed Hart's dispatch to the commissioner "to draw my half pay." He then departed Shanghai for Yokohama and boarded the *Tokio Maru* for San Francisco, where he checked into the Palace Hotel until the next train from Oakland departed. Having arranged to meet Jennie in St. Paul, he detrained there in late April and proceeded to the Merchants Hotel, where he "ask[ed] the clerk at the hotel with the greatest gravity and coolness for the number of Mrs. Colonel Lovatt's room."[52]

NOTES

1. WNL to JSL, February 23 and 25, and August 7, 1877. Lovatt's rank remained tidesurveyor and harbormaster.
2. WNL to JSL, February 25 and 27, March 3 and 5, and December 24, 1877.

3. WNL to JSL, February 27, and March 5 and 8, 1877.
4. WNL to JSL, March 8 and 12, and April 5, 1877.
5. WNL to JSL, April 6, and 19, and June 5, 1877.
6. WNL to JSL, March 8, and April 11 and 12, 1877, and January 28, 1878. Emphasis in the original.
7. WNL to JSL, June 5 and October 3, 1877.
8. WNL to JSL, April 19 and July 30 and 31, 1877.
9. WNL to JSL, April 5, 6, and 11 1877.
10. WNL to JSL, April 19, 1877. Emphasis in the original.
11. WNL to JSL, April 5, 11, and 12, 1877.
12. WNL to JSL, May 7 and 8, June 5, July 6, and August 30, 1877. Lovatt wrote a letter about Wuhu that appeared in the *Courier* in early April 1877.
13. WNL to JSL, April 5, 1877.
14. WNL to JSL, July 11 and 30, and October 2, 1877.
15. WNL to JSL, December 18, 1877 and February 10, 1878.
16. WNL to JSL, October 6, 1877.
17. WNL to JSL, May 7, 8, and 20, 1877. The question was never settled, so three different terms for God remained in use—the two used by Protestants, and a third by Catholics who adopted the term *Tianju* [Lord of Heaven].
18. WNL to JSL, May 7, 8, and 20, 1877.
19. WNL to JSL, March 3, 10, and 12, 1877.
20. WNL to JSL, September 14, November 2, 23, and 29, and December 24, 1877, and January 18, 1878.
21. Kwang-Ching Liu, *Anglo-American Steamship Rivalry in China, 1862–1874* (Cambridge: Harvard University Press, 1962), 11; WNL to JSL, April 5, 11, and 12, and June 18, 1877.
22. WNL to JSL, July 10, October 2, and November 29, 1877, and February 15, 1880.
23. WNL to JSL, July 8, and September 6 and 19, 1877.
24. WNL to JSL, June 18 and July 10, 1877 and February 12, 1878.
25. WNL to JSL, February 9, 1878. Emphasis in the original.
26. WNL to JSL, December 19, 1877 and January 27, 1878.
27. WNL to JSL, November 24, and December 12 and 19, 1877. Chen argued that the railroad violated the 1868 Burlingame Treaty and disturbed the *feng-shui*, and pulled up the tracks after a year of operation. It would not be until twenty years later that the railway resumed operation. Its path is now part of the Shanghai metro system.
28. WNL to JSL, December 7, 1877; Paul Richard Bohr, *Famine in China and the Missionary: Timothy Richard as Relief Administrator and Advocate of National Reform, 1876–1884* (Cambridge: Harvard East Asian Monograph 48, 1972). For his actions in Shandong, see particularly 13–16.
29. WNL to JSL, December 7, 1877. Emphasis in the original. Wong Chin-foo (1847–1898) was baptized by American Baptist missionaries and served as an interpreter in Zhenjiang. He went to the United States and became an activist for Chinese American rights, campaigning against the Chinese Exclusion Act and challenging Denis Kearney. See Scott D. Seligman, *The First Chinese American: The Remarkable Life of Wong Chin Foo* (Hong Kong: Hong Kong University Press, 2013).

30. WNL to JSL, no date.

31. WNL to JSL, July 26, 1877.

32. WNL to JSL, April 21, August 30 and 31, September 6, and November 5, 1877, and February 10, 1878.

33. WNL to JSL, July 6, August 31, September 12, and October 2, 1877.

34. WNL to JSL, September 3, 1877. Partly as a result of Kearney's agitation, the United States would enact the Chinese Exclusion Act five years later in 1882.

35. WNL to JSL, March 5 and 8, April 6, 19, and 21, May 31, June 17, and July 10, 1877. Emphasis in the original.

36. WNL to JSL, June 17 and August 7, 1877.

37. WNL to JSL, August 25, 1877. Emphasis in the original.

38. WNL to JSL, August 26, 1877.

39. WNL to JSL, August 26, 30 and 31, 1877.

40. WNL to JSL, September 14, 19, 29, and 30, and October 1, 2, 3, and 4, 1877.

41. WNL to JSL, October 3 and 4, and November 5, 6, and 21, 1877.

42. WNL to JSL, November 25 and December 12, 1877.

43. WNL to JSL, November 29, 1877 and January 7, 1878. Emphasis in the original.

44. WNL to JSL, June 18, October 1, and December 7 and 27, 1877, and February 13, 1878.

45. WNL to JSL, September 30, 1877 and January 18, 1878.

46. WNL to JSL, February 25, March 1 and 8, April 5, and October 4, 1877.

47. WNL to JSL, September 30, 1877.

48. WNL to JSL, January 18, 1878.

49. WNL to JSL, April 11, 1877. Emphasis in the original. This was not the first incident involving this woman. In Jiujiang, Lovatt witnessed an earlier affair involving her and a Mr. A. Weale, who was temporarily stranded there without passage money because "none of the companies will give him a passage to Shanghai so [he] is waiting to see if the captain of the *Hanyang* will let him go down in her." On one of Lovatt's walks, "when we got into the city and coming round the walk at that place where the bushes grow the thickest, we found Mr. Weale and Mrs. King's maid in quiet converse. I don't suppose there was any love making for Mr. Weale is a hardened sinner." Four days later, however, he noted that "Weale is here yet. I hear a rumour that he is engaged himself to Mrs. King's woman. If so, it is all nonsense--he will never think of her after he leaves here." WNL to JSL, October 4 and 8, 1876.

50. WNL to JSL, October 6, November 2, and December 24, 1877, and January 18, 1878.

51. WNL to JSL, December 18 and 24, 1877 and January 10 and February 9, 1878.

52. *North China Herald*, March 14, 1878, 254; WNL to JSL, November 29 and December 24, 1877, and January 20 and February 9, 1878.

Chapter 7

Return to Hankou, 1878–1881

MINNESOTA, ENGLAND, AND SHANGHAI (APRIL 1878 TO FEBRUARY 1880)

Lovatt arrived in Minnesota in late April 1878 to begin his eighteen-month leave. One year into his leave, he received a three-month extension until January 1880, giving him a total of twenty-one months off. After a year and a half in Minnesota, during which their fourth child, Mabel Victoria, was born on January 21, 1879, Lovatt departed for England in what would be his final trip to the country of his birth, arriving in Liverpool aboard the *Wisconsin* in late October 1879. From there he took the train to Portsmouth to visit his sister Sarah and his brother Tom, his other brother Jack having drowned while serving in the British navy. Lovatt departed England for Shanghai on the *Glenfinas* in mid-November, never to return, his loyalties now completely on the other side of the Atlantic: "I have been long enough in England to like America a hundred times more than ever."[1]

Lovatt passed through the "frightfully hot" Suez Canel, transited the Red Sea, Port Said, Malta, and Singapore. Three days after leaving Singapore, "we encountered strong winds and for four days we pitched [and] rolled." Despite the efforts of the captain to make the trip comfortable, "I never was so glad to get clear of any ship as I was of that" when they arrived in Hong Kong on the morning of January 2, 1880. After three days in Hong Kong, the *Glenfinas* departed for the final leg of the journey. By this time, Lovatt had been on board ship for nearly two months: "I shall be heartily glad to finish this long dreary voyage." Arriving in Shanghai on January 11, he checked in as usual at the Astor House.[2]

Lovatt's first order of business was to go to the Shanghai Customs House to pick up his mail and to learn where his next posting would be, but the commissioner had not yet received Lovatt's onward orders from Hart, so Lovatt went to the tailor to be fitted for a uniform, and assumed customs duties there, which were minimal: "Mr. May, who relieved me at Wuhu, is here and is stationed at Hong Ku [Hong Kew] in charge of all the wharves, and I am assisting him. Besides, we have another Tidesurveyor to assist us, and there being very little to do, we find our greatest difficulty in knowing how to put in our time." In fact, "the only thing I have to [do is] get up and report myself at the Custom House at 7 a.m. every morning, and when I get there find little or nothing to do." Lovatt was simply killing time: "I have been sitting in the office all the forenoon talking about customs affairs, left to go to tiffin, and this afternoon I am to go to Hong Ku Wharf and assist Mr. May to do what little he has to do there."[3]

At a loss for ways to occupy himself, during the day he wrote home and walked around the wharf district chatting with colleagues, one of whom was Youngson, an examiner. Always alert to customs colleagues who overindulged in alcohol, "I was grieved to hear from Mr. May that he [Youngson] is addicted to drink, but I do hope not so as to prove injurious to his family. You can hardly imagine how grieved I am, especially [with a] wife and [five] little ones depending on [him]." In the evenings, he socialized, dining with May at his house in Hong Ku on one evening ("the first time I have been out") and with the captain of the *Glenfinas* the next. He also attended a ball where he danced with the wives of the customs staff. After two weeks of that routine, he picked up a rumor that he was to be sent to Hankou: "They knew all about it, but it will be a month before I know officially." Eventually, the dispatch from Hart arrived confirming his posting to the port where he had begun his customs career seventeen years earlier. After six weeks in Shanghai, Lovatt departed for his next post early in the morning on February 22 aboard the *Kuang Paw*.[4]

THE HANKOU SCENE

Lovatt arrived in Hankou in late February 1880, still a tidesurveyor under Commissioner F. W. White and drawing a monthly salary of 150 taels plus a 25-tael housing allowance. Soon after his arrival, Lovatt formed the distinct impression that he was one of Hart's favorites. For one thing, Hankou represented a plum assignment, arousing the envy of his colleagues: "[Goldspink] is frightfully indignant with the Inspector General for giving me Hankow. He thinks he ought to have had the port. May at Shanghai, who is a very nice fellow, thinks he ought to have been sent to Hankow. Anyway, my beloved brethren are all mad about it. I simply obeyed orders and here I am." A second indication that Hart favored him came when Lovatt put in for travel reimbursement: "On my arrival in Hankow I applied to the I. G. to allow me half of my passage money from England. I am glad to say he did so, and yesterday I got an order for Haikwan Taels 121.51. I am only the second member of the staff that has ever got it, so I think the IG must have a kind of sneaking regard for me."[5]

Lovatt initially had to share a house with Halsey, the tidesurveyor he was replacing, and from whom he even borrowed money to make the annual payment on his land in southwestern Minnesota. But Halsey's grating personality, about which he had been forewarned, caused Lovatt to seek out alternate housing arrangements after only two days. Halsey is

> not a nice man, neither is he agreeable, and the more I know of him the less I like him. He is mean beyond anything I ever saw. Then he is bad tempered, prejudiced against everybody, and a regular grumbler and scold. He would make anyone very wretched to live with, grumble, grumble all the time. This you can easily imagine is not pleasant to a fellow who does not often complain.

Moreover, Halsey "has a mania for money and is besides in so many ways very objectionable. I don't wonder at people not liking him." When Halsey finally boarded the steamer at the end of May, "not a soul in Hankow will regret his going away. You can hardly imagine how much he is disliked by the Commissioner and everybody in the Customs, and amongst the community also. [Only] one man besides myself went to see him off."[6]

The confluence of Halsey's imminent departure and the unexpected travel reimbursement was a godsend to Lovatt. He could now take solo occupancy of his house, repay the money he had borrowed from Halsey and buy his furniture worth $120, send 130 Pounds to Jennie, whitewash the house and purchase matting for it, and buy uniforms and summer clothes: "The Taels 121.51 has just put things to right, and lifted all care from my mind."[7]

As in his previous postings, Lovatt attended church services regularly, allowing him to evaluate the ministers. He was particularly taken by an American: "I like Foster the more I hear him. He preaches a most excellent sermon every Sunday, and on the whole I don't think him a bad fellow." By contrast, after hearing a boring sermon by D. Hill, a British missionary who had just arrived from Shansi, he noted that "none of the English parsons can preach as well as any ordinary American. I imagine they don't pay any attention to the art of public speaking."[8]

Performances on Sundays aside, Lovatt found that some of the local missionaries lived up to their dubious reputation: "The people of the missions here are not so social as they are in Kiukiang, and you know we always heard they were somewhat disagreeable." There were exceptions, of course. He had the Scarboroughs over to tea and played croquet with them and the Yankowskys. He also made the rounds of the missions:

> Saturday morning, it being a Chinese holiday, our office was closed, so I dressed myself, took a chair and four coolies and went up to Scarborough's, and there I found Mr. Hill in full Chinese costume, and not at all a bad looking Chinaman. All the Mission were in fact assembled, holding their yearly meeting to suit Hill, who intends returning to Shansi for a few years.[9]

Lovatt was also able to socialize easily with missionaries like the Archibalds, in part because he had met them previously. For example, he had met Mrs. Archibald in Wuhu when she was coming out to get married, and he characterized her as "a very nice, agreeable lady." The same went for her husband: "I don't see much of the missionaries except [Mr.] Archibald, who tramps round selling books. He is a very good fellow indeed." Consequently, Lovatt often had them over: "Last night I had Mr. & Mrs. Archibald to dinner, also Mrs. Scarborough. I like Mr. & Mrs. Archibald very much, they are very pleasant nice people."[10]

The Archibalds were Scottish, as was Burnett of the Scottish National Bible Society, who roomed briefly with Lovatt, causing him to address the combination of nationality and religion. Burnett is "an excitable and, one would think, a very unsuitable man for the position, but he gets on very well with the Chinese." Despite his affinity toward the Archibalds and Burnett, Lovatt had less than kind words for missionaries from Scotland generally: "I have met several of the Scotch missionary characters lately, and they don't impress one very favorably—religious, hard, and unfeeling—[although] I may be doing them injustice. I fear they are not likely to make many converts to Christianity." By contrast, "the Methodists in my opinion are the best [and] the kindliest. They have more sympathy with the Chinese, and manage to impress the natives with their love and affection for them." As for the Anglicans, "my own church, as a missionary church, I look upon as an utter failure, and without any energy or zeal. [Most] are not commendable in zeal or knowledge."[11]

Punctuating his socializing with the missionary community were occasions that broke up the normal routine. Chinese holidays such as the Dragon Festival was one, during which "the shops were all shut and the streets crowded with people in their holiday dress, all very well behaved, and I was never called foreign devil once." Another welcome disruption was the arrival of steamers with news from afar: "The up steamer today brought news of a row at Canton over the French Cathedral there, but the Chinese Governor General there acted with very great promptness in turning out the soldiers and putting down the riot very severely." And a third was the occasional gunboat, one of which was the British gunboat *Foxhound.* Another was the American gunboat, *Ashuelot*:

> I board[ed] her as she finished firing a salute for some Chinese soldiers that were lining the bank, who had come down to salute the Consul General. I boarded

> her in my official capacity as Harbour Master and made the acquaintance of her Officers, who seemed to be a very nice set of fellows, and this morning the ship has gone over to Wuchang to call on the viceroy.[12]

RUMORS OF WAR: THE ILI CRISIS

As always, China's foreign relations was something that Lovatt and the other members of the Western community in Hankou followed closely for the potential to affect them. And in 1880, the most pressing issue was the threat of war between Russia and China over Ili in the northwest, and it involved Chong Hou, with whom Lovatt had dealings fifteen years earlier when he had been training troops in Tianjin. Chong Hou had negotiated a treaty to have Russia return territory it had seized as a result of the Yakub Beg Rebellion in Xinjiang province, but the treaty was highly unfavorable to China because Russia agreed to return only some of the territory. The Chinese government refused to ratify the treaty and demanded that all the seized territory be returned, which Russia refused to do. As a result, "This treaty got Chung How into trouble."[13]

Lovatt wondered, "Will the gentlemen fight?" Because "the war rumours are very conflicting," Lovatt and the others found themselves "very much in the dark here." Stating that "I believe Russia's intentions are hostile," Lovatt indirectly criticized the sorry condition of China's military, saying that Russia's "advance upon China by sea and land will be with a degree of promptness and activity that will perfectly astonish John Chinaman." Reinforcing his opinion was the reported arrival of two Russian admirals in Yokohama and the fact that Russia had eleven battleships in the area, "a stronger force than she has ever had before, and greater than is necessary for the protection of her commerce."[14]

As for China, Lovatt saw not only a weak military but also a lack of will: "I doubt the Celestial. I believe he will back out if he gets a chance." One reason for this was that they were "indifferent to everything that transpires, except where their own local interests are involved." And when Lovatt queried the traders he dealt with, he found that "the Chinese merchants are all satisfied that China will not go to war." If China were "foolish enough to go to war," it would also impinge on the interests of other major powers, including England, that could be counted on to side with China, support seemingly confirmed when Lovatt learned that his former comrade-in-arms, Charles Gordon, had left England for China.[15]

Since he had been twice ordered by Hart to assist the Chinese militarily, first against the Nian and then against the Japanese, Lovatt knew he could be tapped a third time. Knowing that his family in America were reading the "many disquieting rumours" in the newspapers, he moved to reassure them:

"I will not under any circumstances have anything to do with military matters between Russia and China, not even if I am asked, which I have not been, and I don't think I am likely to be. They want younger men with more recent knowledge of war than I have." This he reconfirmed a month later, when he "promised to have nothing more to do with warlike movements."[16]

By the fall, the war scare abated, although "the news from Peking is still contradictory." For one thing, "the foreign ministers are all on the side of the peace party" and China "may be at last convinced that she has no chance with Russia." As evidence, Lovatt noted that Gordon was on his way back to England. That would of course mean that Hart would not be asking Lovatt to assist China militarily. As for China's ruling circle, "the Mandarins of the Capital continue to fall out and squabble amongst themselves. Most people think that the Russian demands will be conceded in full and then these high and mighty officials will begin business amongst themselves and do lots of head cutting by those who gain the victory, taking the heads of those who opposed them."[17]

CUSTOMS BUSINESS

Lovatt's daily routine was to rise at 5:30 a.m., have tea and toast, write to his wife, or muster the staff, then return to bathe and dress, followed by a breakfast of porridge and milk, a cup of coffee, and a slice of roast beef. He arrived at the office between 8:00 and 9:30 a.m., and stayed until l: 00 p.m., then home for lunch before returning to the office. At 4:00 p.m., his boy brought tea and toast to the office, and at 5:00 p.m. Lovatt left the office to return to the house to rest until dinner at 7:00 p.m. and followed by an hour's walk on the bund. At 9:00 p.m. he visited the ships in the port followed by one more turn on the bund at which point he returns home to read until 11:00 p.m. His routine was carried out with the help of his two servants: "The cook is a very good one, but he can't make coffee. My boy is quite a young fellow . . . and very good. I give him *five* dollars per month and he boards himself. The cook *seven*."[18]

Lovatt routinely had to confiscate contraband. For example, once he had to supervise the sale of three hundred pounds of silk. Perishable items had to be disposed of more quickly:

> I sold 2700 [duck] eggs (fresh) yesterday at auction for $2.25, about three dollars. And 3000 for $2.75, about 2 cash each. The officers seize them on board of the outgoing steamers, and as they will not keep, I sell them at once. I spoke in Chinese, and some of the bidders got mad and bid against each other so that the 12 baskets, 3600 eggs, sold for $6.00.[19]

Another routine assignment was occasionally to go downriver to inspect the beacon lights. These trips offered him the opportunity to stop in Jiujiang to look in on his friends, the local Chinese, and the house

> where we spent so many happy days and where three little pledges of our love were born. The Chinese were very anxious to hear of you and the children. Many old boys and coolies called to see me, all anxious that I should get them something to do. Poor fellows, not many foreigners are friendly to them. The old boatmen seemed especially glad to see me.[20]

Of course, Hankou had the usual petty annoyances. One was "a lot of musquitos. Hankow is a frightful place for them." Another was overly talkative local officials who interrupted his daily routine: "A wretched Chinese official called and talked and talked until two o'clock while I was waiting to have my tiffin. Then I got one of the officers to invite him outside to drink tea that I might have my tiffin while he was gone."[21]

The slow pace of Lovatt's daily routine was upended in the spring with the advent of tea season, when Hankou became much busier than his previous posting: "You who know the quiet and rather slow kind of life at Kiukiang would be surprised at the difference there is between the two ports. There is any amount of work here just now, and Hankow is nearly as lively as Shanghai." The reason for all the activity was new season's tea crop: "The place is full of people, Cantonese as well as foreigners. The Cantonese are teamen or middle men, and besides a lot of men who come up as stevedores, that is, men for the proper packing of tea in the tea ships, and ships come to supply them with provisions."[22]

When the tea season began in May, "the very numerous duties of my office" necessitated that Lovatt work overtime. On one day, ten tea steamers were in port and Lovatt had to board and berth every one. To do that he awoke at five in the morning and went to bed at 10.30 p.m., with "each moment of that pretty long day fully occupied." The market for Ning Chow and Oolung teas were going for 41 to 52 taels per cattie. Describing the loading process of one of the tea steamers, the *Glencoe*, "her sides are surrounded with cargo boats, and tea chests form one string at different points by the continuous stream of tea chests going up her sides into the ship." That process was replicated for the "hundreds of tea boats in the river and arriving daily." Despite the increased workload, Lovatt did not mind: "I like Hankow very much for the simple reason I am so very busy."[23]

By June, the first wave of the tea crop had been processed, easing some of the pressure on Lovatt: "This month will see [my duties] very much lightened. I have no Assistant and I muster the staff at 6 a.m. myself, and generally make the last rounds at 9 p.m., a pretty long work day, but then the days come and go so fast. By last night's steamer a lot of the tea men left for Shanghai and home, that is, men who only buy of the first crop."[24]

Even before the tea season had commenced, Lovatt noted that "the Commissioner and I get on very well so far." So when Lovatt competently handled the first wave of the tea crop, he earned kudos from White who said that "he was very satisfied with the way the work was done, and he left it in my hands entirely. I assure you I have worked very hard on purpose to please the Commissioner, and I am very happy to say I have succeeded, and I intend to keep his good opinion." This was no small accomplishment because Commissioner White had the reputation of being "one of the hardest men in the service" and yet he "has especially thanked me three times."[25]

Not only did Lovatt throw himself into his work, but he also went beyond the call of duty, efforts that did not pass unnoticed by Commissioner White. One such effort involved measuring a

> beast of [an old Butterfield and Swire] hulk for tonnage, and it is an appaling job. It took three of us all Saturday afternoon to measure the old tub, and it took me all Sunday to work out the calculations, and each one I did twice to be sure I was right. When I gave the form to the Commissioner completely filled in he seemed to be astonished at the elaborate calculations the measurements necessitated and seemed equally pleased.

Another initiative undertaken by Lovatt was authoring a twenty-page essay on silk culture "which [the Commissioner] was good enough to say was very good and very interesting." In sum, Lovatt had made a good impression on his boss, and the contrast with his predecessor was unmistakable: "You would be astounded at the difference of his treatment of me and Mr. Halsey. To me, he's all kindness and politeness."[26]

Making a good impression would presumably bring rewards, since commissioners had to submit a "Confidential Report on Staff" every six months to Hart, leading Lovatt to hope he would "get promoted, or rather my pay increased." Of course, that ultimately depended on the IG: "Bob seems to move mighty slow, but don't be discouraged, *we shall pull through*." Hope for a promotion increased with the advent of a new year: "We are *as usual* looking forward to lots of changes in the spring, and every one of us looking anxiously for promotion, and feeling we deserve it, and that if Hart don't promote all of us, he is a mean cuss."[27]

As the frenetic pace of the tea season came to an end, Lovatt resumed his normal routine until one day in March 1881 when on the way to the office as usual, "I met someone [who] asked me if I was all ready to leave for Tientsin. He said he had heard at the Custom House that I was transferred." Upon arriving at the office, the commissioner "said he had news for me and then told me about the transfer. He was good enough to say that he was sorry I was going away, but the dispatch said distinctly on promotion." His impending relocation triggered a bittersweet reaction: "In many ways I'm sorry to leave Hankow. Yet the promotion is what I have worked for, for in getting it I am getting nearer you and home." The promotion also came with a raise to 200 taels per month. Lovatt's reference to going home to Minnesota was fleeting, however, for just five days later he pointedly omitted the word "home": "I am feeling pretty thankful over the promotion, for it will help us so much, and bring the time more quickly for us to be together." Lovatt was planning for Jennie to join him in Asia.[28]

In the short term, however, Lovatt looked forward to returning to Tianjin where he had served a dozen years earlier. For one, the weather would be better: "One of the advantages will be my getting out of the long hot summer, for Tientsin is much cooler than this place and while summer is pretty hot for about six weeks, the nights are much cooler." Moreover, the infrastructure had improved significantly: "The mail arrangements at Tientsin are much better now than they were formerly, as there is a courier leaving once a week during winter." And third, the threat of disease did not deter him: "The plague are all over the north of China, but I know better how to deal with them." Fourth and finally, he looked forward to being reunited with his friends who were still there: "I shall expect to find Tientsin very much altered and changed with very many new people there, but some of my old friends are there. I have no doubt of a warm welcome from my friends."[29]

All that was left was to make arrangements to leave. Lovatt had his mail held in Shanghai, and withdrew the 2,000 taels he had in the customs bank in Hankou, which had been drawing 12 taels a month in interest, to transfer it to the Hong Kong and Shanghai Bank in Shanghai. His replacement, Moorehead, and his family arrived from Jiujiang on April 3, Lovatt noting that "it will take two or three days to hand over charge to him, so I will be here for the races." After thirteen months in Hankou, Lovatt departed on April 8, 1881, arrived in Shanghai on April 12, where he spent three days, departed on April 15, and arrived in Tianjin on April 22 to take up his duties.[30]

NOTES

1. James H. Hart, Commissioner of Customs, to Lovatt (Tidesurveyor on leave), Customs House, No. 4, Shanghai, June 25, 1879 (in Lakeland, Washington County); *Service List, 1878*, 13; WNL to JSL, April 18 and 21, 1877 and October 27, and November 2, 3, 5, and 8, 1879, and January 5, 1889. Sarah "has a good many trials" because her husband Edward, who served aboard a ship that carried tea from Shanghai to England, while "a kind good husband, [is] without brains or ability," so Sarah

"has to manage everything." Tom served aboard the British warship *Excellent*. Tom's one flaw was "the bane of the British navy, he drinks, so I am afraid he will never do himself much good." Lovatt's other brother Jack had drowned while also serving in the British navy. In London while waiting to set off, Lovatt visited an old army buddy, Clifton Trollope, "the man with whom I spent so many of my young years in the tented field, and on the long and weary march through India and Northern China. We were always the best of friends." Trollope died nine years later, in 1888.

2. WNL to JSL, January 3 (*S.S. Glenfinas*, Hong Kong), 12, and 16, and August 13, 1880.

3. WNL to JSL, January 12, 13, 14, 15, and 16, 1880.

4. WNL to JSL, January 16 and 23, and February 22, 1880.

5. WNL to JSL, April 15 and May 12, 1880, and March 18, 1882. Lovatt's correspondence is missing for July and the first half of August, 1880, and also February and early March, 1881; *Service List, 1880*, 14, 66. Goldspink had joined the customs service six months before Lovatt. Serving with Lovatt was First Class Tidewaiter E. Brandon and Second Class Tidewaiter L. Oesterholm (Swedish), who died on the job early in 1881: "He has been failing ever since he was in Kuikiang, but as the winter set in he gradually fell into a decline and became so weak and feeble that he died without any pain. We buried him in the churchyard last evening." WNL to JSL, January 18, 1881.

6. WNL to JSL, April 12, 1880.

7. WNL to JSL, April 12, May 12 and 30, June 4 and 15, and September 30, 1880.

8. WNL to JSL, April 19 and October 31, 1880.

9. WNL to JSL, May 10, June 11 and 14, August 21, and November 2, 1880. Hill left Hankou in November.

10. WNL to JSL, April 20, May 10 and June 4, 1880.

11. WNL to JSL, July 21, 1880.

12. WNL to JSL, June 12, 14, and 15, and September 26, 1880.

13. WNL to JSL, June 23, 1880.

14. WNL to JSL, June 23 and July 21, 1880.

15. WNL to JSL, April 20, June 23, July 21, September 26, and November 14, 1880.

16. WNL to JSL, November 2, 3, and 5, 1879 (In Portsmouth), and April 24, May 10, June 4, 11, 12, and 25, and July 21, 1880.

17. WNL to JSL, August 21, October 31, and November 14, 1880.

18. WNL to JSL, April 20, June 12, and August 13, 1880. Emphasis in the original.

19. WNL to JSL, August 21 and November 2, 1880.

20. WNL to JSL, April 24, May 8, and November 15, 1880.

21. WNL to JSL, June 25, 1880.

22. WNL to JSL, May 10, 12, and 18, 1880.

23. WNL to JSL, May 18, and June 4 and 25, 1880.

24. WNL to JSL, June 4, 1880.

25. WNL to JSL, May 10, June 15, and August 21, 1880.

26. WNL to JSL, May 10 and 18, June 15, and August 21, 1880. Emphasis in the original. Foolscap refers to a paper size standard in England at the time.

27. King, 49; WNL to JSL, June 15 and August 21, 1880, and January 23, 1881. Emphasis in the original.

28. WNL to JSL, March 22 and 27, 1881. His promotion did not mean that he was now a commissioner. There were several grades of tidesurveyor, each of which came with a different pay grade. So his new rank raised his monthly salary to 200 *taels*. He had originally attained the rank of tidesurveyor in October of 1867.

29. WNL to JSL, March 22, 1881. Hankou [Wuhan] is regarded as one of China's four "furnaces."

30. WNL to JSL, March 22, 27, and 29, and April 2, 1881; *Service List*, 1881, 18 and 73.

Chapter 8

Resignation

Tianjin, 1881–1883

PILLAR OF THE COMMUNITY

When Lovatt arrived in Tianjin in late April 1881, it marked his fourth time in that city. The first two times had been brief, as a soldier en route to and from the siege of Beijing in the summer of 1860. His third time in the city was a more extensive three-year period from 1865 to 1868, primarily as a trainer of Qing cavalry. Now there as tidesurveyor and harbor master, he would serve under three commissioners, beginning with Gustav Detring, followed in 1882 by W. H. Jamieson, and finally in 1883 by Herbert E. Hobson.[1]

Lovatt had now been in China for more than two decades, and had acquired a modicum of respect for China's culture and its people. Yet his Euro-American biases still revealed themselves on occasion. For example, in his discussion of the hot summer sun, he commented that many Chinese did not wear hats: "Many hardened sinners here appear to enjoy the summer and revel in the heat, especially the heathen Chinese, who unblushingly face the sun in all his noonday glory with uncovered head. It is easy in that case to clearly understand their final destination [hell]. I of course take the most charitable view, but fear it is hoping against hope." Moreover, he still did not regard Chinese as equal to Westerners: "I read the account of the war in Egypt. All the eastern people appear to be born cruel and bloodthirsty. This war may teach them a lesson, and in future make them show a higher respect and appreciation for European life. The sad thing about it is that many valuable lives will be lost in teaching these savages how to behave."[2]

Nonetheless, Lovatt generally got along with the Chinese and for the most part endured the petty annoyances that Tianjin threw at him. Weather was one. While he mostly liked the winter because it never got very cold, he did not care for the other seasons: "Spring here is very backward, no real cold days, but cloudy gloomy days, and we get to be such children of the sun that a gloomy day or two is depressing." And in the summer, "you have to wear a sun hat to protect your head from the sun." Moreover, the lack of humidity "seems to affect people's nerves a good deal, and many people get very irritable." Another annoyance was Tianjin's famous dust, which "beats anything you ever saw for that article—real genuine dust that blows so thick you can hardly see across the road." Sand flies were yet another annoyance, as they are "numerous . . . , very persistent, and silent, also invisible in their attacks and raise quite large blisters." Lack of proper sanitation and drainage also annoyed Lovatt: "This glorious country is one grand, abominable stink—fresh air or ventilation is abomination of abomination to a Chinaman. Still, they live, flourish, and grow fat. I would like to live away from smells." And there was the threat of small pox, but then "it is always about Chinese streets."[3]

Lovatt quickly fell into a routine. He adopted another feline companion who had been starved by his former Chinese owners. His "boy," Hsiung, prepared his lunch which he ate at the office. Dinner at 7:30 p.m. was oftentimes a communal affair, assisted by "pleasant conversation at dinner and a game of cards after dinner to pass a very pleasant evening. I often spend my last hour of an evening when taking my last smoke [of a Manila cigar]."[4]

Lovatt soon established himself as a leading member of the expatriate community in Tianjin. In addition to his duties at the customs house, Lovatt tried his hand at publishing a newspaper—the *Northern Post*—charging 1 tael a month ($1.40). Initially, he was pleased with his work that took the pulse of the expatriate community: "It is only a half sheet, but I think we get it up very well." He combined his role of newspaper editor with that of an active civic-minded community member concerned with improving the city, with an additional eye on benefiting financially: "The meeting at the Consulate today is to take into consideration . . . the advisability of forming a gas company to light the [foreign] settlement and a portion of the Chinese town. I shall attend the meeting, and if it is formed, I shall also subscribe for a number of shares, for it is going to be a very paying investment, and think it will be the best in China."[5]

Editing the local newspaper brought him to the attention of some of Yung Wing's protégés:

> The Chinese students that were educated in America [Hartford, Connecticut] have been to me and want me to help them get up a newspaper. I am going to write to Shanghai and see if the [*Shanghai*] *Courier* [*and China Gazette*] will not help them. I think [the editor] will, the lads are very nice and pleasant, and are really American in every way.

But his good opinion of that editor soon soured, for when Lovatt sent him a story, the *Courier* did not publish it, so "I feel mad and look with contempt on all newspaper men now." When two months more passed without his story appearing, "I have given up writing to the *Courier*," his decision made easier by the fact that "being in the Customs, I might easily get into a row by writing of things that the I. G. might take offense at."[6]

Eventually the responsibilities of publishing the newspaper became too much for Lovatt: "I am going to finish up the paper on the 28th February and shall feel a good deal of responsibility has been taken off my shoulders." He also revisited his contempt for newspaper men:

> I have the kindliest sympathy for Editors now after my own experience, for although I took special pains never to say an unkind word of anybody or allow anyone to speak unkindly of anyone in it, yet I fear I made a few stupid people dislike me because I did not compliment them or did not compliment them enough, but it does not matter, I am determined never to be an Editor again.[7]

Although he gave up the newspaper, Lovatt was still one of the most prominent members of Tianjin because he also directed a theater troupe, giving performances to the sailors on the gunships as well as to the "refined and cultivated" foreign community. His position as theater director opened many doors for him: "I was at dinner with Mr. Pelldram, the German Consul, who had invited all the theatrical troupe to his house. We spent a very pleasant evening. Mr. Pelldram is quite rich and lives in great style." But like his stint as newspaper editor, Lovatt also soon tired of his role as theater director, and soon "determined never to be a theatrical manager again."[8]

TIANJIN SOCIETY

In Lovatt's social circle, horses figured prominently, and he had his own mount, Smiling Morn, who "jumps very well and carries me, and I am a little heavy [238 pounds]." Lovatt took him on fox hunts, but on one such outing, "with my heavy weight I soon had to pull up and give my pony a rest." Since Tianjin boasted a race track, Lovatt took his horse there for exercise "to keep him from getting too fat, but there is not much fear of that with me on his back." And, of course, there were the usual horse races at the track.[9]

Lovatt was soon on the lookout for a race horse of his own. When a horse dealer from Beijing brought a "nice looking" pony,

> young Mr. Lyall, an assistant of ours, a thoroughly nice fellow, was anxious that I should go in with him for a pony that I agreed to do so out of my liking for

> him, and so we went to the race course and sent the pony round for a half a mile and both of us came to the conclusion he went pretty fast and we consequently decided to buy him.

Then followed a bit of haggling. The horse dealer asked 60 taels

> but we got him for forty and will now train him for the races, and so you see your churchgoing and truly religious husband is going in for horse racing. As Lyall is a little fellow and a very good rider, he will do the training and riding. It will cost us 20 taels each for the pony and the entries, and expenses may make it up to 50 taels each for us.[10]

In addition to horse riding, other opportunities for physical activity abounded, and Lovatt engaged in most of them. During the winter it was ice skating: "It is splendid exercise. I get tired pretty often. I fancy my heavy weight all coming on to my ankles tires me." In the summer it was tennis: "I have felt very well all the summer so far and think that lawn tennis helps to keep me all right. I play every evening [at 4:00 p.m.] somewhere." He lamented that "I would play quite well if I was not quite so stout. I also feel not quite so spry as I once was." Aware that his weight was holding him back, Lovatt did his best not to gain more: "I often try the starvation principle on myself so as to keep from getting too stout, but I only just manage to keep the same weight. I never touch beer. I know the tendency of that liquid element to increase the weight of man."[11]

Other opportunities for exercise included hiking, and there were various destinations and companions from which he could choose: "I am going off with Mr. Clarke ('a real nice fellow') for a walk to the Hai Kwan Su temple." On Sundays, lunch and hiking were often combined: "Today there is a party of us going round the defence wall [a distance of eleven miles] in which we combine a tiffin and a walk." On these excursions, the men walked and the "ladies go in jinrickashas which were introduced into Tientsin last summer, and are much better than chairs, the only drawback being that these Tientsin coolies are such poor, feeble fellows, nothing like those fine fellows [in Japan]."[12]

Entertaining also figured prominently in Tientsin's expatriate community, and Lovatt pulled his share of the load. For example, he hosted a tiffin for the family of Lieutenant Alfred Mahan who stayed until four in the afternoon and "are nice pleasant people." But more often than not, since his wife was not with him, Lovatt was the guest of others, such as at "the Moellendorffs, Mr. and Mrs. Bristow, Dr. Frazier, Dr. Lewen, Mr. Carrale, and yours truly. We had a very pleasant tiffin, laughed and chatted a great deal, and enjoyed ourselves very much." Not all such occasions were as pleasing:

> Last night I went to one of those unsatisfactory parties that has occasionally to be endured, you can't possibly say enjoyed, but imagine ten men, and only two ladies, sitting down to dinner. There were Danes, English, Scotch, Germans, Swiss, and French. Of course, conversation was all in English, only one Swiss gentleman who could not speak English, so we all had a go at him in French, which must have amused him greatly for we nearly all spoke it.[13]

Despite his lack of a formal higher education, Lovatt nonetheless saw himself as somewhat of an intellectual, not only allowing him to mix easily with the various diplomats and missionaries, but also causing him to comment on the apparent lack of appreciation of culture among his colleagues: "The Customs Library is miserably poor, but when our new Commissioner comes I expect to make some great improvements in it." And it was not simply books that were lacking: "I am often astonished at the humdrum tone of people in China. You hardly ever hear them speak of an author, book, or picture, and should you accidentally mention one, or speak of it with pleasure, what a blank look is fixed upon you."[14]

Socializing also took place on the visiting gunships. When the *USS Ashuelot* docked, Lovatt went on board for tiffin and

> had a very enjoyable time. They are an exceedingly nice lot of fellows on board, and every one in Tientsin likes them very much. None of them are western men, nearly all from eastern states. I feel quite at home on board. It makes such a difference to the life and activity of the port, for without the *Ashuelot* we should be very much duller.

Naturally, he was sorry when it weighed anchor: "The good ship *Ashuelot* left this forenoon with all the good fellows on board of her that have helped us to pass so pleasant a winter." As a result, "our port looks quite deserted now two of our gun boats have gone." When a British gunboat arrived four months later, it stopped only briefly: "they only stop a week in port now; that is the new rule."[15]

Impromptu occasions for socializing also occurred when one of their number departed for another post. When the news arrived that Commissioner Detring was being transferred, a public dinner was planned before he left, "this I think is the very least that the community do, considering all that he has done for them." The plan soon came to fruition: "Last night some forty of us sat down to the table, and enjoyed a very good dinner. He [Detring] is certainly the most popular Commissioner I have ever known and deserves well of everybody, for he is a good & kindly hearted man." Lovatt and his colleagues also gave him a parting gift—a silver cup—"this being solely contributed by the members of the staff." In similar fashion, Lovatt and his colleagues planned a farewell when one of their favorite diplomats, the Russian Consul Karl Waeber, was transferred to Beijing. Since "he has been here some sixteen years and always more or less connected with the club, the members propose giving him a dinner tonight."[16]

Because Tianjin was so near to Beijing, visiting dignitaries and diplomats often appeared either on their way to or from the capital, providing an opportunity for socializing with them. These included, for example, the American minister to China John Russell Young, who "appears to be very agreeable. I met him and was introduced to him by General [Alexander C.] Jones, the American consul at Nagasaki." It also included General Robert E. Lee's daughter who was invited to dinner at the British consulate: "A friend of mine who was present says she amused them very much. She has just returned from Peking and says all the armies of China could not put her out of the country, with her fan and a pair of scissors she would keep them all at bay."[17]

Holidays provided another excuse for socializing, as etiquette required that Lovatt make courtesy calls on the other members of the expatriate community: "Yesterday, the whole of the day was spent in making New Year's calls. I think I called upon every lady in the community. The German ladies were very nice and kind."[18]

Sundays were given over to church services, with varying degrees of enjoyment. On one occasion, "There was twenty of us, sixteen missionaries, and four sinners. The parson was extremely feeble and the singing positively weak." At other times the services were more pleasing: "I heard the Rev. Mr. Walter preach a very good sermon." Oftentimes, his Sundays combined church, socializing over lunch or dinner, and exercise:

> Yesterday being Sunday I was pretty busy, went to church twice—morning when Stanley preached a dull old sermon for three quarters of an hour and set us all to sleep. Then in the afternoon I went for a walk with Ensign Oliver of the *Ashuelot*, an extremely nice fellow, and on our return went to skate at the rink for an hour or two, and then in the evening went to hear Mr. Smith. He preaches very well indeed—a man full of thought and ability—the church was quite full. After church I went with Clarke to dinner.[19]

GOSSIP

Gossip was a staple of Lovatt's existence and often revolved around changes in customs personnel. Although there was talk about changes at lower levels, it was those at the top that provided the most grist for the rumor mill. When it became known in early 1882 that Detring was leaving, there was not only regret but also intense speculation on who would replace him. In the end, Detring was replaced by W. H. Jamieson who "is a very nice quiet fellow, and we all like him very much." But Jamieson stayed for only five months before being transferred to Shantou, replaced by Herbert E. Hobson who was coming from Tamsui. Although Lovatt found the constant turnover annoying, he did like the commissioners: "This changing of Commissioners is not very agreeable, but we are getting a very good man in Mr. Jamieson's place. He [Hobson] seems very nice and I think will be very popular. I like him better than the one just leaving today, Mr. Jamieson."[20]

Gossip extended beyond customs service changes to highly personal matters. Lovatt had noticed that during the German Consul Peldram's party for his theatrical troupe, the host paid particular attention to the "young and pretty" wife of US consul James C. Zuck. That might have been the end of it, except that five months later it took on a life of its own:

> Last night, to celebrate the 4th July, I called at the American Consulate to pay my respects to Mr. Zuck and then went for a walk with them. While at the consulate an incident occurred which was somewhat painful and I let you into the secret. Mrs. Zuck is young, tall, and very stylish. She is a California girl born and bred, rough in her ways and masculine in her manners, a kind of woman that men don't mind meeting and joking with, but would hate to have any of those they love act like her. I think her very fond of dress, but I believe her to be a true, upright, and honorable woman. Well, the German Consul who relieved Moellendorff, Mr. Pelldram, has paid great attention to her [and], being rich, he has entertained the Zucks in a very stylish way. Well, Pelldram has tagged Mrs. Zuck round a good deal, and some months ago he took to coming to church to gaze upon her to the amusement of everybody, and the flirtation had become somewhat marked. Mr. Zuck is much older than his wife. In fact, she is his second wife, and is a quiet steady sensible man. Still, he is a good, kind hearted fellow, fond of his wife and children. Well, the day before, I hear, Mr. Pelldram and Mrs. Zuck were out in the Park walking together, a pair of awful swells, she dresses well and knows she looks well. What transpired I don't know, but when I called at the Consulate I was chatting with Mr. and Mrs. Zuck while Zuck was opening a fresh box of cigars, when in came Pelldram and congratulated Mrs. Zuck, while Mr. Zuck seeing him coming, walked away, but soon came back. When Pelldram offered to shake hands, Zuck quietly declined the proffered hand. When Pelldram said, "will you not give me your hand?" Zuck said "no." When Pelldram walked away, Mrs. Zuck sat there in the most unconcerned manner possible. After this we started for a walk. I am glad to think it will bring this terrific flirtation to a close. I think Mrs. Zuck is silly. She has never met before the honeyed and monied men of the world and no doubt thought them nice fellows. She is bright and sharp in everything else, and pleasant. I have heard nothing more about it, and of course have not mentioned to anyone the scene I was accidentally a witness to.[21]

In the course of his duties, Lovatt interacted with the local Chinese residents and, being fluent in Chinese, could pick up gossip and rumors from that quarter. Some pertained to the recently departed Detring who, it was rumored, wanted Viceroy Li Hongzhang to give him an order for a gunboat, which would net Detring a large commission. But since Li did not, "the Chinese think he has not treated Detring very handsomely in the matter, but again rumour has it that the Government in Peking are down on the Viceroy for spending so much money." Since Tianjin was now Li's headquarters, when "the great Li Hung Chang has left us, there is little or no news stirring amongst the Chinese."[22]

Other rumors circulating among the local Chinese that Lovatt picked up revolved around foreign enemies, real or imagined. One was the Japanese: "[The Chinese] get up a little idea of their own that the Japanese want to fight them, and they fluster and bluster a good deal for a short time and then settle down as if nothing occurred." Another was the Russians: "[The Chinese] occasionally start a story that Russia is moving immense armies towards their frontier, and intends to take away half the empire." And rumors about French designs in Vietnam, a Chinese territory, were beginning to surface.[23]

Lovatt's contacts among the Chinese revealed the fitful progress of China's modernization and attitudes at the local level. When the emperor ordered the Kaiping Coal Mines closed on account of the death of the Western Empress, the local Chinese commented that the "old fokies of Pekin have come to the conclusion that the opening of the bowels of mother earth let out bad fung shui [geomancy] on the capital, and now they are stopping it. Fung shui must not be interfered with."[24]

In addition to national issues, Lovatt got the inside scoop on local events from his Chinese contacts. For example, "when a fire breaks out and burns a street of houses down, that interests all of them, especially the fellows who steal, and they are not a few." Murders also aroused local interest: "The commital of some atrocious crime by some rascal causes a nine days wonder until they have heard that he is beheaded, and then they kindly remark that it was the wrong man."[25]

One topic seemingly in short supply was antiforeignism, notable given that the infamous Tianjin Massacre had occurred only a dozen years earlier. In fact, during the entire year of 1882, there was only one report, that not only did not involve Tianjin but also one that Lovatt immediately discounted: "The only thing was a report that several missionaries belonging to Chefoo [Yantai] were killed by a mob of lawless heathens, but I don't believe there is a word of truth in it." And in the following year, he noted only two occurrences, neither of which involved Tianjin. One was in Yantai where "a boatman belonging to a foreign Hong [business] struck another Chinaman in a native lighter and killed him. The foreigner took his own Chinaman's part and has sent him away. This has enraged the people at Chefoo, and now the foreigner has to remain on board a gunboat." The other occurred in Hankou where "a secret society intended to set fire to the three cities [Hankou, Wuchang, and Hanyang], and then rob the banks and shops, and so causing general destruction with the hope of raising a rebellion."[26]

INFRASTRUCTURE

Located roughly halfway between the capital and the coast at Dagu, the issue of infrastructure was salient since Lovatt had the occasion to visit both. When he took a two-week leave to visit Beijing, about 90 miles away, to visit the Great Wall and the surrounding mountains, and, of course, to pay a courtesy call on Hart, it took him two days to get there. It was possible to make the trip in nine hours, as Detring had, but he had four ponies stationed along the way. One could also come and go to Beijing on the Peiho, but that route was often problematical. When Hart and his family came by boat from Beijing to Tianjin, Lovatt was concerned that the lack of water would pose a problem: "All the steamers get stuck this spring [and] whether this old ditch called the Peiho is really going to dry up or not I don't know, but there is precious little water in it." Sure enough,

> the I. G. and family yesterday went on board the S. S. *Taku* and when the *Taku* tried to get away she lay right across the river and would not budge until high water in the middle of the night, and then she just got round and stuck on the bank that had formed by the steamer laying across the river, and while I am writing this she lays in the stream opposite my office window, waiting for the tide.[27]

The Peiho could also become jammed by the barges coming up the Grand Canal:

> My righteous soul is being vexed within me by the arrival in the river of some 200 monstrous junks laden with rice from the south, and this little bit of a wet ditch is just choked up with them, and consequently captains of steamers vent their wrath on me as if I was to blame, and collisions are disagreeably numerous. I have sent down an officer who will attend to it in future, and try to get these wretched junks into line.[28]

As part of his duties, Lovatt on a regular basis had to travel in the other direction to Dagu, an aspect of his job that he enjoyed. Hart had directed the Harbormaster to visit the buoys and beacons once a month, so for Lovatt "it is a nice three or four day holiday." This was especially true during the summer, "for it is an agreeable change from the heat of Tientsin to the cool sea breeze of Taku." Even when he felt under the weather, a trip to Dagu was therapeutic: "I am still feeling pretty seedy. I am going to the office this morning and will see the Commissioner and tell him I will go to Taku for a change."[29]

As with Beijing, the trip to Dagu could be made either by river or by road. The distance by river was 53 miles and could be covered by steam launch in five or six hours, so if conditions were good it was the preferable mode of conveyance. However, traveling by boat also had the same potential problem of low water levels as between Tianjin and Beijing: "I have been on my monthly tour of inspection to Taku and only returned this morning by the steamer *Sin Nan Zing* [when] we got stuck last night in the river and had to remain."[30]

At other times he went to Dagu by "a real bad [36-mile] road. I left Tientsin the day before yesterday in a cart for the lively and exhilarating spot, with the definite object in view of remeasuring all the lighters that are here laid up for the winter. I had only one old mattress in the cart." Due to the rigors of traveling overland, he was happy to arrive at his assistant's place in Dagu where "I found a warm welcome from Mr. & Mrs. [William F.] Stevenson, and a nice warm room, that and a good dinner soon made me feel allright again."[31]

Although he normally enjoyed his monthly trips to Dagu, that was not always the case. Not only did he have to inspect and verify the position of the buoys and beacons, but he also had "an awful tedious job measuring sixteen vessels for Tonnage, and I shall be glad when finished." And when the weather did not cooperate, "Taku is one sea of mud." Given the bad roads he often endured in Dagu, "I will be glad to get back to [Tianjin's] good roads."[32]

Lovatt departed Tianjin in the late summer of 1883 to assume the position of commissioner of Customs in Pusan, Korea, his appointment due to his friend Paul Georg von Möllendorff who had been appointed chief commissioner of the Korean Customs Service the previous year. Lovatt would serve there until 1886 when he was forced out by Sir Robert Hart.[33]

NOTES

1. *Service List, 1881*, 18, 73; *Service List, 1882*, 19, 82; *Service List, 1883*, 19, 88. Serving underneath Lovatt was William F. Stevenson as Assistant Tidesurveyor in Dagu, and C. C. de Castro as Examiner. Most of his correspondence between April and December of 1881 and November and December of 1882 is missing.

2. WNL to JSL, July 7 and September 24, 1882.

3. WNL to JSL, June 22, July 7 and 24, and August 1, 1882, and March 2 and April 16, 1883. The stench Lovatt refers to came from the soap boiling works. Charles King, Nicholas Belfield Dennys, and William Frederick Mayers, *The Treaty Ports of China and Japan: A Complete Guide to the Open Ports of Those Countries, Together*

with Peking, Yedo, Hongkong and Macao, Forming a Guide Book and Vade Mecum for Travellers, Merchants, and Residents in General (London: Trubner and Co., and Hong Kong: Shortrede and Co., 1867), 473–474.

4. WNL to JSL, January 4, August 23, and September 11, 1882, and February 25, 1883.

5. WNL to JSL, January 13, 17, and 24, and February 7, 1882.

6. WNL to JSL, January 27, February 8, July 2, and September 21, 1882.

7. WNL to JSL, February 7 and March 6, 1882.

8. WNL to JSL, February 4 and 12, and March 6, 1882.

9. WNL to JSL, January 1 and 16, March 22, and April 5, 1882.

10. WNL to JSL, April 7, 1882.

11. WNL to JSL, February 4, July 29, August 9, and October 10, 1882.

12. The party included Lieutenant Alfred and Mrs. Mahan, the U.S. Consul James C. Zuck, Pelldram, the German Consul, Mr. Clarke, Mr. Lyall, and Dr. Greene. WNL to JSL, January 29, February 5 and 10, and July 13, 1882.

13. WNL to JSL, September 5, 1881, January 1, 1882, and April 22, 1883.

14. WNL to JSL, February 7 and March 20, 1882.

15. WNL to JSL, January 4, March 15, and July 15, 1882. By this time, Lovatt, married to an American and having expressed on several occasions his admiration of the country, decided that he would become a naturalized American on his next home leave. In a rather bold statement to his Irish I. G. when he paid a courtesy call on him at his office in Beijing, Lovatt told him that he would become an American citizen when he returned. WNL (in Beijing) to JSL, March 4, 1882. Lovatt returned to the United States in 1886, but there is no evidence that he became a naturalized citizen.

16. WNL to JSL, March 15, 16, and 20, and April 5, 7, 9, and 11, 1882. Detring was liked not only by his subordinates but also by Hart:

> "The Commissioner has received a dispatch from the I. G. in which the I. G. compliments him and says in consideration of his important services in Tientsin he grants him his two years leave on *full pay*. Taels 500 per month for two years for wandering about Europe. I wish Mr. Detring very much to enjoy it, and hope he will, for he deserves all of it."

WNL to JSL, November 4, 1882.

17. WNL to JSL, November 8, 1882 and May 22, 1883. Young (1840–1899) served as US minister to China from 1882 to 1885.

18. WNL to JSL, January 3 and June 20, 1882. And since Lovatt was a Mason, he had the companionship of his fellow members on a regular basis: "Our Masonic lodge is to be consecrated this evening and a general assembly of the brethren will take place."

19. WNL to JSL, January 10 and 22, July 2, and October 16, 1882.

20. WNL to JSL, February 5 and 23, September 24 and 29, and October 2, 1882; *Service List, 1882*, 19, 82; *Service List, 1883*, 19, 88. Hobson had served as Charles Gordon's interpreter.

21. WNL to JSL, February 12 and July 5, 1882.

22. WNL to JSL, January 4, April 9 and July 7, 1882.

23. WNL to JSL, February 8, 1882 and May 19 to July 30, 1883, various letters.

24. WNL to JSL, March 11, 1882 and March 2, 1883. Emphasis in the original.

25. WNL to JSL, February 8 and July 7, 1882.

26. WNL to JSL, June 26, 1882, and May 9 and 19, 1883.

27. WNL to JSL, February 7, 10, and 23, and March 4, 6, 9, 15, 16, 22, 24, 26, 28, and 30, 1882; see the description in *The Treaty Ports of China and Japan,* 482–483.

28. WNL to JSL, March 12, 1883.

29. WNL to JSL, July 17, August 14, and September 14, 1882.

30. WNL to JSL, June 18, August 14, and September 19, 1882.

31. WNL to JSL, November 4, 1882 and February 15, 1883. The British secretary of the Imperial Naval Yard at Dagu, Stevenson (1843–1904), had been married three months earlier to Annie Alice Frith and had just moved in to his new house, built by the naval yard for him, where he "seems to be very happy." He died in Shanghai and is buried there. Correspondence from his great-grandson, Peter Hodge, 2014.

32. WNL to JSL, August 14, 1882, and February 21 and March 12, 1883. The only third-party record of Lovatt's official duties is contained in a letter from Commissioner W. H. Jamieson, to A. M. Bisbee, Coast Inspector in Shanghai, June 9, 1882: "I beg now to forward enclosed, a list, supplied by Mr. Tidesurveyor and Harbour Master Lovatt, of Instruments and Books belonging to his Department at this port." The list included a rain gauge, barometer, compass, and thermometer. *Tianjin. Correspondence to and from Outposts*, Number 679. Second Historical Archives, Nanjing.

33. Lovatt's service in Korea is described in full in my book *In the Service of His Korean Majesty: William Nelson Lovatt, the Pusan Customs, and Sino-Korean Relations, 1876–1888* (Berkeley: University of California Institute of East Asian Studies Korea Research Monograph 35, 2012).

Chapter 9

Commissioner in Korea

1883–1888

PUSAN, AUGUST 1883 TO JUNE 1886

During his time in Jiujiang from 1870 to 1877, Lovatt had befriended another member of the Customs Service, the German Paul Georg von Möllendorff. Möllendorff eventually resigned from the Chinese customs and moved to Tianjin where he served as German vice-consul before resigning to work for Li Hongzhang. In 1882, when Korea asked Li for advice on how to set up its own Customs Service, Li advised them to do what the Chinese had done—hire a Westerner like Hart. Li then sent Möllendorff to Korea to establish its Customs Service as well as to act as Korea's principal foreign policy adviser to make sure that country did not come under the influence of Japan or Russia. Meanwhile, Lovatt, after a posting in Wuhu, home leave, and a stint in Hankou, arrived in Tianjin in the spring of 1881 and was witness to his friend's appointment to Korea. Initially, he was skeptical that Möllendorff could succeed, and predicted that if it did not work out, he "could always come back to the [Chinese] customs, of course in a junior capacity." In other words, if Hart took Möllendorff back, it would no doubt be at a lower rank (figure 9.1).[1]

That hypothetical future for his friend became more than merely academic for Lovatt in Tianjin when Möllendorff offered him the post of customs commissioner in Pusan, causing Lovatt to weigh his options. On the one hand, if he rejected the offer and remained in China, there was the possibility that he would be promoted to commissioner. But promotion depended on Hart, and Lovatt now sensed that the IG did not particularly like him, recalling a

Figure 9.1 Paul Georg von Mollendorff in Chinese Clothing in Jiujang. Courtesy: The Bancroft Library, University of California, Berkeley.

conversation the two had had in Beijing the previous winter when Hart said, "I suppose when you go home on leave next time you will remain." This offhand remark surprised Lovatt and led him to conclude that "I have about all the promotion I am likely to get."[2]

On the other hand, if he accepted Möllendorff's offer, he would attain the higher rank of commissioner and a higher salary of 300 taels, a substantial increase from his current tidesurveyor salary of 200 taels. But that course of action also carried with it the risk that if he resigned from the Chinese customs, Hart would view him as disloyal, precluding any return to China should the Korean customs collapse. That is, he would be in the same hypothetical situation as Möllendorff: "It would never do to ask the I. G. to rejoin the service after I once leave it, and I could not bear to ask it or to accept some inferior position in it unless it was a case of absolute necessity, and I hope it will never come to that."[3]

After mulling it over for nearly a year, Lovatt finally accepted Möllendorff's offer. So as not to burn his bridges in case the Korean customs did not pan out, Lovatt, "after mature consideration, [wrote] a private note to Sir Robert Hart telling him of Moellendorff's offer and my desire to accept it, and asking his approval and permission to retire from the service." Aware that Hart might be upset, he crafted his letter "in a manner which I do not think can possibly offend him." Hart's reply was not long in coming, and if Lovatt had hopes that the IG would beg him to stay on, pronounce him indispensable, indicate that he was next in line for a commissionership, or promise him an increase in salary, he was sorely disappointed. Rather, Lovatt characterized Hart's response as, "you may go if you wish." In effect, the IG had told him not to let the door hit him on his way out! Seeing that he now had little choice, Lovatt sent in his formal letter of resignation. And so in late August 1883, the forty-five-year-old Lovatt departed Tianjin and the Chinese service for Korea.[4]

For the next two and a half years, Lovatt proved to be a capable commissioner of customs in Pusan, running the port efficiently and keeping it in the black financially, unlike the commissioners in the other two treaty ports of Inch'ŏn and Wŏnsan. Joining him there for nearly two years were Jennie and Mabel, until Jennie's pregnancy required that she and Mabel return to Minnesota to give birth. Lovatt liked his job, and it appeared that he would remain in that post for the foreseeable future. However, in the summer of 1885, Möllendorff angered Li Hongzhang by approaching Russia to supplant China as Korea's protector, prompting Li to demand that Korea dismiss him. Now that there was a vacancy at the head of the Korean customs,

Figure 9.2 Lovatt's Family in 1883. Seated from Left: Jennie, Mabel, and John. Standing from Left: Helen [Nellie] and Ida. Courtesy: Dorothy Shaw Gillette.

Figure 9.3 Portrait of Henry F. Merrill in the Harvard College Class of 1874 50th Anniversary Report. Courtesy: HUD 274.50 A, Harvard University Archives.

Hart saw an opportunity to extend his and China's influence over Korea by hatching a secret plan to annex the Korean customs. When Li asked Hart for advice on who should replace Möllendorff, Hart recommended his subordinate, the American Henry F. Merrill, who would follow Hart's orders. Before Merrill departed China, Hart informed him of his plan to annex the Korean customs, which included dismissing the three commissioners, including Lovatt, and swore him to secrecy (figure 9.3).

When Merrill arrived in Seoul, his first priority was to determine the level of efficiency of the Korean Customs. He soon concluded that "*with the exception of Mr. Lovatt,* [the commissioners do] not appear to have administered their offices satisfactorily," and informed Hart that Lovatt did not deserve to be fired. But Hart quickly overruled Merrill: "Lovatt is a very decent fellow, but he is not the stamp of man to have charge of a port: an excellent Tidesurveyor, but that's all!" Not only was Lovatt's career in Korea over, but also if he were ever to return to China, Hart would never promote him to the rank of commissioner. Not privy to this correspondence, Lovatt remained unaware of Hart's disparaging opinion of him for the rest of his life.[5]

Consequently, in early 1886, Merrill reluctantly informed Lovatt that he was being let go and, with Hart's approval, offered him a severance package—a choice between, on the one hand $3,500 and unemployment, or on the other hand $1,500 and a position in the Chinese customs. But unbeknownst to Hart and Merrill, Merrill's assistant had leaked Hart's secret plan to annex the Korean customs to Lovatt. Armed with this inside information, Lovatt decided to carve out a golden parachute for himself, demanding a financial settlement much larger than $3,500, a return to the Chinese Customs at the rank of commissioner, a long paid leave of absence, resignation rather than termination, and a positive letter of reference before resigning. Merrill and Hart, still unaware that Lovatt knew about the secret plan, agreed to raise his retirement allowance to $4,500 if he chose unemployment. But Lovatt responded that was still not enough and suggested that a disinterested neutral third party determine the appropriate amount, and the person he suggested was Robert Hart! It was immediately obvious to Merrill and Hart that Lovatt not only knew about Hart's plan to annex the Korean customs but also by making those demands was implying that he might blow the whistle and reveal the secret annexation plan to the anti-Chinese faction in the Korean government and/or to the mostly anti-Chinese Western representatives in Seoul. If the secret were exposed, Hart would not only be unable to annex the Korean customs but China's influence in Korea would also be crippled. In short, Lovatt was blackmailing Hart to get the golden parachute he was seeking.

In order to get Lovatt to go quietly without revealing Hart's secret plan to annex the Korean customs, Hart and Merrill agreed to allow him to resign, sent him a glowing letter of recommendation, gave him an eighteen-month leave of absence at half-pay for the first six months, and offered him a choice of his old position of tidesurveyor in the Chinese service plus $1,500, or $6,000 if he chose not to return to China. Since Hart would not take him back at the rank of commissioner, Lovatt opted for the $6,000 and agreed to leave without revealing the secret. Lovatt had succeeded in getting most of his demands met, but in the process he had angered Hart, first by jumping ship from the Chinese customs to take the position in Korea, and then by blackmailing him to get a generous settlement to leave Korea quietly.

Lovatt departed Korea in June 1886. Although he had received his golden parachute, he nonetheless blamed Hart for his dismissal and was "boiling over with rage" on his arrival in Yokohama. From there he took the *Gaelic* to San Francisco, boarded the train back to Minnesota, and arrived home in July 1886. Awaiting him was his family, including its newest member, William Harold [Willie], who had been born the previous December.[6]

MINNESOTA AND HONG KONG/CANTON (GUANGZHOU), JULY 1886 TO JUNE 1888

For the next eighteen months Lovatt remained in Minnesota with his family. But when his one year of unpaid leave expired and his resignation took effect at the end of 1887, Lovatt began to reconsider his refusal to return to the Chinese customs. One reason was his continued distaste for the harsh climate. Referring to "those two awful winters of 86–87, 87–88," Lovatt swore that "I certainly do not wish ever to put in another winter in Minnesota." A second reason was a marked deterioration in their finances. His real estate investments had proved unsuccessful, such that "everything was going out and nothing was coming in." For these reasons, Lovatt swallowed his pride and sought reemployment in China, a step he had earlier sworn he would never take.[7]

Lovatt faced a potential snag, however, because Hart's offer of reemployment had been made only at the time of his forced resignation from the Korean customs in June 1886 and only if Lovatt would accept $1,500 in severance pay. There was no guarantee that Hart would honor that commitment now, particularly after Lovatt had blackmailed him for severance pay four times that amount. So Lovatt in December 1887 decided to send a formal application for reinstatement not to Hart in Beijing but rather to Merrill in Seoul with the expectation that he would intercede with the IG because he knew that Merrill felt guilty for terminating him. As expected, Merrill forwarded Lovatt's application to Hart with the recommendation that he be rehired. But even if Lovatt were rehired by Hart, it was not clear at what rank. Although he had at one time declared that he would accept nothing less than a commissionership, he now asked Merrill to persuade Hart not only to rehire him but also to rehire him at his former rank of tidesurveyor. In his reply, Merrill was silent on the rank, but he assured Lovatt that he would be rehired and advised him to go directly to China to receive his orders from Hart.[8]

Lovatt departed Lakeland by train on a "raw, cold" afternoon of May 7, 1888, leaving so quickly that he barely had time to say goodbye to his wife Jennie, his children at their schoolhouse, his in-laws, and their friends. In St. Paul, he caught a train to Omaha, where he changed trains, arrived in San Francisco on May 11, and checked into the Palace Hotel. Since there was a possibility that he would be assigned to a port in South China, he purchased a ticket to Hong Kong since the fare of $200 was the same as the fare to Yokohama, and he departed on the *Belgie* the next day.[9]

As Lovatt steamed toward Yokohama, still unsure if he would be rehired, where he would be posted, or what his rank and salary would be, he was pessimistic: "I fear from [the IG's] vindictiveness he will not be willing to do much for us," he wrote his wife, adding, "our future looks dim now." In fact, his future had already been determined. While Lovatt was on the train to California, Hart sent Merrill a telegram confirming that he would rehire Lovatt and spelled out Lovatt's rank, salary, and posting. Merrill in turn sent a letter containing Hart's telegram to Yokohama to await Lovatt's arrival. As he approached Japan, unaware that Hart had already decided his fate, Lovatt speculated on "what the grand arbitrator of the Customs has for me to do" and hoped that it was not "some cheerless duty in some out of the way port."[10]

When the *Belgie* arrived in Yokohama on the evening of May 29, Lovatt checked into the Geoma Hotel and the next morning picked up Merrill's letter containing the long-awaited news. The enclosed telegram from Hart showed that Lovatt's premonition had been correct: "Lovatt may rejoin as *Assistant* Tidesurveyor at Foochow from 1st July—salary one hundred haikwan taels." Although he had been rehired, it was at a reduced rank, with a salary only one-third that of a commissioner and one-half that of a first-class tidesurveyor. Disappointed, and intent on refusing the appointment, Lovatt immediately started a letter to Merrill: "I arrived here last night in the *Belgie*, and on calling on Mr. Morse received yours of May 10th. I am afraid the I. G. is feeling somewhat hard towards me." But he never finished the letter.[11]

Instead, on that same day, Lovatt penned a second letter, this time to Jennie, breaking the bad news to her and knowing that she too would be disappointed: "I fear you will be grieved over it. The position and pay seems almost an insult, but you know Sir Robert Hart is very bitter and he evidently intends I shall eat humble pie and be a warning to other members of the service." But in the same letter, Lovatt also revealed that he had had a change of heart: "Let us make the best of it. Fortunately, I took my passage for Hong Kong, so I shall go there. It will be so much saved in expense." Still, he confessed, "I am feeling somewhat unhappy."[12]

Why did Lovatt not follow his initial instincts and reject the appointment? In fact, he acknowledged that he would have declined had he learned of it earlier: "If I had received Mr. Merrill's letter in America I would never have returned to China to occupy so subordinate a position and such small pay, but now I am here, and in debt will of course make the best of it." What swayed him was what Merrill told him in his letter containing Hart's telegram:

> This is not what I expected to be given you, and perhaps your impulse will be to decline the appointment. My advice is to think well before letting this offer pass, unless you are sure of something better. I openly believe that it will be only a matter of a few months before you would be restored to your old rank [tidesurveyor] in the Service if you would consent to begin where the I. G. makes the opening. I am very sorry that you are not offered your old rank at the outset. If pride is the only thing that stands in the way, I hope you will overcome it and accept what is now offered in the confident hope of speedy promotion.

So instead of finishing and posting his original letter to Merrill, Lovatt wrote him a different letter accepting the position, which Merrill then passed on to Hart.[13]

Having swallowed his pride, Lovatt reboarded the *Belgie* for the next leg of his voyage from Yokohama to Hong Kong. Now with plenty of time to reflect on this recent turn of events, he began to speculate on the reasons for Hart's action. His initial thought was that he was being punished for abandoning the Chinese service five years earlier for a higher position in Korea: "The Inspector General would hardly permit one to return without in some outward way manifesting his displeasure at my conduct and showing the members of the service what they may expect if they ever think of leaving." But Lovatt also acknowledged that Hart might have been motivated by a sense of equity. Lovatt had, after all, been offered his former rank of tidesurveyor and a retiring allowance of $1,500. Instead, Lovatt had opted for unemployment, allowing him to negotiate a much higher retiring allowance of $6,000 by threatening to expose Hart's plan to absorb the Korean customs. Lovatt had netted, in effect, an extra $4,500 simply by taking two years off, including six months at half salary. So a reduction in rank and salary actually brought Lovatt closer in line to the settlement received by the other two terminated commissioners.[14]

Here is how Lovatt explained it to his wife:

> [Hart] has fully considered what I got from Corea—retiring pay, six months leave on half pay, and a long [one year] leave without, and putting it all together, he probably came to this conclusion: "Mr. Lovatt, all things considered, you have done much better than if you had remained with me. You have three retiring allowances and a good deal of leave, and now you must eat humble pie. You are a pretty good fellow, you have done me good service, and in Corea you were the only one who acted like an honorable man, showing the result of my excellent system. I don't dislike you for looking after your own interests in an honorable way, but discipline must and shall be maintained, and I will show you that hard is the path of those who oppose me. Let your case be a warning to others. So to Foochow you will go, where you will probably not be so very well known, and where you will not be made to feel so keenly (as you deserve) your change of position. And if the commissioner reports favorable upon you, that you don't give yourself airs, but that you do your duty like the man I think you are, perhaps at the end of six months I will see if I have not some more suitable position for you."

Having put this spin on Hart's reasoning, Lovatt concluded the letter: "After reading Merrill's letter carefully over and giving the subject careful thought, the I. G. may have thought it over in the way I have written above. Consequently, I shall put in an appearance in Foochow, and I shall try and convince the commissioner [Moorhead] there that he never had so good an Assistant Tidesurveyor."[15]

Until a promotion came through, however, money would be tight: "I will live very close and, as you know, the darkest hour is just before the dawn." Luckily, his decision to purchase a steamship ticket to the end of the line was a wise choice: "The easiest thing I have done for a long time was taking my passage to Hong Kong. I just did it because the agents said it was all the same—Yokohama or Hong Kong. It has saved me over $100—$50 to Shanghai and $50 Shanghai to Foochow." But exactly when promotion would come still weighed on his mind.[16]

During that first week of June 1888 en route to Hong Kong on the *Belgie*, captained by his friend Walker, he started planning what he would need to do during his three-week layover there. One was to stock up on appropriate clothing, as "Foochow is very hot until the end of October, [so] I shall have to lay in a stock of white clothing." Short on cash, "I shall get a Chinese tailor to make what things I want and will try and get them on credit." In fact, because of his financial straits and because he wanted to visit nearby Guangzhou, he would need a place to stay: "I intend writing to May at Canton and see if he will put me up for a few days, otherwise I could not afford to visit the old city." As for his financial future, "the I. G. will do nothing for me for 6 months at least, and it is more than probable not for 12 or 18 months. We must try and pull through a year at least, for I fear Sir Robert will not give me an increase in less time."[17]

Lovatt arrived in Hong Kong on the afternoon of June 5 and checked into the "too expensive" Victoria Hotel, where he had a bath, a shave, and a haircut. The next day he went to the tailor to be fitted, went to a photographer's studio to have his picture taken, and then went to the HSBC branch to advance him $200 to pay for his hotel, clothes, and passage to Canton and Fuzhou. He then posted his letters in time for the 2:00 mail to May in Canton and to S. Parkhill, the tidesurveyor in Fuzhou, hoping that he would invite him to stay with him, knowing that "housekeeping or furnishing is out of the question on such a salary [100 *taels*, and] all I can see is to board somewhere."[18]

While waiting for May to reply, Lovatt went sightseeing, on this his first visit to Hong Kong since 1866, visiting the city museum, the public garden, and Macao. At the invitation of Captain Walker, he took tiffin on board the *Belgie*, after which the two hired chairs to go to the newly constructed tram up Victoria Peak. At the top they met the engineer who built the Tram, and who then treated Walker and Lovatt to dinner at the Peak Hotel. In all, Lovatt was impressed: "Hong Kong looks to have improved very much."[19]

Meanwhile, May's invitation arrived, so at 8:00 a.m. on June 20, Lovatt boarded the *Honam*, sailed up the Pearl River, and arrived in Canton at 2:45 p.m. for a two-day visit. The Mays lived in the Foreign Settlement—"a beautiful place. It is a low perfectly flat island in the river and very near the left bank about a mile long by half a mile in width, laid out in pretty compounds, filled with large trees, and covered with nice green grass. In fact, it looks exactly like a beautiful park, with nice concrete walks all through it." On the occasion of his visit, Mrs. May gave a dinner party, including guests from the Canton customs, the gunboat currently in port, and foreign firms, which Lovatt found to be "very pleasant, if you allow for it being 90 [degrees] in the dining room." Lovatt left Canton on the *Powan* at 5 p.m. on June 22, arriving in Hong Kong the next morning, and checked in once again at the Victoria Hotel.[20]

During his three weeks in Hong Kong and Canton in June, as seasoned as Lovatt was to the heat in China, he nonetheless complained, and "long[ed] for the cool nights of Minn." Adding to his discomfort was bowel complaints which he attributed to the water, the moist heat, and tinned salmon and cucumbers. To recover, "I have carefully avoided all vegetables and fruit." For a time, he thought he might have contracted cholera because when he had his photograph taken, "I was quite sick at the time. It was awful hot, and the perspiration was pouring down my face." To counteract it, he bought three cholera bells because "cholera is very bad in Hong Kong." In fact, "there has been a good deal of Cholera at all the ports, especially in the early summer arising principally from heat, water, and unripe fruit."[21]

On June 25, Lovatt departed for Fuzhou on the nonstop "finer and larger" Canadian steamer *Aberdeen*, which, unlike the regular coast steamer, was ten dollars cheaper and did not stop at Shantou. Awaiting him there was Commissioner R. B. Moorhead, pleasing Lovatt immensely: "I could not find anyone more kindly disposed towards me or who will be more friendly, so I will probably hear through him what the I. G. intends to do."[22]

NOTES

1. WNL to JSL, September 29, 1882.
2. WNL to JSL, June 20, 1882 and February 3, 1883.
3. WNL to JSL, July 27, 1883.
4. WNL to JSL, July 24 and 30, 1883; *Hart Diaries*, July 23, 1883.
5. Merrill to Hart, October 26, 1885; Hart to Merrill, November, 30, 1885, *Hart Letters*. Emphasis added.
6. WNL to JSL, November 17, 1888. Lovatt's "boy," Hsiung [Shung Yu Ting], stayed in Korea to work for Lovatt's successor and eventually made his way to the United States: "I also received a letter from my old servant *Hsiung* from Washington. He writes in English and is quite amusing." WNL to JSL, November 4, 1889.
7. WNL to JSL, May 18 and 31, 1888, and February 28, 1890.
8. WNL to Merrill, December 5, 1887; Merrill to WNL, February 8, 1888. *Merrill Letters*. Lovatt had initially departed Minnesota in late February, 1888, but upon arriving in California learned that Jennie had taken ill, causing him to return to Minnesota until she recovered later that spring.

9. WNL to JSL, May 11 (Palace Hotel, San Francisco), June 5 (Hong Kong), July 19, and September 8, 1888 (Fuzhou), and May 7, 1890. *1885 Minnesota State Census Records*: Washington County, Roll 45, Stillwater Public Library.

10. WNL to JSL, May 12, 13, 14, 15, 16, 20, and 26, 1888; Merrill to Hart, May 23, 1888. *Merrill Letters*.

11. WNL to Merrill, May 30, 1888. Emphasis added. Although Lovatt never sent the letter, it nonetheless remains among Lovatt's correspondence.

12. WNL to JSL, May 30 and September 8, 1888.

13. Merrill to WNL, May 10, 1888, and Merrill to Hart, July 3, 1888, *Merrill Letters*; WNL to JSL, September 8, 1888.

14. WNL to JSL, May 31, 1888.

15. WNL to JSL, May 31, 1888.

16. WNL to JSL, May 31, 1888.

17. WNL to JSL, At Sea. *Belgie*, May 31 and June 4, and (in Hong Kong) June 12 and 23, 1888.

18. WNL to JSL, May 31, and June 4, 5, 6, 7, 10, and 24, 1888.

19. WNL to JSL, June 10, 12, and 16, 1888. Among other activities, he hired a rickshaw to take a turn around Happy Valley and watch a bayonet drill by the Northamptonshire Regiment.

20. WNL to JSL, (Canton) June 20 and 23, 1888. While in Canton, Lovatt made the usual rounds, calling on the British consul Alabaster and also on the "very popular" American consul, Seymour, who had been the editor of a La Crosse (Wisconsin) newspaper.

21. WNL to JSL, June 12, 23, and 24, July 3, September 23, and December 22, 1888.

22. WNL to JSL, June 20, 23, and 24, 1888. On his last two days in Hong Kong, he went swimming at the boat club, had tiffin with May's son who was apprenticing as an engineer, and picked up his clothes from the tailor: six white jackets, ten pairs of white trousers, and three white waistcoats for 42 pounds, one helmet for 3.45 pounds, one straw hat for 1.50 pounds, and an umbrella and sunshade for 8.75 pounds. Shantou was known as Swatow at the time.

Chapter 10

Return to China on Demotion

Fuzhou, 1888–1889

Lovatt arrived in Fuzhou from Hong Kong aboard the *Aberdeen* on June 28, still miffed by his unjust termination from Korea two years earlier: "Having been Chief of a port and losing it only through the I. G.'s will does not fit one to go back cheerfully or willingly to a smaller port." Nonetheless, the British commissioner Moorhead "received me very kindly." Since Parkhill had not extended an invitation to board with him, Lovatt put up at the "comfortable enough" Hong Kong Hotel at $60 per month which, "altho it is dear, it is the cheaper and better way, for if I took a house I would have to have at least a boy and coolie." But his financial picture still remained shaky, being 1,200 taels in debt to the bank, and commented wryly that "on the whole my financial transactions have not been an unalloyed success." And the short-term outlook did not look particularly promising: "Two dispatches came yesterday, promoting one fellow, transferring one more, but no dispatch about your Will." Still, he remained optimistic: "I also hope that this is our darkest hour, just before the dawn of better things."[1]

Lovatt began his duties as assistant tidesurveyor officially on the first of July and spent the first ten days "pretty busy getting the run of things in general, so that I have not left the office until half past five o'clock every evening." Since "my duties bring me here at 8 am," he was actually logging more time than the 10 a.m. to 5 p.m. summer hours that Hart had recently decreed. Despite the fact that "the hours are somewhat long, owing to having to make up the mails late and send them down to the [Pagoda] anchorage to be delivered to the steamer," Lovatt declared that "my position is comfortable and independent enough, I am the Chief of my own department, I have a good office, and the work is not heavy."[2]

The city of Fuzhou was located in Fujian Province on the delta of the Min River, about 25 miles from the coast and 9 miles from the Pagoda Achorage, which could be reached by oceangoing vessels. Opened as a treaty port in 1844, the Fuzhou customs was divided into two sections, connected by the customs launch. One section was the Pagoda Anchorage where the steamers docked and where the harbormaster, tidesurveyor, and tidewaiters were located. Assistant tidesurveyor Lovatt worked in the other section of the customs in the city itself, 9 miles away, with the commissioner, deputy commissioner, assistants, and examiners, along with the various foreign consuls and merchants. There, Lovatt found "the young men of the staff a very agreeable lot." Most important, of course, was Commissioner Moorhead, who "is very good and all that is kind and pleasant." Since the tidesurveyor Parkhill worked downriver at the Pagoda Anchorage, "I have only the Commissioner as Boss and you know he is the kindest man in the service and [he has] a good deal of confidence in me." Moorhead was in addition generous in giving Lovatt time off with benefits. In August, for example, "the office was closed and Mr. Moorhead very kindly offered me his houseboat [the *Wulung* or *Five Dragons*] for this holiday and also kindly throwing Saturday in."[3]

Unlike the other treaty ports where Lovatt had served and where there was a concentrated foreign settlement, the foreign community in Fuzhou was scattered over the surrounding hills in houses that "are all large." As a result, despite the existence of the Club, "it is anything but lively. The place looks, feels, and is dull owing partly to the absence of a settlement."[4]

Being on the coast had both advantages and disadvantages. One advantage was that there was regular mail service—one or two steamers per week to Hong Kong, and from there a steamer every week either to San Francisco or Vancouver, with postage at five cents per ounce via Shanghai and paid for by the Customs, unlike the British Post Office that charged twice as much. One disadvantage was the frequency of typhoons, such as the one in mid-August that not only blew a hole in the roof of Lovatt's hotel but also increased his workload: "my work has been making out estimates and setting the contractors to work. The repairs are all owing to the recent typhoon."[5]

In the course of his duties, Lovatt interacted with officials at the yamen. One amusing encounter occurred that fall when

> the local magistrate came in to see me about an empty old trunk from Shanghai, which he said was of no value, but being sent to him he would like to have it. He was a very chatty old fellow and sucked at the stump of an old cigar, looking at it and then at me, most comically, but my [cigar] case being unfortunately empty, I could not come to his relief. He asked me what countryman I was. I told him English-American. "Ah," he said, "that is a fine country; we have never had a fight with that country." He deserved a cigar, but I had none with me.[6]

As a newcomer, Lovatt initially socialized with the two people he had known previously, and frequented the Club. Aside from Moorhead, the only other person he knew was Reverend John R. Wolfe of the London Missionary Society who he had met in Korea several years earlier, and who invited Lovatt to tea at his house soon after his arrival. At the Club, Lovatt shared in the conviviality of good times: "The teamen are full of joy. I hear Champagne was running like water at the club yesterday on the arrival of a telegram from London saying the tea from here, by SS *Gleneagle* was bringing a clear profit of seven taels per picul. No wonder the teamen were wild with joy."[7]

By the end of his first summer, Lovatt had become friends with several of his colleagues, some of whom became his companions on various excursions. One was hiking up the nearby "famous" 3,000-foot Kushan Mountain, often accompanied by First Assistant Onia Tiberii. Another one of his frequent excursions involved borrowing the commissioner's houseboat, and taking it downriver where "I [can] swim and breathe the fresh pure sea air." On other occasions, he went upriver: "I am leaving with Mr. Tiberii in one of our houseboats for a trip up the country. We are going up the main river—the Min. The scenery here is very beautiful, the finest I have seen in China. A pleasant trip up river with my Italian friend and perhaps a shot or two at a pheasant" (figure 10.1).[8]

One such excursion is described in some detail:

> I returned to Foochow last night just before the clock struck twelve after a very pleasant excursion up the Min River. Today is Thursday, and Monday, Tuesday and Wednesday being nice days, Mr. Tiberii and myself decided that a trip in a houseboat would be far preferable to attending the race meeting, and having got one of our comfortable boats from the Commissioner, we made all our arrangements last Saturday. I dined with Tiberii that evening, and after dinner we got on board our boat and left with the flood tide for the higher reaches of the Min River. I engaged a cook and with plenty of provisions we started up the river, and by daylight on Sunday morning reached the upper bridge. After breakfast we went on shore for a walk and I have nowhere else in China seen such lovely scenery. The river a beautiful clear emerald green. Mountains on both sides from 500 feet to 2500 in height. In the bends of the river were large flats from 50 to 500 yards in width which were filled with large trees. There are very many picturesque temples, comfortable farm houses, and decent villages. The whole aspect of the country and people are in very striking contrast to those on the Yangztze, and the barren looking north.

The only downside to the trip was communicating: "I had considerable difficulty in understanding what was said, as the boatman's English was limited to about ten words, and his small vocabulary had to be very much twisted to get any information at all. The local [Fujian] Chinese dialect is about the worst I have ever heard. I can hardly understand a word."[9]

Other excursions went overland, and his description of one in particular gives an insight into the lives and behavior of chair bearers, beggars, and Buddhist monks. First, the chair bearers:

Figure 10.1 Picnic Party in Fuzhou, February 17, 1889. Lovatt Standing Lower Left with Tiberii, Bjornson, Moorhead Jr., Moorhead Sr., and Mortinson. Courtesy: The Bancroft Library, University of California, Berkeley.

I was bound to have a trip into the country, and so taking my tiffin I got into my chair with four coolies and started for the city. The bridge across the river Min is very long and added to which is two smaller bridges connecting with the large bridge from two little islands. The bridge is built of stone and appears to have stood a great number of years. The life and animation on the bridge, and through

> the long street extending over a mile and a half, is wonderful. The street was crowded with movement and blocks of course, in such a narrow thoroughfare, but all met very good humouredly. The chairmen are especially noisy, and call out, "look out, clear the way," constantly. The people of this part of Fookien are industrious and frugal, and look better than those further north. I also noticed very few scowling faces in the crowd through which I passed. Most seemed pleasantly disposed towards me, very different to what a large crowd would be in any large city on the Yangtze.

The trip also included encounters with beggars:

> The bridge is crowded with travelling cook shops, hucksters, and beggars. The latter appear to divide the bridge into equal portions, and each one of them begs from you a certain distance, then he drops you, when you are immediately importuned by a fresh one. Strange to say, many of the beggars speak very good Mandarin; evidently they are men of travel and experience. They all possess a good deal of philosophy, for they take the many rebuffs they meet with very calmly and grim pleasure.

He also encountered a Buddhist monk on his trip:

> As soon as I reached the far side [of the bridge] I got down out of my chair and walked out to a large temple, the Abbott of which met me and did the honors. He was quite a traveled priest. He had been twice to Hongkong and also to Singapore and Penang. The temple, a fine one, is quite new; the Government re-built it five or six years ago. It now contains two hundred priests and service is regularly performed. The Abbott mourned the utter indifference of the people toward religion. There was a fine library on an upper floor, a present from the Emperor. I had a very nice cup of tea with the Abbott, [and] told him the foreign news, which he seemed pleased to hear, and left him.

At the end of his trip,

> the day was awful hot, and the road was long, and those flagstone paths are extremely tiresome to walk on. I finally got to a tea house and had some tea, and was only able to have a little tiffin. Then at three o'clock I started for Foochow and had another long walk, reaching the hotel about 5:30 p.m. in the evening where a cup of tea greatly revived me.[10]

As Lovatt was settling into his routine, he learned that Jennie had relocated the family that fall from the "lonely" farm in rural Lakeland to a rented house in the more urban setting of Stillwater 9 miles to the north. Lovatt approved, writing that "our Stillwater friends are very kind nice people," "city life is much pleasanter," and "that farm was too much hard and laborious work."

More importantly, it meant an end to rural isolation, exacerbated by the long winters. The move was, however, not easy for Jennie since it meant not only leaving the home they had lived in for nearly twenty years but also leaving behind her parents who lived on the adjacent property, particularly since her mother was exhibiting signs of dementia. Additionally, being separated from her husband yet again caused her to lament that their "life [is] all shadow." Lovatt, from afar, did what he could to cheer her up, countering that "I think we have had a vast amount more of sunshine than of shadow."[11]

Contributing to those "shadows" were the ever-present financial difficulties. After six months, Lovatt had managed to reduce his indebtedness to the bank almost by half to 650 taels, although he acknowledged that "it is slow work saving out of small pay" and his expenses "has kept me poor." He briefly entertained hopes of going into the tea export business with his St. Paul attorney, to whom he had sent twenty boxes of tea when he first arrived in Fuzhou, but he soon concluded that "it is no use our trying the tea business." Rather, his key to solvency was promotion back to the rank of tidesurveyor, with an accompanying increase in pay. After three months in Fuzhou, he entertained the notion of gently nudging Moorhead for news and perhaps a helping hand: "I have not asked the Commissioner lately if there is any despatch [from Hart] come to hand about me, for I don't like pushing myself too prominently forward, but I will do so when some favorable opportunity offers." But Lovatt did not even need to ask, because "I am sure he would tell me if he did." When the next steamer arrived from Shanghai, "I should have dearly liked to have told you he [Hart] had acted generously, but not a single dispatch from Peking is to hand." From the time of his arrival in Fuzhou, this hope was constant, as nearly every letter attests.[12]

As the year end approached, Lovatt ruefully concluded that a quick promotion was not in the cards because he had not been punished enough for his past misdeeds:

> I presume the I. G. will keep me here until he thinks I have done penance enough, and perhaps when some Tidesurveyor goes home on leave, he may give me his port with a little increase. He may do better for me, of course, and I hope he will, but it is better not to build too much on his generosity. Let us wait, and something will turn up.

The year's end also saw him mellow a bit toward Hart:

> You must not be indignant with Sir Robert Hart, my dear. I left the [Chinese] service of my own free will and accord. He paid me all I could justly claim. It is true he crowded me out of Corea, but he was not bound to re-engage me [in China after taking two years off]. And if you will only consider the retiring allowance I have had [$6,000 plus six months at half salary] and then glance at

> the position of my contemporaries, you will find that your William is still a long way ahead. True, I often feel bitter now, but then I want to be fair and just, and I do look forward to his doing something for me next spring owing to his unfair conduct in forcing me to leave the Corean Service.[13]

With only silence from the IG, Lovatt cynically groused about how others wangled promotions:

> Sir Robert Hart is now known as Henry VIII. It appears all the men who are pretty well up in the service and also in years, when they go home generally look out for some very pretty woman, a good French scholar, and certainly musical, [a] good voice indispensable. A concert at Shanghai, or somewhere else, makes known the new talent and then the order comes—appointed to Peking—and it is said now all the new Deputy Commissioners are indebted to their wives for their appointments. Anyway, Bob acts in a way that evidently gives rise to a good deal of scandal, and China you know is full of it.[14]

Since only a transfer would bring with it a promotion, Lovatt was willing to give up his current posting, even if it took him to a less desirable port. Indeed, after six months in Fuzhou, Lovatt had concluded that it "is not a bad place," where "the climate is so delightful," with a "very pleasant winter," although the summer heat is "unbearable." As for the work load, it is "a very easy port," since "I have any amount of leisure," and the "good natured" commissioner "certainly makes my place very pleasant for me." Clearly, rank and salary were more important to him than location.[15]

As 1888 drew to a close with no word from Hart, Lovatt engaged in speculation about his future, predictions that would turn out to be surprisingly accurate. For example, he surmised that "I shall be packed off up the Yangtze next spring, and if it brings an increase in pay I shall not complain." Moreover, he heard a rumor that Chungking (Chongqing) in Sichuan was about to be opened and "the I. G. may send me there. He may think I am adapted from roughing it. I am prepared for anything rather than to be left without notice to stagnate in my present comfortable but insignificant position." He was also able, again with surprising accuracy, to predict the long term future of his family in China, telling Jennie that "I wish I had you here and Willie," and that Ida "wants to see the world and she will never be happy until she is out here, eating young frogs and other choice delicacies. I shall certainly have her in China."[16]

As Lovatt awaited word from Beijing, the Christmas holiday season arrived with its usual round of socializing, and Lovatt had several invitations to juggle: "The Commissioner asked me to dine with him on Christmas day, but I have already promised to dine with Mrs. Parkhill. Mr. Wolfe has just sent me an invitation, so I am not likely to go without my dinner." And the following week brought another round, including an invitation to a New Year's Eve ball at Mr. de Roza's, a Portuguese merchant and

> a very nice fellow. Then I dressed and breakfasted and started on my New Year calls. When I got to Archdeacon Wolfe's I remained to tiffin with them. I called on the [American] Consul, all the Customs people, and Mr. Wilcox of the Methodist Mission. I also called on [Nathan] and Mrs. Plumb of the same mission. Then I called on [Commissioner] Moorhead with whom I am going to dine, and from there I went on to Mr. and Mrs. Lord, our Chief Assistant.

The commissioner's dinner "passed off all right. He is pretty savage against the Russians and the French, but you know the kind of after dinner talk in China, generally on some international questions, and if not very serious, is amusing."[17]

The new year of 1889 brought with it the usual transfers. Given that Fuzhou was so comfortable for Lovatt, there was the potential that some of the transfers would diminish its attractiveness. The most important change was at the top: "The Commissioner goes home on two years leave from the 1st April." Replacing him was "Mr. Palm, our new commissioner, [who] is very polite, and I like him for one thing—he leaves at 4 p.m. sharp. Mr. Moorhead generally commenced his letters then and kept two or three of us to 5 or 6 o'clock, but then he was awful good about leave, and in lots of other things." On the other hand, "Mr. Moorhouse from Peking is coming here as Deputy Com., a very peculiar beggar, and will make life very uncomfortable for a lot about the Custom House." Another of his good friends was transferred to Shanghai: "I am sorry Mr. Lord is going, for Mrs. Lord and himself have shown me many acts of kindness since my arrival." The new year's changes renewed Lovatt's anticipation that he might be next: "we must see what the I. G. will do this spring." Although he had earlier hesitated to enlist the commissioner's assistance, now he changed his mind: "I asked Mr. Moorhead last Monday if he would write to the I. G. for me. He said he would, but he would have to do it privately. I am sure he will, and I hope by April to be in a better position."[18]

When April finally arrived, Lovatt was filled with anticipation: "We are expecting a few service movements here some time this month [and] am hoping we shall have good news soon." When the dispatches arrived from Beijing, however, they contained "no changes, no promotions." As April turned to May, Lovatt remained optimistic: "I hope to soon to be able to tell you I am going to another port." Finally, in early June, after a year in Fuzhou, Lovatt received the dispatch that he had been awaiting, transferring him to Jiujiang, where he had served from 1870 to 1877, and promoting him to acting tidesurveyor and harbormaster with a raise of 25 taels per month. Before leaving, he had to break in his obnoxious replacement, Walker, who "was not the nicest fellow in the world, altho I went to a good deal of trouble in posting him well up in local affairs." Lovatt departed for Shanghai in late June, transferred there to the up steamer, and arrived in Jiujiang on Sunday, June 30, in time to begin his duties the next morning.[19]

NOTES

1. S. S. Aberdeen, Custom House, Fuzhou, June 29, July 3, 10, and 19, September 8, and December 8, 1888. Lovatt would later relocate to the Foochow Hotel.

2. WNL to JSL, July 10 and September 8, 1888; *Service List, 1888*. 23, 118.

3. WNL to JSL, August 7 and 25, and September 8, 1888.

4. WNL to JSL, July 19 and August 25, 1888.

5. WNL to JSL, August 18 and 25, 1888.

6. WNL to JSL, October 17, 1888.

7. WNL to JSL, July 3, 10, and 14, 1888. But a month later, the good cheer had dissipated:

> "Things are very bad in China. The tea trade is pretty nearly ruined by the competition of the Indian teas, and our revenue shows it accordingly. Two years ago 90 million pounds of tea from China to London, last year 60 million, and this year only 50 million. The very finest teas this year were profitable, but later advices from London show a great decline."

WNL to JSL, August 15, 1888.

8. WNL to JSL, September 23, November 17, and December 15, 1888, and February 11 and June 4, 1889.

9. WNL to JSL, December 20, 1888.

10. WNL to JSL, October 17, 1888.

11. WNL to JSL, August 18 and 28, September 8 and 13, October 12, November 3, 16, 17, 23, and 26, and December 4, 15, and 22, 1888, and January 9, and April 18 and 24, 1889.

12. WNL to JSL, August 7 and 25, September 8, 13, and 23, October 12 and 23, and November 3, 17, and 23, 1888, and January 9, late February (n.d.), April 10, May 1, and August 2, 1889. Paradoxically, while pleading poverty, he continued to play the Manila lottery and speculate in the stock market, and was willing to increase his debt to do so: "I have just written to the bank in Shanghai to borrow Tls. 15,000 and with that sum I intend purchasing 60 more shares in the Hong Kong and Shanghai Bank. I think the shares are likely to go high, and with 100 shares every rise of a tael or two means a very substantial gain."

In August, "the steamers are in from Shanghai [but] there are no official dispatches, so it is a case of wait and hope." Later that month, "I have no news from our friend Sir Robert." In October, "no news from the north." And later that same month, "Parkhill was promoted the other day. If the I. G. will only give me a lift we will be all right." In November, "Sir Robert will not do anything for me before the spring I fear. He may at the end of December, but I doubt it."

13. WNL to JSL, November 3 and 17, 1888.

14. WNL to JSL, December 4, 1888.

15. WNL to JSL, January 2, 9, and 24, and June 4, 1889.

16. WNL to JSL, November 3, 16, 17, and 23, 1888. Emphasis in the original.

17. WNL to JSL, December 20 and 28, 1888, and January 1 and 2, 1889.

18. WNL to JSL, December 15 and 28, 1888, and January 9 and 24, February 4 and 18, April 10, May 1, and June 4, 1889.

19. WNL to JSL, April 10, 18, and 27, May 1, June 4, and August 7, 1889; *Service List, 1889*, 25, 119. Lovatt's correspondence for May 2 to June 3 and from June 5 to July 1, 1889, is missing.

Chapter 11

Hoping for a Promotion

Jiujiang, 1889–1890

RETURN TO JIUJIANG

On the morning of Monday, July 1, Lovatt "at once went on duty," meeting for the first time his new boss, Commissioner A. Mouillesaux de Bernieres, "a very nice fellow this Frenchman—good hearted and straightforward—more like an Englishman," a favorable first impression that increased over time: "The Commissioner is extremely nice, and since we have got to know each other, no one could be kinder." The British colleague he was replacing, J. H. C. Gunther, was auctioning off his belongings, so Lovatt bought his bed and other furnishings for his "extremely modest" house located on a sandbank 600 yards long and 300 yards wide. Even though he was now earning an extra 25 taels per month, or 125 taels, he lamented that he was no better off because now he needed a house boy and a cook, expenses that he did not have in his hotel in Fuzhou: "I live very quietly and never at so small expense, my largest single item being servants $19—cook, boy and coolie."[1]

Lovatt found Jiujiang "very much the same as when I left it, with, of course, a few improvements." One improvement was that "it is much drier and healthier now than then." There were also additional houses, more brick tea factories, some Russian firms, as well as the tea firm of Anderson and Company. The China Inland Mission had grown considerably, including "a large property in the city, with several fine buildings, and a boy's school containing 80 students." The transportation infrastructure had also improved, with four steamer lines, resulting in his receiving a letter from home only twenty-nine days after it had been mailed.[2]

Infrastructure improvements were not confined to Jiujiang. Downriver, passenger service from Shanghai saw dramatic fare reductions, with passage to Vancouver only $100, causing Lovatt to muse: "I wonder [why] everybody, myself included, don't clear out, and take the pleasant voyage." Upriver, Hankou, where Lovatt was destined to return, was on the brink of a major transportation upgrade when the new viceroy, Zhang Zhidong, who "is putting things through properly," planned a rail line to Beijing. Noting the "enormous increase of steamer traffic on the river," Lovatt predicted that the confluence of these two transportation modes would see Hankou become "a very great port." Developments such as this prompted Lovatt to write about China's future:

> Here in China we are moving on in the path of progress and civilization, but so slow as to be almost imperceptible to all but the most lynx-eyed observers, but that you can easily conceive is owing to the vast mass of ignorance, prejudice and conservatism that has to be moved. That it is moved at all is satisfactory and moving in the right direction as the vast mass gets leavened more and more with modern, or rather western, ideas.[3]

Many of the same people were still in Jiujiang, and "all seemed pleased to see me." One of those was "poor old Sengkee," the carpenter who two weeks later "ate his dinner last afternoon, walked out of the room, and fell down dead." Another was their former and now "very poor" amah who was cleaning bathrooms and who asked him for a job. In the missionary community, Hykes was still there, as was Miss Howe, who "has become quite stout."[4]

One thing that had not changed about Jiujiang was the extreme heat. From the time of his arrival in July, Lovatt complained that it "has been awful hot, and walking in to the city is a little too much." As a consequence, Lovatt limited his physical activity: "I am keeping pretty quiet. I do not go home to tiffin, but have it brought down. It is fried fish, stewed fruit and rice, breakfast and dinner much the same." Despite his precautions, the heat took its toll, raising boils that "made any position but that of *Stand to Attention* a painful one." Making matters worse were "the mosquitos [that] will not let you do anything at night" to keep cool.[5]

The heat was not only uncomfortable but also potentially life-threatening: "Three of the staff is on the sick list and one or two are very feeble looking." Even more serious was when the British steamer *W. C. deVries* arrived from Shanghai with her flag at half-mast because its engineer had died of cholera that afternoon after a few hours' illness and was buried in Jiujiang, "cast[ing] a shadow over us for some time." Lovatt explained that the heat was part of the problem: "Cholera is prevalent in the hot weather in the large cities owing to the filthy habits of the people and their utter lack of all sanitary arrangements."[6]

There were ways for Lovatt to beat the heat besides limiting his physical activity. At the office, "I started the punkah coolie to work." Another was the liberal use of ice, which was fine as long as the supply lasted. When the ice runs out, "there is woe and lamentation throughout the Settlement, but we are getting some from Hankow [where] there is a very good ice house." The following summer saw a repetition: "I hope you are cool, with plenty of ice, neither of which is to be found in Kiukiang." The shortage affected his diet, as "we have very little to eat owing to having no ice [and] by the end of August it gets serious and leaves you weak."[7]

For a longer spell of relief from the heat, Lovatt and his colleagues could go to the customs bungalow in Lushan three hours away, and he often availed himself of that privilege. Those trips followed more or less the same pattern: leave Jiujiang in the late afternoon taking the gig downriver where chairs would be waiting to take them up the mountain, manned by "capital coolies [who] rattled us out in great style" to the bungalow where

> at 6:30 pm I found myself in this quiet retreat, a drink from the mountain stream, and a plunge into the charming pool was decidedly refreshing. Meal: soup, boiled eels, chicken pie with some nice oxford sausages, stewed pears and rice, a cup of coffee, a cigar. Breakfast: bacon and eggs, toast and marmalade, stewed pears, and rice with a cup of good tea.

On the return trip they would sometimes walk about an hour downhill, Lovatt describing the route with a touch of sarcasm: "The road is still the rough and stony road it ever was, and the villages smell as sweetly as they always did." At the two arches they got into their chairs, whose "coolies were good ones and stepped out manfully," taking them to the river where the boatmen were waiting to take them back to Jiujiang.[8]

While the customs bungalow was nice, Lovatt and his colleagues preferred Kiufeng where the Russians had a bungalow. And so, Lovatt sometimes would avail himself of that opportunity: "On Sunday I went to Kiufeng. I felt the climb took it out of me a good deal. On our arrival I tripped and tumbled into the pool, the water was icy cold. I took dry clothes with me and felt quite a new man after it. The Russians have a beautiful bungalow there now, where we had a good tiffin." So nice was that site that de Bernieres asked Hart for permission to construct a customs bungalow there. When Hart approved, Lovatt was assigned to meet with the local district magistrate to survey the area, but the official dragged his feet: "it was a pity we did not start our new bungalow two months ago so that we might have the benefit of it during the present hot weather, but the Chinese are so long settling about the ground that the summer will be nearly over before we have it habitable." When the official finally approved, "the Commissioner feels very happy. He has got a piece of ground in the gorge. I am to go tomorrow and close the bargain"[9] (see figures 11.1 and 11.2).

Figure 11.1 Mountains above Jiujiang, April, 1890, with Russian Bungalow in the rear. Lovatt in the center with Mme. de Bernieres on the left and Wade, the Accountant on right. Courtesy: de Carbonel Family.

Lovatt had always prided himself on his health and physical prowess, but now at the age of fifty-one, he acknowledged that he was slowing down: "I play a game of tennis now and then, and with one or two turns on the bund find I have quite enough exercise." An inveterate walker, Lovatt slowed down in that area as well: "On Sunday I went with three other men out to the [customs] bungalow. I can still walk out and back, but not at the fast pace I once could." And "going up the mountains and back takes it out of me, doing it the same day." During the winter he came down with bronchitis, and the doctor predicted that would make him more susceptible to colds. As the doctor predicted, "I have had a couple of severe colds which seem to affect my bronchial tubes, which I attribute to the great changes of temperature."[10]

In addition to the summer heat was the torrential rain that produced flooding so severe that it ranked among the worst in China's modern history. Lovatt noted it first in northern China, where "the Yellow River has again broken its banks and is once more wandering at its own sweet will over the northern provinces carrying famine and disease in its track." And the following month saw more of the same from "China's Sorrow" that was "committing great ravages, and thousands of the poor Chinese are to suffer

Figure 11.2 Lovatt, seated with Mme. de Bernieres and daughter at a pool in the mountains above Jiujiang. June, 1890. Courtesy: de Carbonel Family.

considerably." As bad as it was in north China, it was the Yangzi River valley flooding that Lovatt experienced firsthand.[11]

Jiujiang was no stranger to flooding, and the first reference to it came when Lovatt wrote that "the river came over the bund yesterday morning." But a week later it was clear that this was not business as usual: "The present height of the river [is] higher at this season than has been known for a generation of mankind, the water mark registers 42'.6." The community took precautions, for example, by raising the cook houses. The cause of the flooding, of course, was what Lovatt termed an "overdose" of rain: "It has rained for 30 days more or less." Moreover, "the rain extends all along the valley of the Yangtze and has made things very dismal [downriver] in Shanghai." Upriver, "the river is still higher in Hankow. The whole of the settlement there is under water." Lovatt, however, saw it as little more than an inconvenience:

> Yesterday morning the Commissioner came in to my office and said there is a wild boar on the hill just at the back of the settlement and asked me to go with him, Allen the [US] Consul, and Smith our Senior Asst. It immediately began to rain, but as it had rained more or less for the past fifty days, we did not mind it. We are kind of used to it now, and are feeling somewhat amphibious.

However, for others, the consequences were more serious.[12]

The constant rain had dire consequences: "The country is flooded and many crops destroyed." Referring specifically to one crop, "the rain for the last month has about ruined the cotton crop." It also affected the tea trade adversely: "The China trade is in a state of collapse almost owing to the wholesale way in which Indian tea has taken the English market, and what with the floods during this summer, lasting as they have all through the autumn." However, the flooding did help the price of one crop: "the rice crop was a very abundant one and [it was] gathered before the floods came. There is a great demand for rice in the south, and the present price is double that of ordinary times, so farmer John Chinaman who has any to sell will do well this year." Overall, however, "the people along the valley of the Yangtze are in the greatest distress, and this is likely to be a severe winter for the poor."[13]

The rain and flooding also had a deleterious effect on boat traffic and trade: "Another rainy day, owing to the whole of the country being in flood, and [with] the nights dark the steamers cannot very well travel, and to get on shore at this season is very dangerous as they might spend the winter there." Even when tied up on shore, the changing water level had dire consequences: "The river has fallen rapidly and left two Chinese junks on the bund who did not expect to see the water vanish from under them." The unpredictable water level combined with the torrential rains also led to junks running aground: "The river was falling slowly at the time, which made the situation still more dangerous. Then a storm came on—the poles, boards, and coffinwood were scattered—the junk broken into four pieces and floated past Kiukiang—no lives lost—a great deal of profanity in Mandarin, and a wholesome fear of the owner in Hankow." That accident also had its human element:

> Two Chinamen came in and told me their story. One was the old Junk Captain, the other was the Supercargo. Ten days ago, coming down the river and when about ten miles above Kiukiang, the Captain left the deck, giving the helm to another sailor, while he went below to eat his dinner with the Supercargo. The man at the helm was not attending to his business, but allowed the junk to go aground in shallow water.[14]

The rain and flooding along the Yangzi in the summer and fall of 1889 were not isolated weather extremes. The following year saw more of the same, prompting Lovatt to see it in Biblical proportions and at the same time take a swipe at Hart: "I think the wickedness of man, and especially the I. G., has got so great that the Noahic flood is to be repeated. If this rain goes on we shall have the biggest flood that was ever known. The river is nearly up to the top of the bund, and it is only the middle of June." As a result, the same problems that vexed transportation the previous year repeated itself: "One of

Figure 11.3 British Consul Allen, Senior Assistant Frank Smith, Lovatt, and de Bernieres boarding a gig via plank due to flooding of the Yangzi River over the Jiujiang Bund on their way to hunt wild boar. November, 1889. Courtesy: de Carbonel Family.

the steamers is on shore very badly up the river. The country is flooded, and it is difficult to tell which is the main river from the flooded land. I never knew the river to be so high at so early a date. If it should continue to rise I fancy we would be confined to the upper stories of our houses" (figure 11.3).[15]

In sum, while conditions in Jiujiang had improved since Lovatt had last served there, natural forces such as heat, rain, and flooding remained constant reminders of the hazards that accompanied service in the Chinese customs service, and which also signally affected the lives of the Chinese around him.

THE JIUJIANG ROUTINE

Lovatt soon established a routine of working from 10:00 a.m. until 4:00 p.m., then reading until 5:30 p.m., after which he played lawn tennis until 7:00 p.m., then went to the Club, where he read the papers and played billiards. Dinner was at 8: 00 p.m., and he was in bed by 11:00 p.m. During the summer tea season he was busy weighing and collecting duty: "Two hundred half chests of tea went up to Hankow last night, so we can say the market is now open, the tea men have all passed up, and there will be tea steamers here."

Charged with preventing dutiable cargo from slipping by undetected, Lovatt was vigilant, since "the Chinese are sly in their stealing." When he caught them, confiscation was the usual protocol:

> I am sitting here in the office surrounded by Chinese, some kneeling, some very sorrowful, others indifferent, but all desirous of wheedling out of me the things seized on board the steamer. I do give back a good many, in fact pretty near all, so that some of the foreign officers feel a little sore over it. Still, the Chinaman has a right to his things.[16]

Unlike Fuzhou, where there was nary a word of antiforeignism, news of disturbances came down from the upper reaches of the Yangzi River soon after Lovatt's arrival:

> The down steamer from today brought word of a row in the [Hankou] settlement. Some Chinese students from Wuchang were over in the settlement and had a row with the police, and then the mob began to be very unruly and swarmed into the settlement and attacked the police, but there is lithographic communication now with Shanghai at all the river fronts. The Chinese authorities move with much more promptitude now to keep things in order than they did formerly.[17]

Soon thereafter, two potential incidents occurred in Jiujiang itself, the first of which Lovatt termed "quite a sensation." An Englishman on one of the gunboats got drunk and fired his rifle into the air. Unfortunately, one of the bullets hit a little boy, causing the daotai sent three midnight dispatches to British consul Hurst indicating that he might not be able to prevent the local students from rioting and looting the foreign settlement. Consequently, the next morning Hurst wired to Hankou requesting that the British gunboat *Porpoise* come to Jiujiang, and the ship, which could travel at 22 miles an hour, arrived nine hours later. That same morning, Hurst went in to see the daotai, who said that he had settled the whole affair and had given the family 100 dollars out of his own pocket. Hurst said "all right" and let the matter drop. Hurst then urged the sailor who had fired the shot to offer the daotai fifty dollars, a sum that the sailor thought was too much but who nonetheless agreed to pay it. Although it was not clear if the sailor paid up, a few days later the daotai requested that Hurst reimburse him the full hundred dollars. Hurst replied, "No, you settled it without consulting me in the matter—directly contrary to treaty [that provided for extra territoriality]—but you can charge [the sailor] in my court and I will settle it in accordance with our law." Shortly thereafter, another episode involving the recently arrived British gunboat took place: "One of our Jack Tars knocked a Chinaman down the other day. Three of the Porpoises got tight when in the Chinese street and had a high old time, trying to paint the town red, but the Chinese run them in to the consulate so Jack will be fined and get his leave stopped for a month or two."[18]

Lovatt relayed this episode to his wife because he thought that "a few sensational things" might appear in her local newspaper, but "as you are now in possession of all the details you will not in any case be alarmed." In fact, he asserted that "the place was never more quiet or the people more peaceful." And since few Chinese knew of the two incidents, "any fear of a row is too absurd for anything." Even less problematical was the January visit of the American gunboat *Monocacy* that had passed through Jiujiang en route upriver to Hankou and then returned to Jiujiang where it remained for a week. Naturally, Lovatt went on board to meet Captain Johnston and his passenger, the American consul Franklin. Unlike the rowdy British sailors, he found the American sailors to be "a nice pleasant lot."[19]

Summoning gunboats to quell antiforeign disturbances was not always called for, however, as Lovatt chronicled one egregious false alarm. One day he had gone to the club "to smoke my cigar and see what was the latest rate of exchange" when he received a telegram from the French consul at the Lushan customs bungalow. Lovatt in turn sent the telegram to the French consul general in Shanghai. The message asked for a gunboat because the French mission was threatened. The telegram ended with "Hope everything." Lovatt said:

> I could not help laughing as I wrote out the message in a big round hand for the Chinese Clerk. Here am I living in the place, who know nothing about any row, the Consul is at the hills, has not been in for a week, and does not know a word of Chinese anyway, and thinks so little that he fails to come in himself, but sends this war-like telegram to Shanghai. I am disgusted with Officials. They only appear to think what Kudos they can get out of anything that turns up.[20]

After Lovatt forwarded the telegram, he decided to investigate this "threat" of a riot:

> As you know, I have many Chinese from whom I can get any information. One told me there was no row, but some of the native tea dealers had been making a row about a Catholic tea merchant bolting and not paying for the tea he got from them. In fact, one of the creditors threw himself into the pond at the back of the Mission and was drowned. The Chinese tea dealers say the Catholic priests have the man secreted and will not give him up because he is a Catholic. The priests wrote and told the Consul the Mission was *menaced*. The Consul sends the war-like telegram, but does not come in. The Br. Consul left on Saturday to spend a week with his friend, and his constable sends him a wire to come back. A nice kettle of fish.

When the French consul finally returned from the bungalow a few days later, Lovatt briefed him "and I think he is satisfied [that] no disturbance is intended by the Chinese."[21]

While the threat of antiforeignism was ever-present, Lovatt was able to remain coolheaded in the face of potentially serious incidents. However, the threats would continue to grow and Lovatt would have to confront them more directly in his next posting.

SOCIAL LIFE IN JIUJIANG

In Jiujiang, Lovatt's social life revolved in part around the local diplomatic community. He often dined with the Hursts, who were the first to invite him when he arrived, and he often joined them at the holidays, such as at Christmas when he dined with them and "we passed a fairly pleasant evening." When he learned that fall that Hurst was going away on twelve months' leave, the effect on his social life was on his mind. He hoped Hurst would be replaced by Holland who he knew from Fuzhou and who was married. When he subsequently learned that the new consul would not be Holland but rather a bachelor, he lamented, "I am sorry, for I knew [Holland], and a married man would help to make the place more agreeable and sociable." In addition to Hurst's imminent departure was the news in January that US consul Allen, with whom Lovatt often socialized, was also leaving.[22]

Lovatt's social life also revolved around his colleagues in the customs, chief of whom was the commissioner and his wife. During the holidays, he was among those invited to Madame de Bernieres' "fancy dress ball." He also often dined with them, and found the commissioner to be "very kind and pleasant. Madame de Bernieres is also very agreeable." Dinners had their own protocol, usually beginning at eight in the evening. If at a house with a lady, he went in evening dress; if a bachelor, in white. Oftentimes there was an international guest list, with Germans, Danes, French, English, and Americans, all of whom sat under a punkah, with sherry, claret, and beer being the beverages of choice. Despite this formality, Lovatt sometimes preferred to dine alone, such as Sunday tiffins that "are big affairs and I preferred the quiet of my own house" (figures 11.4-11.7).[23]

Lovatt also socialized with the missionaries, many of whom he knew from his previous posting in that port. For example, he hobnobbed with the Hykes, Miss Howe and Miss Wheeler, his familiarity with them making him privy to the latest missionary gossip. For example,

> Hykes often comes in. He told the latest news from America was that [Virgil] Hart has joined a new missionary organization—The Christian Alliance—and is expected to return to China next year. He seemed to have fallen out with Hykes and the Mission board. Poor old fellow, to sever his connection with the church of his youth will be very trying to him.

Figure 11.4 Lovatt, left, proposing a toast, the de Bernieres at right, and Chinese servants to his left. Jiujiang, 1890. Courtesy: de Carbonel Family.

Figure 11.5 Rear of Customs House, Jiujiang, May 7, 1890. Lovatt, second from right, with customs personnel and families. Courtesy: de Carbonel Family.

Figure 11.6 The daotai and his retinue visiting the Jiujiang Custom House. Lovatt's office is in the lower right. March, 1890. Courtesy: de Carbonel Family.

Figure 11.7 Walking down the Jiujiang Bund to the Steamer, May, 1890. Courtesy: de Carbonel Family.

Sometimes new faces appeared, including Catholic missionaries, one of whom made a rare appearance in Jiujiang: "I turned out this morning at 6 o'clock, and did the bund for an hour and a half, very pleasant. A fine old priest, an Italian gentleman, joined me, and as he did not know one word of English, I had to struggle along in French, but we managed to do a fair amount of talking and to understand each other."[24]

The gossip, complaints, and news during these social gatherings were often more than Lovatt really wanted to know. One French customs worker "commenced telling me what a talented, brilliant fellow he was, and how badly the I. G. had treated him, and there I had to listen for over one hour to his grievances. He made me feel as if I did not want to see him again for another 15 years." Other gossip involved his friends: "I hear my old friend Molloy, who is Tidesurveyor [in Wuhu], has got into some row and is being [demoted] in rank and pay. Poor Mrs. Molloy will be heart-broken." The gossip turned out to be true two days later: "A circular from the I. G. giving the reason of his action for disrating Mr. Molloy to Assistant Tidesurveyor says it is for inefficiency, but I fancy it is rather for debt. Molloy is a very extravagant fellow." Other customs news was more serious:

> We have had startling news from Chefoo. Mr. Colin Jamieson, who has just been sent there as Commissioner, went out for a walk one evening after office hours and never returned. There are two rumours about him. One rumour is that he may have fallen over the cliffs and killed. Another rumour is that he might have been taken ill, gone into a Chinaman's house, and died suddenly. The Chinese, being alarmed at his sudden death, may have buried him to save themselves from what they feared would be the consequence of his sudden death in their house. Of course, all this is conjecture. Everything is being done both by Chinese and foreigners to find him.[25]

Although Lovatt was on record that he had enjoyed his previous posting of Fuzhou, after several months in Jiujiang he admitted that "I like the old port much better than Foochow." He acknowledged that it was "a sleepy old place, but I like it for many reasons," one of which was his congenial colleagues: "We have a very good lot here now, and I am not in a hurry to see any of the Staff changed." Still, changes were inevitable, and sometimes led to friends being transferred. One was the Danish senior assistant Oisen: "I am sorry he is going away. He is a very nice fellow. We were together in Tientsin and have always been the best of friends." In another unwelcome transfer, "a despatch yesterday from the I. G. grants Mr. Haut, the Boat Officer here, one year's leave from the 1st April on half pay. I shall be sorry to lose Haut."[26]

While alive to the ever-present transfers, there was one in particular that caught his attention: "Mr. Hobson is appointed to *Ichang*, but it is supposed his final destination will be Chung King in the province of Szechuin, indicating that the Chinese have decided to let the steamer go up and try to reach Chung King." Indeed, just two days later, Hobson passed through on his way to Ichang, leading Lovatt to conclude that Chongqing might be opened as a treaty port as early as that summer (1890) because Hart had also sent a long list of questions regarding junks and travel on the upper Yangzi between Hankou, Yichang, and Chongqing, showing "which way the wind is blowing."[27]

Lovatt's intuition told him that the news might affect him, and initially at least, he hoped that it would not: "I hope I am not sent [to Chongqing]," in part because of the three weeks it took for a letter to go from Yichang to Chongqing by junk, and also because "I am tired of changing." On the other hand, he allowed that he would "be glad of more pay, if the I. G. will only give me back my old [tidesurveyor] pay, taels 200," which could only come if he were transferred. With no indication that a transfer was imminent, he resigned himself "to becom[ing] one of the institutions of this old port [Jiujiang]."[28]

But unbeknownst to Lovatt, just two days before resigning himself to Jiujiang, the Chinese government and the inspector general had made the decision that would result in Lovatt's transfer: "Yesterday the [Zongli] Yamen instructed me [Hart] to establish Customs, etc. at Chungking, so I am sending Hobson. It was for that port that I originally sent him to Ichang so that he might study local conditions from the Ichang end of the Chungking-Ichang line." Lovatt, of course, was unaware of this decision in Beijing, and as July passed into August, Lovatt sighed that "there is no news." Within a matter of days, however, the bombshell news arrived.[29]

Hart's dispatch read, "Mr. Lovatt is transferred [on promotion to Tidesurveyor and Harbormaster] and is to report at Chung King by the 1st September." Despite his earlier misgivings, Lovatt was pleased with the transfer. For one, he had finally been promoted. For another, his new colleagues were friends with whom he had formerly worked, including his former boss in Tianjin, Hobson, who was going there as commissioner, Stebbins as chief examiner, and Creck, his former colleague at Fuzhou, as examiner. Third, he was pleased that he had been included with those three tasked with opening the new treaty port, "so you see we are all big swells going to Chung King, none of the Juniors or small fry allowed to go." For his part, Hart saw it as a hardship post, since none of them had wives with them, Lovatt telling Jennie, "he would not have sent me if you had been with me." Lovatt saw this as a sign that the IG had confidence in him and sent a note to Hart thanking him. Jennie, on the other hand, was "indignant at my being sent to Western China."[30]

Her indignation was spurred not only because Lovatt was not coming home but he was additionally going farther away upriver, making communication by mail even more difficult. When Jennie asked him about their future, Lovatt replied that he had no plans to retire anytime soon, declaring that "the Customs is the best thing after all." Another indication that retirement was not in the offing was his desire to bring her and Willie to China because "I feel so tired of living alone."[31]

Since Hart's dispatch did not indicate what salary increase came with the promotion, Lovatt wrote to his soon-to-be commissioner Hobson, hoping that he would be restored to the full tidesurveyor's salary he had been drawing before resigning to become a commissioner in Korea rather than the measly 25 taels he had received when he had been transferred to Jiujiang. Unfortunately, the increase was only 25 taels a month: "[I received] Hobson's answer to my letter. I did hope I was to have two hundred per month, but alas it is only 150. When I am transferred from Chung King he will probably give me the 200."[32]

Lovatt then began to prepare for his departure. He ordered some stoves from Shanghai since he had heard that they were terribly expensive in Chongqing. And he had his boy pack up all his furniture except for the wardrobe and desk because he would need "a furnished house when you and Willie come out." He also had to hire a new boy and cook, since "my old ones will not leave home." Another logistical issue was how to get to his new post, since conditions along the Yangzi made it obvious that he would be unable to arrive in time: "The River is over the bund and I fancy the great current pouring through the gorges will prevent anyone going up for some time yet. I think if we get there by Christmas we shall do very well. It is a long and tedious voyage by junk."[33]

During his final week he engaged in leave-taking, with farewell dinners with his friends, including the British consul. Friday, August 28, was his last day on the job, and on Saturday he had a farewell dinner with Commissioner de Bernieres. Lovatt had made many friends during his year in Jiujiang, where "everybody is very kind, and all express their regret at my departure." The highlight of his leave-taking came when "the staff here presented me with a beautiful silver cup. It is very handsome." Since Hykes was returning to the United States the following month, Lovatt asked him to take it back with him, as "my present to my son Willie when I die." On his last morning, Sunday, August 30, he said goodbye to Miss Wheeler and Miss Howe, who said that Chongqing was "a charming place." He departed for Hankou that same afternoon.[34]

NOTES

1. WNL to JSL, July 2 and 6, August 19 and 23, and October 8 and 26, 1889, and February 6, 1890; *Service List, 1889*, 25, 119. Second Historical Archives, Nanjing. Although he was now acting tidesurveyor and harbormaster, having been appointed in June 1889, technically he was still an assistant tidesurveyor. Despite a year of frugal living arrangements, Lovatt decided that even that arrangement was too costly: "I have told the Commissioner I can't keep up a house on my present pay, as after paying all expenses it does not leave me enough to send to my family. I think I will probably arrange to live and mess in Anderson's house on the bund. It will reduce my expenses greatly." He never acted on that because a few days later he was notified that he would be transferred. WNL to JSL, August 3, 1890.

2. WNL to JSL, July 6 and 29, 1889, and April 8, June 3 and 16, and July 8, 1890. The mail went via Yokohama and Shanghai.

3. WNL to JSL, February 11 and 26, March 29, and July 22 and 30, 1890; WNL to Father Shaw, August 3, 1890.

4. WNL to JSL, July 6 and 19, 1889.

5. WNL to JSL, July 6, August 7, and October 5, 1889, and July 8, 1890. Emphasis in the original.

6. WNL to JSL July 30, 1890; WNL to Father Shaw, August 3, 1890.

7. WNL to JSL, August 12 and 16, 1889, and June 27 and July 8, 1890.

8. WNL to JSL, August 12, 16, 17, and 27, 1889, and February 15 and June 24, 1890.

9. WNL to JSL, July 19 and November 4, 1889, and March 29, May 7 and 26, July 11, and n.d., 1890. Emphasis in the original.

10. WNL to JSL, August 7, 1889, and February 4, 19, 26, and 28, and May 7, 1890.

11. WNL to JSL, August 16 and September 3, 1889.

12. WNL to JSL, October 5, 12, 14, 21, and 29, 1889.

13. WNL to JSL, October 12 and 21, and November 15, 1889.

14. WNL to JSL, August 19, and October 21 and 22, 1889.

15. WNL to JSL, June 16 and 20, 1890.

16. WNL to JSL, November 19, 1889, and March 25, May 2 and 7, and July 22, 1890; WNL to Father Shaw, August 3, 1890.

17. WNL to JSL, July 6, 1889.

18. WNL to JSL, October 5, 12, and n.d., 1889.

19. WNL to JSL, October 5, 1889, and January 14 and 22, 1890.

20. WNL to JSL, June 30, 1890.

21. WNL to JSL, June 30 and early July (n.d.), 1890. Emphasis in the original.

22. WNL to JSL, July 6, August 7, September 4, October 12, and December 30, 1889, and January 25 and 28, and February 11 and 14, 1890. Lovatt had been friends with Holland from his previous posting in Fuzhou. The bachelor Hopkins arrived in mid-March 1890. Lovatt described one dinner with the American consul:

> Yesterday I had an invitation from Mrs. Allen to go up and join them at dinner to eat a portion of pheasant, one which I sent them, so at seven and a half o'clock I put in an appearance with Mr. Deacon, our Oxford man. I whiled away the evening until nearly

eleven o'clock when we left. I had one of our tidewaiters with me, Mr. Lewis, a very nice fellow who was once a lieutenant in the 21st North British Fusiliers. He has never seen service, but is a pleasant fellow and a very gentlemanly man.

Other members of the dinner party were St. Croix, the agent for the China Navigation Co., Munter, and Currie.

23. WNL to JSL, December 30, 1889, and March 22, and July 8, 1890; WNL to Father Shaw, August 3, 1890.

24. WNL to JSL, August 23, 1889, and January 22, March 11, and June 10, 1890.

25. WNL to JSL, November 12 and December 18, 1889, and July 28 and 30, 1890.

26. WNL to JSL, August 23, October 14 and n.d., and December 30, 1889, and January 28 and February 11, 1890.

27. WNL to JSL, November 12 and 15, 1889, and March 20, 1890. Emphasis in the original.

28. When Moorehead transited Jiujiang en route from Hankou to Shanghai on twenty days' leave early in 1890, Lovatt learned that his former commissioner desired a transfer to Shanghai, and if that were to happen, he predicted that "it is possible I may go to Hankow. I would, however, prefer Tientsin." When six more months went by without any news, in July 1890 he toyed with the idea of going in person to see Hart: "Sometimes I think I will go up to Peking and see the IG, [but] alas! the expense also makes me but pause." WNL to JSL, August 23 and 31, and November 19, 1889, and March 10 and 14, and July 22, 1890. Emphasis in the original.

29. WNL to JSL, February 11, July 22, and August 3, 1890; Hart to Campbell, July 20, 1890. Hobson was commissioner at Yichang during 1889–1890.

30. *Service List, 1891*, 20; WNL to JSL, August 7 and 25, and December 8, 1890.

31. WNL to JSL, November 3 and December 22, 1888, and January 18 and 25, March 3, April 24, June 3, July 19, August 13, 16, 23, 26, and 31, September 3, October 4, 5, 8, 14, 15, 21, 26, and 29, and November 4, 15, and 19, 1889, and January 4, 18, and 25, February 4 and 6, March 11, 22, and 29, April 5, 24, and 30, May 2, 13, and 26, June 10, July 15, 22, and 30, and September 30, 1890; WNL to Father Shaw, August 3, 1890.

Although Lovatt continued to complain about his finances, he nonetheless continued to dabble in the stock market, buying additional shares in the Sheridan Mining Company of Colorado.

Adding to Jennie's concerns was her mother's dementia that had become worse, making her care increasingly difficult for her seventy-two-year-old husband.

32. WNL to JSL, August 7, 19, and 25, 1890.

33. WNL to JSL, August 7, 11, and 27, and September 18, 1890. He told Jennie to get Archibald Little's book, *The Gorges of the Yangstze,* and Hart's *Western China* to follow his travels up the Yangtze.

34. WNL to JSL, August 11, 15, 19, 25, and 27, and September 1, 1890. Great-grandson William de Carbonel has the silver cup given to Lovatt upon his departure from Jiujiang in 1890.

Chapter 12

Opening a New Customs Station

Chongqing, 1890–1894

HANKOU AND YICHANG, SEPTEMBER–OCTOBER 1890

Lovatt arrived in Hankou, the first stop on his journey to his new posting, on Monday, September 1, 1890. Since it was little more than a stopover, his socializing was limited to a short nine days. He stayed with the Mooreheads who "have been very kind indeed to me," went across the river to Wuchang with Foster, called on Hill who "always came to see me in Kiukiang," and went to a party at the US consulate ("everybody was there"). Perhaps the most utilitarian aspect of his socializing came during his Saturday evening tennis match with the newly assigned British consul to Chongqing, Henry Fulford, "a very nice fellow." Fulford had been perusing the reports of the previous consul, who had spent over three years in that city, and he shared the "very interesting" contents with Lovatt. This included information on the foggy winter weather and the good beef and vegetables. However, foreign goods were very expensive, and anything from Shanghai took at least three months to arrive.[1]

Lovatt's next leg from Hankou to Yichang depended on the steamer schedule and the height of the river. The *Kiangloong* had arrived in Hankou on September 4 and now that the river was slowly falling, it was able to depart on the morning of September 9. As he left Hankou, Lovatt began to have second thoughts about his wife and youngest son joining him in Chongqing. After reiterating that he could never return permanently to Minnesota, he now said that "when transferred to another port I should like to meet you there. You and Willie join me." His reasoning was that "here in China we can be comfortable and happy without the labor and care-worn toil of life at home. My pay by next year will be T[aels] 200 and here are comforts that we can't have at home."[2]

Lovatt arrived in Yichang on the morning of September 12 and immediately reported to Hobson, who had assembled a flotilla of three junks to take them to Chongqing. But while the water level had receded sufficiently to make the trip from Hankou to Yichang, it had not receded enough for the more arduous forty-day 400-mile journey upriver to Chongqing through the gorges and their rapids. So, although the plan was to stay only eight days in Yichang, it was clear that he would be there longer. Since this was his first time there, he took note of the surroundings, calling it "the usual dirty Chinese city without anything in particular to note, a poor miserable city and about as dull as a Chinese city can be." As usual, he made the rounds of the expatriate community, calling on British consul Fraser, Dr. Aldridge, and Henry and Mrs. Cockbourne, who he had known from his posting in Hankou and who invited Lovatt to stay with them, commenting that they "are very kind to me, and have made me very comfortable."[3]

On September 20, the day originally scheduled for departure, the *Kiang-loong* returned, bringing with it Fulford from Hankou and Lovatt's furnishings from Jiujiang. But conditions were still unsatisfactory: "when the river falls a little more we shall make a start." More favorable conditions a week later meant that "we shall leave here on Friday the 3rd instant enroute for Chung King, the river is falling rapidly, and the current is not near so strong, so that the rapids will be quite negotiable by the time we get there."[4]

As Lovatt prepared to depart, two problems surfaced. One was a delay in receiving a traveling allowance from Hart: "I told [Hobson] we would all be ruined if we did not get it, for one can hardly go a month's journey in a boat without supplies, or to a place like Chung King without foreign shops, then when you write from Chung King for anything to Shanghai, it takes three months, often six months, before you get anything." In preparation, Lovatt took enough butter, coffee, tea, and sugar to last six months, and "with care I can make them go longer, but so large an outlay leaves many bills unpaid." A second problem was an onset of illness. An inveterate exerciser, Lovatt anticipated that spending forty days in a junk "cannot be very enjoyable to an active man," so five days after his arrival he climbed an 800-foot hill known as "The Pyramid." But the climb took so much out of him that the next day, uncharacteristically, "I do not feel like taking exercise." Lovatt initially blamed his lethargy on the rigors of travel from Jiujiang to Hankou and Hankou to Yichang and on a cold that he caught in Hankou. But when he failed to improve, two days before departure, "Mr. Cockbourne and I decided I had probably malaria, so took a large dose of quinine last night and another this morning." On the day of departure, Lovatt dragged himself to a farewell tiffin, despite being under the weather, after which he and his colleagues departed.[5]

YICHANG TO CHONGQING, OCTOBER–NOVEMBER 1890

The three-junk flotilla left Yichang on October 3, a sampan attached to each junk, and a Chinese gunboat escort with a 3-pound iron gun mounted on the bow. Lovatt and Littledale had hiked through there twenty-seven years earlier, but this was the first time that he had traversed the area by boat. Consequently, he had ample opportunity to observe the boatmen manning the junks and the twenty trackers from Sichuan province, who were "not tall, but slim and wiry without a particle of superfluous flesh." Since they worked naked during the heat of the day, Lovatt predicted that this would "make the voyage to Chungking for ladies frightfully disagreeable." Needless to say, the trackers did not have an easy job. Many of the places they traversed did not have a tracking path, particularly through the Yichang and Ninkan gorges that produced "dangerous rapids," so the going was slow at only 5 miles per day. Their compensation was minimal, at eight cash (less than one cent) per day plus food, consisting of hot rice garnished with a little salted cabbage or boiled beans. As Lovatt noted, "Unlimited population does not always bring blessings; there are plenty of coolies to be had even cheaper."[6]

Lovatt initially found traversing the rapids and the gorges "an awful journey," prompting him to take a few shots at Hart and at the British government for good measure: "Our Irish I. G. has increased the wrath of God against him by sending me on this miserable trip. Eight days doing 40 miles, but what a forty, so we may hope to reach Chung Ching by Christmas." And since foreign steamers were not allowed to go to Chongqing, he felt that the British government had been had: "One of the reasons the [Chinese] government objected to steamers on the upper Yangstze was that the monkeys in the gorges might throw stones down on the steamers as they passed up, and this reasoning the sapient British Minister at Peking allowed to influence him and to surrender the right of foreigners to send steamers to Chung Ching." Sarcastically, Lovatt added, "By the way, I have so far seen no monkeys, and hardly think they can throw stones a hundred yards."[7]

After nearly two weeks, they finally entered Sichuan and put in at Kweifu (Guifu), "the usual dirty old Chinese city," on the evening of October 15 for two nights. At this halfway point, they were met by two gunboats sent by the Chongqing *daotai* to escort them the rest of the way, they sent their mail through a Chinese postal firm back to Yichang, changed boats and trackers, and paid the junk captains and crew. Now in a different province, Lovatt was able to learn something about local officialdom. The local district magistrate, Wang, who had held the position for four years, had just been promoted to a position in the capital of Chengdu, and "leaves to the regret of all classes who say he was a good and just man," to be replaced by a Mr. Tang from

Chongqing. Wang, apparently, was one of the few honest officials in a district that "is considered one of the most money making of any in the Empire." But others were less honest.[8]

Lovatt witnessed firsthand two attempts at extortion while in Guifu. One was that "all junks, either upward or downward bound, must stop and report to the [likin] customs here and pay duty, [and] even to do that the agents must square [bribe] the underlings of the yamens or else suffer ruinous detention." Consequently,

> in the evening a man from the [yamen] came and said it was his duty to search the junks, but he would not do it if he was paid twenty cents. Of course, Hobson would pay him nothing. Then he begged for a piece of candle for his lantern, which he got and left. Think of the bare-faced effrontery of them trying to squeeze the Custom's junks! What must merchants suffer at their hands!

In the second attempt, "Just before leaving, one of the gunboat captains called to say one of his men, in pushing off the gunboat from the shore, fell overboard and was drowned. He wanted Hobson to remain another day, and also asked him for ten thousand cash [$10] to buy a coffin, both of which were refused." Hobson told him he could stay and look after the body, but the captain declined, since his orders were to accompany them to Chongqing.[9]

The convoy departed Guiifu on October 17 and five days later arrived at the next transit point, the walled city of Wanxian and the seat of the district magistrate's yamen, 120 miles from their destination. Here again, Lovatt noted official corruption and the measures taken by the merchants to protect themselves:

> Nearly all classes of the Chinese, especially the merchants and men of wealth, try to avoid living in the city, the principal reasons being that the gates are shut at an inconvenient early hour and the underlings [runners] of the officials are always prying into their private affairs. But where they live in the suburbs they come and go as they like, live in the neighborhood of each other, and can unite to oppose any act of tyranny or oppression that the officials might be inclined to exercise for the purpose of extorting money from isolated individuals living in the city and close to their own yamens.[10]

Although the party was scheduled to spend only one night in Wanxian, they ended up spending two. According to the junk captain, the reason was that the next set of junks had arrived too late due to the rapids ahead. But Lovatt, who understood Chinese, overheard him saying that opium was cheap there and that there was a theatrical performance at the dedication of a local temple, so most of the crew attended the performance. The behavior of the junk crews at these transit stations thus came under Lovatt's scrutiny—"an unmistakable air about them of leading vile, dissolute lives during the intervals between the completion of one voyage and the beginning of another."[11]

That opium was a key factor in the "dissolute" lives prompted Lovatt to expound on its evils, noting that it is "everywhere" and that all the riverside shanties sell it already prepared for smoking. Specifically in Sichuan, "all classes here smoke, many with sickly looking faces," and he cited its addictive properties: "the opium smoker, like a drunkard, will give his last cash for his favorite poison." He admitted, however, that the strong crew members also smoked opium with fewer ill effects: "a good deal depends on the quantity of food eaten; where the men eat plenty, their few pipes of opium does not apparently affect their health, but with little and poor food the sad effects are too plainly visible." Lovatt then launched into policy prescription: "I think everything ought to be done to stop the growth and the cultivation of the drug. Its use is killing the people slowly but surely." Unfortunately, the addiction rate was worse in Sichuan because the local crop was less expensive than foreign opium. Lovatt attributed this to corrupt officials, "not one of [whom] care a copper cash, only so far as it affects their pockets." This lack of concern extended all the way up to Li Hongzhang himself, whose negotiations with British minister Wade resulted in high duties on foreign opium and made it more worthwhile for Chinese to grow opium: "The poppy was grown all around Tientsin and along the banks of the Peiho right under the nose of the Viceroy [Li] who derived advantage from it in the increase of his revenue."[12]

In contrast to venal officials, Lovatt gave high marks to the ordinary Chinese he met on the journey, noting that "the country people we met were very nice, quiet, and civil." His positive opinion was seconded by one of the China Inland missionaries he met along the way, Harold Hayward, who said that the local "people treated him with much civility." To Lovatt, not only were they "very civil," they were also "always ready for a chat," particularly about their desire that the Yangtze be fully opened: "The people along the river here are anxious to see the advent of steamers. They want cheap cotton goods and believe the arrival of the foreign vessels would be good for trade."[13]

As the convoy was tracking up the right bank on approach to Chongqing, A. E. Von Rosthorn, who had eschewed the junk in favor of hiking the entire 400 miles from Yichang, appeared in a sampan from Chongqing in the afternoon of November 2 bringing mail. He had made the overland trip in less than four weeks, arriving on October 31. As the end of the trip was now in sight, Lovatt could look back on what he had initially said was an awful journey and say that "with the exception of one day, we have had lovely weather, and now the trip is over I can only say on the whole it has been pleasant, especially at all rapids and the other exciting incidents."[14]

CHONGQING, NOVEMBER 1890 TO MAY 1894

Lovatt arrived in Chongqing on the morning of November 4, 1890, after a journey of one month from Yichang, along with his traveling companions: Commissioner Hobson, who had been in Yichang; First Class Tidewaiter J. P. Strong from Zhenjiang; and Third Class Tidewaiter L. L. Stockwell, also from Zhenjiang. Awaiting them was Third Assistant von Rosthorn. Soon thereafter, Chief Examiner Stebbins from Tianjin arrived for a total of six. Their duty was to prepare that city for its official opening as a treaty port and to establish a customs office. Upon his arrival, Lovatt speculated, again with surprising accuracy, that "Our friend Bob may have meant to do me a friendly turn by sending me here [Chongqing], making it the reason for giving me a promotion and preparing the way for another, but I fear he will not make me a Commissioner."[15]

After their junks tied up at the third gate, the *Taiping-men* (Great Peace Gate), Lovatt had his first look at the city. He was initially impressed by its size, using phrases like "very large" and "enormous," and speaking comparatively, "with the exception of Nanking and Peking, it is the largest Chinese city I have seen." Additionally, since the Taiping rebels had not been there, it had many old buildings. Surrounding Chongqing was a city wall about 6 miles in circumference, with nine gates, five opening to the Yangtze, three to the small Jialing River, and one landward. Its inhabitants were "comfortably dressed, easy going and fond of pleasure, polite and courteous." The shops were "numerous" and offered "every kind and variety of goods." Five Christian missions had preceded them: American Methodist, Episcopal—London, China Inland, Friends, and the Catholic Foreign Mission of Paris.[16]

Lovatt's first task was to find a place to live, so the next morning he went to the China Inland Mission, as they were familiar with the city: "I have been round with Mr. Lewis looking for a house, as we will have to live right in the city crowded with houses and brimful of Chinese." For the next three days, members of that mission "very kindly went round with me to look at several houses, but all of which were too filthy to think of taking." After four days, he was exhausted, and took Sunday off: "the day of rest is very welcome." His housing quest resumed on Monday and for the next two days followed a similar routine. It was not until Thursday that he took another break, but predicted that "some Chinaman will be sure to come along and say he has a palace to let, and then take me tramping through the city and show me some dirty old pig sty of a place."[17]

Since he had no house, he and his compatriots were stuck on the river: "It is a dull rainy day, and we are confined of course to our junk, and I need hardly say I am tired of our Noah's ark of a dwelling place, and I see no immediate prospect of leaving it." This continued for the next three weeks. But his luck was about to change.[18]

After three weeks of house hunting, Lovatt finally hit pay dirt: "I have at last found a fine house, in a good position, which we will take if the Taotai does not provide us with a place soon." His new address was Wang Chia Yuen Ken Teng Kai, or as Lovatt rendered it, "The Court of the Wang Family on the Heavenly Lamp Street." The house was large and roomy, with court yards and gardens, in "the brightest part of the city," and close to the Inland Mission, "all [of whose] members have done all they could to help me about a house." The rent was 20 taels per month for six months with an option to extend, to be paid in advance since "John Chinaman shows no favours to foreigners when he is boss." On his first night in his new house, his neighbors kept him awake with a "hideous" racket because of a lunar eclipse "by the beating of gongs, and the firing of guns and [fire]crackers to drive away the dragon from devouring the *Fair Regent of the Heavens*." Lovatt's house would serve as temporary housing for the other five customs officers until the Daotai provided housing for them.[19]

Indeed, while Lovatt was searching for a house, Hobson had been unsuccessfully asking the Daotai for a house. Since that meant that the customs staff would be living with him, Lovatt had to renovate the house, supervising carpenters, masons, painters, and whitewashers making a "frightful din . . . to make the place habitable [because] Chung Ching is a very damp place." Because he was "busy all day long" dealing with Chinese contractors, he had to stay alert, as the "worst job of all [is] trying to keep the wily Chinese from squeezing too much cash out of the different contracts."[20]

After little more than a month in the city, Lovatt had come to dislike Chongqing's climate, as "gloomy days, thick fog, and rain appears to be the rule, and you know that kind of weather, would, if continued, make anyone mad, billious, and disagreeable." As he wrote to his former commissioner, de Bernieres, "one would not come here from choice." His opinion was shared by the others: "Pretty near the whole staff are longing to get away. The Chinese Prefect who called yesterday said if anyone lived in Chung Ching they must eat plenty of chillies and other hot things to keep out the damp, and that spoils digestion. So it is a choice of evils." And since Jennie continued to ask about joining him, Lovatt used the weather in part to dissuade her: "I would not have the heart to ask you to face the climate of Chung Ching." In fact, the only positive thing he could say about the climate was that the winter "is not near so cold as at Hankow and Kiukiang."[21]

Despite his complaints, Lovatt did not second-guess his decision to leave America three years earlier: "on the farm we were constantly losing capital, besides doing a lot of hard work and drudgery, and not much prospect of things improving." Nor was he eager to return to try another line of work:

"There is no use my trying to get anything in America. I am too old, and not used to hard labour, so it would be no use. Farming I tried, and you know the result." So the plan remained to have Jennie join him in China, but only after leaving Chongqing.[22]

Once he had found a place to live and had resigned himself to the disagreeable weather, Lovatt began to settle into a routine. That routine had little to do with customs duties since the port was not officially open, and would likely not open any time soon. Since there were no official duties, Lovatt decided to renew his Chinese language study: "I have engaged a teacher . . . [W]ith my residence in Corea and at home, then a year at Foochow, which is another dialect altogether, I found my Chinese was not improving, [so] I propose devoting the forenoons to Chinese." So every morning, "I peg away at Chinese" and by mid-January he had read twenty-five lessons. In doing so, Lovatt appreciated that Chinese "is twice as hard as the most difficult Greek." And he acknowledged his own limitations, likening himself to some missionaries who "will learn to speak a little bad Chinese as we all do. I am sure one must study Chinese when young if anyone is to become a proper Chinese scholar."[23]

With his mornings devoted to language study, his afternoons were given over in part to writing, not only letters but also a forty-page account of his recent "perilous and exciting voyage" from Yichang to Chongqing, accompanied by a map and chart with "a list of the *rapids, rocks,* and *dangers* of the upper *Yangstze.*" He was hoping to impress the IG, because "I fancy he liked the style of my reports on the Kiukiang lights last year [and] perhaps that is one reason he sent me here. My report was the only one he ordered to be published." It might even result in a promotion: "I hope Robert will acknowledge the labour, even if he doubts the literary ability with which it is written."[24]

Another way Lovatt passed his afternoons in addition to his writing was to hike, usually with others. One frequent companion was his commissioner, sometimes doing the two-hour hike around the city walls. At other times they headed out of town: "Hobson and I have just been out for a walk. The hills all round the outside of the city is the grave yard. I never saw so many graves." Lovatt got to know his commissioner better on these walks, as he wrote to his former commissioner, de Bernieres, "I like Hobson very much indeed, but as you know, he is not much of a talker." And as a former commissioner in Korea himself, Lovatt was able to empathize with Hobson's responsibilities: "He . . . actually grumbles because it is near pay day, a matter to me of inexpressible delight. Still, I feel for him—a large staff [and] little money." Another one of his companions was the inveterate hiker von Rosthorn:

> This has been for Chung Ching a pretty fine day, so von Rosthorn and myself left for an afternoon walk. We went out at the Tung yuin men [gate] and took the

great stone road that leads to the capital of the province, Chung tu [Chengdu], and walked out to the Fu to Kuan, Buddha's Fortress, and had a look at the country, very hilly, all the slopes terraced into rice fields.[25]

Another hike was longer and sometimes involved an overnight stay: "I invited [Methodist missionaries] Dr. and Mrs. McCartney, also my friend [British Consul Harry] Fulford, to go with me to the Pagoda for a picnic, [where] the view over the city and the two rivers was splendid from our altitude of 1300 feet." At other times, he went alone: "Two days rest in a temple on the summit, and my lungs full of pure air. [After] a few months in a reeking Chinese city, mountain air feels good to one after that amount of residence." On one such trip, he chatted with the Buddhist priest:

> The old boy was making yellow official envelopes by day and writing official letters at night. When I asked him why he wrote the characters so small, he said, one must be humble when addressing heaven, and yellow is the heavenly colour. These letters are messages to peoples departed friends, which the priest writes at so much a despatch. The despatches are then burned and the message ascends in smoke. The old man was very kind to me.[26]

In addition to hikes were longer excursions on the Yangzi River, often with the British consul.

> I left here on Saturday morning with Fulford in his house boat for a trip down river to the Tung lo (Brass Gong) Gorge. It is the first gorge below Chung King, the current took us down in about two hours and, having found a good anchorage, we remained until the evening when we took a walk down through the gorge on the trackers path, which forms an excellent road, and enjoyed the cool pleasant breeze.

That particular trek exposed Lovatt once again to the addictive scourge plaguing China:

> While walking through the gorge I noticed a man at work scarifying the poppy heads. After the poppy has flowered and the head goes to seed, it forms a ball like a small tomato and when hard, the cultivator comes along with a little instrument like a small knife. It has four sharp points like the points of pine, he takes the head of the poppy in his left hand, and with a neat little stroke, makes a mark from the poppy head to the stem, which is four lines, nothing more than delicate scratches, and through these scratches the poppy juice exudes a white glutinous substance which he scrapes off with a knife. You can easily imagine there is not much and scrapes the knife on a little box made out of a hollow bamboo. This thick glue-like stuff, when boiled down, is the famous opium.[27]

As might be expected, when Lovatt and his companions went out, they ran the risk of harassment from the locals. On one particular hike with Fulford along the Yangzi, the two encountered "a rough class" of boatmen who "made various uncomplimentary remarks about our appearance, dress, and our whole outfit, and the boys were inclined to be very insolent." Lovatt attributed this unruly behavior to the fact that while "there is no doubt the Chinese very much dislike foreigners, those in the older treaty ports . . . are accustomed to our presence and have at different times been taught to behave themselves by high handed measures, about the only way to make them behave." By contrast, foreigners were few and relatively new in Chongqing. Still, this unpleasant encounter along the hike appeared to be an exception.[28]

Lovatt's afternoon outings were usually relatively pleasant affairs: "I took a long walk through the city and brought up at the [British] Consulate and had a chat with Fulford. The people were very civil. Here you are not called *Foreign Devil* very much. The Chinese have a superstitious feeling about using the word *devil*, but *Foreign Dog* is a very favourite expression of theirs." And a trip to the other side of the Yangzi engendered no unpleasantness: "I have been across the river, and on my return met a company of soldiers. They looked very much surprised to see me, but were fairly civil." The overall lack of hostility on the part of the local population toward Lovatt and the other Westerners may have been due in part to official edicts:

> The old Taotai and Magistrate has issued proclamations saying we are here on the service of the Emperor and requested the people to treat us with politeness, as we have not come to take anything from them. A queer way of putting things, but anyway the people are very civil to me, and I have been out all over the city nearly every day since I have been here.[29]

After his afternoon excursions, Lovatt's evenings had their own routine as well: "We dine at 7, and by 8:30, smoke, and I settle down to a long evening reading." Most of his reading came courtesy of Hobson who "is quite obliging [and] has very fair taste in books." Appropriate to the frontier nature of his posting, Lovatt's reading tended toward travel in western China. When he ran out of travel books, he chose Shakespeare, of whose plays "I have read a good deal." Bedtime in the warmer months was at midnight but moved up to ten in the winter because "the house is too cold to sit up in."[30]

While studying, reading, writing, and hiking helped pass the time, Lovatt sought more in the way of human contact. Naturally, closest to him were his five customs colleagues, but given their small number, if one departed, a void was created. When the Chief Examiner was transferred on promotion to tide-surveyor, Lovatt ruefully noted that "Stebbins leaves the day after tomorrow for Ichang [and] we are not likely to get anyone in his place." Five months later, "the mail brought Von Rosthorn's leave, three months, so when he goes, life will be lonelier than ever here, and it is dull." With few colleagues and with no duties to perform, Lovatt compared his life to that of the Chinese gentry: "The daily round of our dull monotonous life here [is] that one eats, sleeps, and thinks, much about the same every day. Action. Without it, we are no better than the Chinese and we are three months here and all we have done is to make ourselves comfortable."[31]

Moreover, because Chongqing had not yet been opened as a treaty port, there were no foreign businessmen for Lovatt to associate with. And so reports of the imminent arrival of Western traders were welcome news. The first to make their way westward was his friend Archibald Little and his wife, who was on his way with two compradores to start a business: "I shall be glad to see him. A new face or two not belonging to the Customs will be very welcome," and would provide a break from the "the usual very quiet, dull" social scene. They arrived in March 1891, and "last evening I went round to dine with Mr. Fulford at the consulate and there met Mr. and Mrs. Little. Mrs. Little was very bright and pleasant [and] planned a picnic to *Lao Ching tung* for tomorrow to which she had invited Mr. Hobson and myself." Little also floated an offer for Lovatt to join him in his business venture, the China Western Transport Company, with a capital investment of 40,000 taels, but Lovatt said "I will have nothing to do with it. There would be any amount of worry and annoyance."[32]

After thirty years in the service, Lovatt knew Hart's preferences. One was that he did not like his employees to write for the newspapers, and Archibald Little caused Lovatt inadvertently to run afoul of that maxim. When portions of a letter he had written to Little appeared under his name in the *North China Herald*, Lovatt decided not to write to him again because "I know the I. G. does not like it." A second preference of Hart was that his employees not attempt to flatter or bribe him, and Lovatt knew that any attempt along those lines would be counterproductive, a lesson not yet learned by one junior officer: "One of our service toadys got up a scheme to present a diamond necklet to Lady Hart. The I. G. heard of it and wrote to the individual, saying he was to do nothing of the sort. The I. G. did not wish peoples resources to be taxed for him or anybody else." But this lame attempt to attract Hart's notice was by no means the most egregious.[33]

Charles Mason, a fourth assistant at Zhenjiang, in 1891 decided to join the anti-Qing Elder Brother Society (*Gelaohui*), ostensibly to learn its secrets. Lovatt was contemptuous of his blatant attempt to curry favor: "[Mason] has gone into the whole thing hoping to make a name and so get the I. G. to promote him out of the ordinary run of promotion." Aware of Hart's proclivities, Lovatt knew that Mason had "gone too far, and in his eagerness has lost his sense of what an honorable man may do. He will lose his position, and the British government may put him on trial for conspiring against the peace of the Emperor of China, with whom the [British] government is at peace." Coming at a time when "the country is full of rumours over the fear that there is a rebellion brewing," Lovatt concluded that Mason was "mad," and predicted accurately that he would soon be put on trial in Shanghai.[34]

More important for Lovatt was how this episode would affect the IG personally and, more broadly, the customs service institutionally. He felt sure that Hart "is feeling pretty bad over the Mason affair, a man of his own selection who he was taking up to Pekin to act as a professor of English." Institutionally, "this act will do more to injure the Customs Service and Sir R. Hart's position than anything" because Hart's rivals saw an opportunity: "Li Hung Chang and his set of Chinese officials are trying to make capital out of the Mason affair, . . . suggesting [his] removal on account of his appointing a . . . traitorous foreigner to the Customs Service." If he were removed, jealous high officials, "especially the Chinese who have been abroad," would appoint "the men now being educated in America on their return . . . and so gradually take the place of foreigners," including Lovatt. But Lovatt predicted that Hart would weather the storm because the Empress Dowager (*Cixi*) "has a very high opinion of the I. G., who has served them long and well." Lovatt prided himself on the fact that unlike Mason and others, his attempt to attract Hart's notice by preparing an account of the trip upriver to Chongqing was above reproach.[35]

MISSIONARIES AND CHRISTIANITY

Since the customs and business community was so small, Lovatt had to look elsewhere for opportunities to socialize. It was missionaries, mostly Protestants from America, England, and Canada, who filled the gaps in his social calendar. Sichuan had a small group of them, some of whom had preceded the customs party. Indeed, within the first few days of his arrival, Lovatt had made the rounds of the various missionary establishments, calling on the London Mission and the "prosperous" China Inland Mission which boasted "quite a large piece of property" housing a hospital and a boys and girls school.[36]

The missionary presence in Sichuan continued to grow while Lovatt was there. The Methodists were about to open a new mission in Chengdu, with three new missionaries. And the customs doctor, "now on his way up river," was an American attached to the Methodist mission in Chongqing, "so things are moving even in these far away places." The Quakers had a presence in Chongqing and were about to open a mission in Chengdu. And the China Inland Mission in Chongqing also had an infusion of new missionaries. Given

Lovatt's long residence in China, he was often acquainted with some of those veteran missionaries who were en route, learning, for instance, that Virgil Hart, along with his wife and daughter of the Canadian Methodist Church, was coming to Chengdu with nine other missionaries to open their first mission there, "so I am looking forward with pleasure to seeing our old friend once more."[37]

Getting to Sichuan was no easy matter, as Lovatt knew from firsthand experience. He knew the language and was accustomed to the rigors of travel in China, but most of the missionaries were new to the country and to traveling in the interior, and did not know the language. So the experience, especially for female missionaries, could be daunting: "Ten Missionary ladies belonging to the China Inland Mission now on their way from Ichang, all in one junk, must be having a warm and crowded time of it, and can't be very comfortable tracking up against the present frightful current." Lovatt then described the conditions on the boat:

> The junk may have three and a half little rooms, the servants cooking, the captain who generally has his wife, and twenty trackers, besides a crew of eight, one of whom is a cook who prepares four meals of boiling rice. No use calling for the Steward or Stewardess; there is none. Beds on floor, fleas, to say nothing of grey dragoons. Red coated Soldiers, or Rats, gambol round you through the soft and still watches of the night. The coolies snore and smell, the river boils and rages past you.[38]

Knowing what the women were in for, the more seasoned male missionaries often made the four-day trip downriver to meet them in Yichang to escort them upriver. Hart, for example, will "bring up the other members of the mission and his wife." As for the local missions, "most of our community are now on the river on their way back to Chung King with new missionaries. There is some sixteen missionaries between here and Ichang, five of them young ladies." To Lovatt's astonishment, despite the rigors of the journey, the women were quite resilient, "rest[ing] here two or three days, and are all off again, this time in chairs to distant cities. The young ladies rather enjoyed the trip." And as bad as the trip upriver might be, traveling overland was even worse: "Traveling by boat is so much more comfortable for the ladies than doing long distances in chairs and having to put up with Chinese inns."[39]

Chongqing served as a staging area for missionary forays into even more remote areas of the province and western China, where travel was even more daunting. One group from the China Inland Mission left for Yunnan, twenty-nine days away, "an awful journey, and I think they will have to cross two high mountain ranges." Lovatt met another woman from that mission and "we talked about her long journey to *Ya li fu*. Miss Anderson and her brother leave for there about the end of this month." And they were not the only ones going there: "The Chinese junk with seven young missionary ladies arrived here yesterday. Two are to proceed to Ya li fu, a frightful journey at this [winter] season of the year." Lovatt was impressed by the willingness of the women to endure hardship:

> 52 days journey from here by land. The ladies went in chairs. Are they not brave girls to face such a long journey and the wretched accommodations of Chinese Inns? I think they only get a mail once in six weeks. Anyway, all arrived safe and well, and appear to like the place very well. Ya Li fu is very healthy and the Chinese there are quite friendly to the missionaries.[40]

Lovatt made it a point to socialize with these new arrivals. At the Methodist Mission, "yesterday afternoon I went down by special invitation of Mrs. Cameron to take a cup of tea with them, and I met a great many of our missionary community there, and quite enjoyed the change." At the Quaker mission, "I called on Mr. J. Davidson, where I had a cup of tea and then I tramped back by the city wall." And at the London Mission, "I went round yesterday and called on Mr. Wilson and his wife, [and] Dr. Davenport." Always on the lookout for hiking companions, Lovatt enlisted the newly arrived missionaries for that purpose: "Yesterday I asked Mr. and Mrs. Wilson, also Dr. Davenport, to go for a walk. We went out by the west gate, and had a nice afternoon's stroll, and then they came back here to tea with me."[41]

In addition to tea and hiking excursions, Lovatt took part in more formal social gatherings, as he and his customs colleagues started hosting dinner parties for the new arrivals: "We have three ladies and four gentlemen coming to dinner tonight—all missionaries—our first ladies." A week later, they threw a second dinner for another group: "We are having all the China Inland Mission to dinner tonight, ladies and gentlemen in Chinese clothes."[42]

Lovatt was impressed by the missionaries, not only because of their willingness to endure the rigors of travel by boat and chair but also because of their willingness to get by on so little. The Inland Mission people "live upon the bare necessaries of life," and for the females, "it is a rough life, but they all seem to like it." He also noted that the pain was shared equally between husband and wife: "They only get about T[aels] 20 a month. The married T[aels] 40. The lady is entitled to as much as a man—the fairest thing about the mission." Charitably characterizing that stipend as "not very enticing" and "somewhat limited," Lovatt admitted that

> still they live very comfortably with two or three servants, and many of them have families. Everything is of course native, flour, beef, mutton, vegetables, tea, sugar, rice. I believe they indulge in foreign butter and jam—also soap. I

need hardly say they buy things at prices no other foreigners do, and wages to servants are something like 1000 [copper] cash a month and rice.[43]

He was also impressed with their work ethic. "I was down at the China Inland Mission making a call the other day. The ladies do a great deal of work, Women's Meetings, Bible Classes, and visiting." An American woman affiliated with that group who had just arrived from his new hometown near the twin cities of Minnesapolis/St. Paul and who is "full of go" caught his attention as someone who "will wake up and astonish the Chinese." And the seven women in her group "will become nice, agreeable teachers." Consequently, "the China Inland Mission is very successful here. They have some sixty converts and the Chinese like Dr. Cameron very much." They are "truly a hard working body." Although Lovatt had been critical in the past, "I am rapidly changing my opinion of the China Inland Missionaries. They are much better people than the original crowd that Hudson Taylor brought out."[44]

He had the same positive opinion of the Methodists. When they opened a new hospital, Lovatt described it as "a fine, large, roomy building, no pretense to architecture, but admirably suited for the purpose. The Dr. [McCartney] has made quite a reputation here as a very skillful surgeon. He is a very nice fellow, and will be a very able man when he has had more experience." The local Chinese shared the same impression, according to Lovatt: "The Methodists in my opinion are the best, the kindliest. They have more sympathy with the Chinese and manage to impress the natives with their love and affection for them." Clearly, Lovatt supported their efforts: "I have called round on all our missionary friends and am pleased to say they are all flourishing."[45]

Moreover, Lovatt liked the missionaries personally. He found the Quakers to be "nice people." The London Mission had "very nice pleasant people" who lived so close that Lovatt could hear them: "they were having a very joyous time last evening, singing hymns and Salvation Army songs." Consequently, he often visited them. "Yesterday I went round to the London Mission. . . . They are very nice people and I always enjoy a visit there." As for the China Inland Mission, Lovatt found that "many of the men were very agreeable [and] the ladies were all extremely nice. They are about the most select crowd of the whole service, and a pretty good tempered lot, or otherwise life would be pretty miserable." This despite the fact that they did not live nearby: "if we only lived nearer to each other it would be very pleasant, but all are at least 20 minutes distance from us in a crowded Chinese city." Due to his relative isolation, Lovatt appreciated just how much these missionaries contributed to his own quality of life.[46]

While Lovatt admired most of the rank and file members of the China Inland Mission, the same could not be said for its leader: "One of the young ladies that applied for leave to be engaged has been refused by the Director of the Mission. She was to have married a man belonging to another mission, and Hudson Taylor would not grant permission. He is a regular old tyrant from all I hear." He also noted Hudson Taylor's clumsy financial skills:

> There is a good deal of dissatisfaction with the management of the China Inland Mission. They are constantly adding numbers to the Mission, the last lot from Sweden and Norway, but I believe the funds do not roll in in proportion, and if men and women come from these countries on much lower pay, this is bringing down the pay of the others, and so a good deal of feeling is around, and the English portion think too much English pay goes to foreigners.

Lovatt also took him to task for poor recruiting: "Hudson Taylor is pouring all kinds of missionaries—Swedes, Danes, and Norwegians, besides lots of inferior men from England and Australia—a class of men who could never learn their Greek Testament, and how are they ever to preach an intelligent Gospel in [Chinese]?" When Lovatt learned that Hudson Taylor was "sending two hundred Swedes [upriver] at a very cheap rate to become missionaries," he wondered, "how can such people ever do any good amongst the Chinese?"[47]

It was not only the nationality of some of the missionaries that Lovatt thought less than suitable. He also detected a generational gap:

> There is a younger, more pushing, class of missionaries who preach with less consideration or regard for the feelings of the heathen than the old and more highly educated missionaries did. The present race of young missionaries are often loud, vulgar, and rude to the educated Chinese, and I am not sure if they do not feel they have done a good thing in stirring up a riot.

Lovatt associated many of these brash younger missionaries with one mission in particular: "All it wants now to have a general sweep of Missions is to send out a good crowd of the Salvation Army. That would stir up the Chinese properly." Clearly, Lovatt was sensitive to the delicate nature of the missionary relationship with Chinese that could erupt in antiforeign riots.[48]

Lovatt sometimes questioned missionary tactics, particularly their attempts to maintain a low profile: "The Am. Mission here are all very quiet and keep very much to themselves. In fact, owing to the long distances we live from each other, there is not much visiting, the missionaries always go about in closed chairs." This was especially the case with the females, who "are by far too much confined to the house. Here in Chung King it is very seldom they go out, and if they do, it is in a closed chair." This strategy included dressing in Chinese rather than Western clothes. Doing so on an occasional basis, such as at a wedding or a dinner party, was understandable to Lovatt, but not on a daily basis: "One of the advantages of dressing in Chinese is that less attention is attracted, but then it is largely qualified by the remarks of the Chinese—*there goes a false foreigner*. On the whole, I think missionaries are wise who keep to their own dress."[49]

Despite his admiration for missionaries, Lovatt thought there was an inordinate number of them. Regarding females,

> I really fail to see the advisability of sending so many young ladies to mission work in China. It would be so much better if they would work amongst the poorer classes of their own country. One does not like saying unkind things of missionaries, for they do a certain amount of good, but we have a large number of heathens in all the big cities of the world.

That included the country of his birth: "in my opinion, London is the place for all British missionaries." On the other hand, having a lot of single female missionaries provided marriage partners for single male missionaries. In fact, several marriages took place during Lovatt's tenure, providing additional opportunities over and above the usual social events. During his first summer in the city, wedding plans for one couple belonging to the China Inland Mission had been set, according to a notice at the British consulate. The wedding finally came off in August: "The first marriage in Chung King tomorrow—Mr. Faers to Miss Hook. Bride and Bridegroom wear Chinese clothes and will be married at the [British] Consulate. Then we go to Mrs. Davidson's. I will represent the Customs. I expect all the foreigners of Chungking will be gathered on that occasion."[50]

Other nuptials soon followed.

> A couple of the China Inland Missionaries are going to unite their fortune. The lady, Miss Hinge, comes all the way from the province of Yunnan—24 days stages to a town on the river, four days from here, where she will take a boat and come down to Chung King. The gentleman [Mr. Pollard] comes from Yunnanfoo, the Capital of Yunnan that is 28 stages from here. The inns are not over good, but love endures everything.

This second ceremony also took place at the British consulate in mid-December, after which the newlyweds "will leave by junk tonight for up river, and again take to the road for Yunnanfoo," a route that Lovatt described as a "three weeks journey [on] a very bad road." A third involved the Society of Friends: "I am going to the Quakers to offer my congratulations to the bride and bridegroom, Mr. & Mrs. Wigham [nee Miss Southall], who I presume have been married by this time at the consulate. I hear they are going up the small river [Jialing] in a junk to spend their honeymoon."[51]

By now, Lovatt was in the habit of sizing up newly-arrived single female missionaries for marriageability: "Did I tell you the seven maiden ladies arrived for the China Inland Mission—five weeks from Ichang to Chung King? They did not look a marrying lot. In fact, that is one of the striking peculiarities of the ladies who come out here for the China Inland." What he meant was that they were short on looks: "There are an immense number of ladies come out. Twelve young ladies passed through here not long since—not a pretty girl in the whole crowd."[52]

Catholic missionaries also made their appearance in the region, and although they came to the attention of Lovatt, he rarely socialized with them: "Yesterday eight young priests arrived from France to be distributed over the province. The Roman Catholics are very successful in this province, and also in this city, where they have some three thousand native Christians." Their presence, however, was not without controversy:

> In a city three days journey from here there is a small war going on. During the last Chinese mid-autumn festival (August), the native procession going through the streets of the city stopped at the Catholic Chapel and wanted to go in, and also asked for a subscription towards defraying the expenses, both of which were refused. This led to both a row and riot. The Chapel was destroyed and several, in fact a good many, people lost their lives on both sides. Imperial soldiers have been sent there, and the rioters have attacked them.

Despite the dispatch of the army, Lovatt, recalling the Tianjin Massacre two decades earlier, noted the continued ambivalence of the government toward French missionaries in particular: "There has been a good deal of lukewarmness on the part of the officials, and evidently they do not wish to support the Catholics more than they can help."[53]

Another brouhaha involving Catholic missionaries farther down the Yangzi River also attracted Lovatt's notice because he had previously been stationed there:

> Wuhu has been the scene of operations this time. I hear it arose from some Catholic, whether priest or layman I do not know, picking up in the streets an abandoned baby girl and sending her to the orphanage. This enraged the unwashed, who took it into their heads that the Catholics constantly recruited their orphanage from girls picked up in this way, and the fools consequently burned the building.[54]

Of course, Catholic missionaries were not the only source of instability:

> Dr. McCartney called yesterday and said that they had a letter from their [Methodist] mission in Chengtu in which it said that a beam fell down in the house that [Virgil] Hart is building in that city and killed a man that was stealing shavings. This nearly caused a riot. The officials made Hart give up the land, said it was

> temple ground, and he should not have purchased it, but they would at once compensate him for his loss, which they did, and there was no riot. I am very glad there has been no row. The Chinese officials are getting awfully scared at riots, as they have to pay all damages out of their own pockets.

And sometimes trouble arose from Christianity in general, absent any missionary involvement:

> Last year, in the city of Ta Tsu, [there was a riot] between the native Christians and the people. The former would not contribute as in olden time to one of the yearly heathen festivals, and this led to *wigs upon the green*, which finally developed into murder and outrage. Anyway, all is peace on the left bank of the *Yangtze* now and long may it flourish.[55]

Lest his wife fear for his safety, Lovatt took pains to reassure her: "Dr. Cameron arrived from his long journey. He says he traveled in perfect safety and peace, and was never once asked to produce his passport." Even females traveling alone were safe: "Did I tell you of eleven missionary young ladies now on their way up the river, no man with them, all in one junk, and in charge of an elderly maiden lady? Think of that for the peace and order of China." And they arrived safely, "so you see traveling as a rule is perfectly safe. The junk that carried this large addition to the China Inland Mission was hauled by nearly forty naked coolies." And when there were reports of riots, such as the one at their former port of "good old Kiukiang," Lovatt "doubt[ed] if it will be very serious there, [since] the people are pretty good." Indeed, on an almost weekly basis, his letters exuded optimism, such as "I don't think you need be alarmed at the news you hear from China" and "the wave of riotous feeling that has rolled up the Yangtze valley amongst the natives has about exhausted itself." But Lovatt had spoken too soon.[56]

ANTIFOREIGNISM

Lovatt's reassuring words soon proved illusory because anti-Christian, antiforeign violence (*jiaoan*) continued along the Yangzi, and appeared to be headed upriver toward Lovatt in Chongqing. Many of the riots were responses to reports of alleged depraved action involving children. For example, a rumor in June that missionaries in Wuxue were removing children's eyes for use in photography led to a mob attacking the mission school, looting the building, and killing two Englishmen. On the following day, the violence spread to Jiujiang 25 miles downriver. At another one of Lovatt's former ports, what began as a rumor was confirmed when "the last mail brought us news of a riot not far from Foochow, and a fear that one or two missionaries were either killed or seriously injured."[57]

Antiforeignism had manifested itself soon after Lovatt arrived in China primarily as hostility to Christianity. In 1861 the famous treatise *bixie jishi* (A record of facts to ward off [Christian] heterodoxy) was issued, often attributed to prominent self-strengthener Zeng Guofan in Hunan, to help suppress the appeal of the quasi-Christian Taiping. And nearly a decade later, the Tianjin Massacre occurred soon after Lovatt had returned to China with his new bride. In the years that followed, anti-Christian tracts, posters, and pamphlets continued to circulate, creating an atmosphere that exploded in the early 1890s and served as a precursor to the 1900 Boxer Rebellion. The antiforeign riots placed Qing officials in a dilemma between foreign pressure on the one hand and potential rebellion among the populace on the other.

Indeed, there were varying responses by officials. Some vigorously repressed the disturbances, some fanned the flames, and some were simply paralyzed into inaction. In Sichuan, provincial governor Liu Bingjang had been viewed as antiforeign since his appointment in 1886, and when a Western diplomat made a representation to him, it was "difficult for the governor to abstain from showing his hatred of foreigners." This attitude percolated down to the local level: "This is a new phase of official inertness—foreigners insulted and maltreated, Consul complains to Taotai, Taotai politely declines to interfere."[58]

Some officials actively fanned the flames by giving credence to wild rumors. A disconcerting example of this occurred when antiforeign violence struck relatively nearby in Yichang in early September, indicating that violence might be headed toward Chongqing. Lovatt and the foreign community first learned of it when Fulford received a telegram from Yichang that read: "*Riot* in Ichang, all the missions property burnt down, no lives lost, Customs & Consulate not touched." Lovatt, who had earlier downplayed these incidents, now referred to this riot as "serious" and averred that "the Chinese are brutes indeed when their passions are aroused."[59]

The riot occurred when a rumor, similar to the one in Wuxue, of removing children's eyes, was leveled against the Catholic Sisters of Charity, resulting in the torching of their mission building and forcing most of the entire Western community in Yichang to flee. In the aftermath, the district magistrate there asked French consul d'Arnoux and British consul Fraser to come to his yamen to see evidence of the "frightful offense." As a precaution, the two men brought along the customs doctor to examine the blind children, who had been admitted to the mission hospital out of compassion, and showed the prefect that their eyes were in fact there but that they had been born blind. At that point, the official accused the Catholics of setting fire to their own premises in an attempt to blame the Chinese government, leading Lovatt to comment sarcastically, "a nice sort of a magistrate to have to deal with."[60]

The episode caused Lovatt to believe that official connivance was behind the riot. Because he had received a letter from Stebbins in Yichang dated August 30 that made no mention of any antiforeign feeling, the fact that Stebbins was "totally oblivious" two days before the riot broke out "shows to my mind that the officials are at the bottom of the whole business, and had carefully arranged the whole affair." After reading a follow-up letter from Stebbins, Lovatt concluded that "I don't think it is possible to have a clearer case of a regular organized official riot. It was beautifully got up and admirably carried out by the cowardly scoundrels." From the localized violence in Yichang, Lovatt applied this more widely: "Many high officials are causing the riots at the treaty ports."[61]

While suggesting that some local officials were complicit, either actively or passively, in these outbreaks, Lovatt also acknowledged that officials were sometimes simply helpless. Referring to the "pretty serious row" at Wuhu, Lovatt noted that "[officials] have unfortunately no power when a riot commences; they are really afraid of the people." To get off the hook, sometimes the officials simply shifted the blame, such as an antiforeign incident in nearby Wanxian about which "the authorities here [in Chongjing] say it is all settled, that it is only a band of robbers."[62]

In addition to hostile, passive, or helpless local officials, Lovatt saw larger, more sinister, forces at work: "From the steady way the rows have gone on proceeding up river, there can be no doubt that it is the work of some Secret Society." As for their goals, "the general row along the valley of the Yangtze at Wuhu, Yang Chow [Yangzhou], and Ngan Kin [Nanjing] is supposed to arise from some Secret Society desirous of overthrowing the present dynasty, and their first object is to embroil the country in a foreign war."[63]

That is, antiforeign sentiment was aimed not only at Westerners but also ultimately at the alien Manchus, causing some officials to collude with the secret societies in the hope that if the Qing government became embroiled in a war with Western powers, there would be an opportunity to establish a *Chinese* dynasty, representing a traditional Chinese stratagem of pitting one enemy against another. According to Lovatt, who mingled with the local people, the central government was "unaware what a hold the secret societies have got, especially along the river. The present dynasty is very unpopular from all accounts with the Chinese." Another reason for the anti-Qing sentiment that Lovatt picked up in his conversations with local Chinese was their belief that a male, rather than the Empress Dowager Cixi, should be on the throne, reflecting the Confucian ideal of male superiority.[64]

Much of this agitation seemed to emanate from Hunan Province which had remained a hotbed of anti-Christian, anti-Western sentiment. By the early 1890s, Hunan's "discontented rebels" were "military officers and other officials unemployed, backed up by a large number of discharged soldiers and others." Behind them, "able men are working the movement and I think many men in high positions are in it," or what Lovatt sneeringly referred to as "the so-called literary class." As for their motivation and timing, "the heads of the movement are no doubt hoping to see foreign governments involved in war with the Chinese, and they know that would be the time to strike. So things are being kept as quiet as possible waiting for the opportune moment."[65]

These events caused Lovatt to look for deeper meaning behind the antiforeign attitudes of the literati: "The wide spreading influence of Christian and scientific books is arousing the old conservatism of China. Then it is dawning upon the Chinese that he is not the first in education or civilization, and this rankles like poison." Additionally, Westerners disrupted the harmony at the national as well as at the local level. Chinese "always have to give way before the hated foreigner and the result is increasing hatred to the missionaries who preach doctrines opposed to their ancient classics [and] who withdraw the people from joining their subscription to the great festivals." As a result, he predicted that in the clash between Western and Eastern knowledge, "the latter must go down and with it the present government of China. It is too old to learn so must go down in the crash, and from the ruin will arise a better government." While that was all well and good for the long term, it was the short term that Lovatt had to contend with.[66]

That is, Lovatt wondered if Chongqing might be next. On the one hand, his own reading of the situation indicated that it would not: "I don't see any unfriendly feeling and I do the city twice a day." And a month later, "The people here are very quiet and there is no sign of any ill feeling towards us." In fact, he told his wife that she "would be much amused to see how tame everything is in this crowded city." In his view, only excessive corruption would trigger a riot: "The people are a fun loving lot, [and] only go in for rows when the officials try to squeeze them unmercifully. I feel sure with a moderate degree of caution on the part of foreigners generally there will be no riot here."[67]

On the other hand, he acknowledged that the Yichang uprising "gave us room for thought." And he reckoned that "I should not be surprised when the news comes up and gets properly diffused amongst the tea shops but what we will have a riot here. In fact, Chung King is somewhat famous for its riots." But he qualified that by saying that if there were a riot, it would probably be carried out by outsiders rather than the locals: "We have had two telegrams from Hankow saying to be on the lookout. It is supposed the Hunan rowdies who burnt the foreign residences at Ichang are on their way up river to shake up the foreigners here and plunder their houses." If they did try to come to Chongqing, they would face obstacles: "300 miles either by road or river is no small undertaking, and after entering this province they would be in a trap as it were, and the authorities, if so inclined, could put their hands upon them at any time."[68]

As usual, Lovatt and the other Westerners had mostly rumors to rely on: "The Chinese have their sensational rumours and we foreigners have ours." One of the "wild" rumors was that in three days, it would not be outsiders, but rather "local rowdies anxious to clear out the foreigners and I suppose loot the residences, but as their last outbreak of that kind cost the government some 50,000 taels, I rather think the authorities will see it is not repeated." Indeed, three days later there was no incident:

> This is the day the Chinese were to have cleared us out. I have just come the whole length of the city and through the most crowded streets, and not a soul made use of any uncivil expressions. One or two small boys were not as polite as little boys should be to elderly gentlemen, but they were very much like the little boys found on the streets of big cities of other countries.

Still, the murmurings persisted, which Lovatt could pick up because of his knowledge of the language: "we have heard the talk of the tea shops, but it has only been the excitable gossip of the time. This morning I walked [the 35 minutes] from our house down to the *Taiping gate* [and was] treated in a civil way." But not everyone in Chongqing was as confident in the local security situation: "We have a missionary of the London Mission who is, to put it in a mild form, *very nervous*. Soldiers would call it mortal funk. He goes round frightening the ladies and advising them to clear out. In fact, he wants to go himself, but does not like to go while ladies remain."[69]

If Chongqing was in a relatively safe position, the cities downstream appeared to be less secure: "Things at all the ports appear to be very unsettled. There is no doubt a flood of angry feeling against missionaries in general and all foreigners." This evoked the usual response from the Westerners—gunboats. In the case of the riot in Jiujiang, Captain Marthon of the USS *Palos* sent one of his officers with twenty-two sailors to protect American and British citizens, and as a precaution remained anchored there for the rest of the summer. In the Yichang incident, the British gunboat *Swift* and the French gunboat *Aspic* were close by "so there will soon be ample protection, tho as usual they arrive the day after the affair." Those two gunboats were reinforced by the arrival soon afterward of the British gunboat *Elk*. Hankou was experiencing "the same spirit of general uneasiness that prevails everywhere," despite the fact that Hankou had three gunboats in port. When fears arose of a riot in Nanjing, "the timely arrival of the French gunboat nipped it in the bud." And in Chongqing, "we have four gunboats here to act as guard and today all their flags are flying, it being the Feast of Heavenly Gifts."[70]

In his analysis of antiforeign sentiment, Lovatt drew a distinction between missionaries and people like himself. While acknowledging that Chinese "do not like the missionaries," Lovatt defended them: "the missionaries here are a very good lot and try to help the Chinese in very many ways." In the same breath, he implicitly suggested that their low profile engendered suspicion: "The city is so vast, the missionaries are so little known, and as a rule keep very quiet." What Lovatt was suggesting was that China needed more people like himself—non-missionaries who maintain a public profile: "I pass nearly round the city every day and meet more Chinese than any other foreigner in the place." In return, "the people are very well disposed [and] towards me they always manifest a very friendly feeling." So in the long run, "the arrival of foreigners who are not missionaries and who mix more with the people in a friendly way has done a good deal to create a more tolerant, kindly, feeling. The latter will come with time and better acquaintance."[71]

If having more people like himself in China was a long-term solution, the short-term solution was to prod the Chinese government into action. While Lovatt did not charge Beijing with causing the riots (the emperor had issued a decree on June 13 forbidding them), he did take it to task for negligence, and hoped that the "enormous bill of damages that is accumulating" would awaken the authorities to their responsibilities. At the same time, it was important that the Western governments make the necessary representations: "If the Foreign Ministers at Peking are firm in their demands for the redress of the wrongs committed on foreigners," then the Chinese government will "take very active steps to protect foreigners in future." However, when representations were made to the Zongli Yamen, the results were usually unsatisfactory, with Westerners referring to that body as "a Board of Delay, a Dead Letter Office, an Oriental Circumlocution Office, [or] the great stronghold of Chinese procrastination." Lovatt suggested that one reason that the central government had not been more active was because the riots occurred far from Beijing. When a riot broke out nearer to Beijing by overtaxed gold washers, although not an antiforeign riot *per se*, Lovatt hoped that this would "stir up the government to take more active measures."[72]

Given his sentiments, it was with satisfaction that he noted that the British consul at Hankow and the British minister at Peking "have been most earnest in their efforts to protect foreigners and obtain redress for the injuries," and hoped that "the government finds the safe policy is to take good care of foreigners." Prospects were not as favorable at the local level, where Lovatt acknowledged "the mortal funk the Chinese officials are in." On the one hand, "they have the strictest orders to keep the peace and protect foreigners, and I will say this for them, they are very anxious to do so," adding that "the Mandarins are very strict." On the other hand, "the means at their command is very limited, and they are never very sure if the people will not turn on them." Still, "everything is very quiet in Chung King and the native officials are very desirous that it should be so." Finally, at the individual level, the Chongqing "people are by no means a bad lot" and "are civil and polite to me everywhere." "Don't worry about me," he told his wife, and "never mind the newspapers. They are generally wrong." Knowing that she had read about Yichang, he now said that "on the whole for a riot it was a very moderate one." And if the situation should change, "I shall be on hand if there is any row and, if necessary, give a good account of myself."[73]

In sum, the half measures of the Chinese officialdom at the national as well as the local level ultimately failed to satisfy the foreigners and Lovatt. Nor did it satisfy the Chinese public, causing a loss of confidence in Qing rule. When the government switched sides less than ten years later and supported the antiforeign Boxers, the result was another Western incursion and the beginning of the end of the dynasty.

EVERYDAY LIFE IN CHONGQING

Since Lovatt made it a point of walking nearly everywhere, combined with his ability to speak Chinese and his long residence in China, he was able to make keen observations of everyday life in Chongqing, not just of his own but also of the Chinese residents of the city: "[I have a] quiet, humdrum life here, living in the midst of a teeming city of three or four hundred thousands of people but not of them. They interest me. I watch them and their struggle for existence, their home life, and the thousand and one ways they have of making a cash and the care and thought in spending their hard earned money." And what he saw clearly depressed him. Their homes were "dark, gloomy, and cheerless." Once inside, "the grumbling begins, for a Chinese home appears absolutely comfortless." Expanding on that metaphor, he described "gloom and stillness that settles down on the city at night, the shops close, there are no lights, very different from the life, light, and animation of a foreign city." Chongqing was also dirty and "odorous," such that "one is so glad when Sunday comes to get out of this evil smelling city." Rain brought only temporary relief: "The smells of this city are very strong, and we badly need a downpour, but in spite of the absence of all sanitary or hygienic arrangements, the Chinese live and flourish." Their "dull" daily routine consisted of "shop[ing] day after day, no news, no papers, no interest but to sell day after day. No wonder a foreigner walking through their streets creates a sensation."[74]

Chongqing had its share of animals, pests, and rodents. At the annoying end of the spectrum was "our greatest plague, a small black sand fly, which silently bites or stings, and raises considerable sized lumps on face and hands." Also annoying were the rats, so large that "I should think home cats would be afraid to tackle them." As a result, there was a market for large cats that were then tethered by a string around their necks. And since cats were in demand, there were the inevitable cat thieves. In addition to cats, other animals frequently inhabited homes, and "live amongst the children, in the house and out of it, and form part of the family." These included geese that stood outside of the door all day watching the people go by: "My chair in passing one poor goose gave him a knock on the head. The goose had lowered his head to let the chair pass but not low enough, so when he got a rap on the head he gave a squawk of indignation, but kept his place." Lovatt remarked also that the geese, cocks, hens, and pigs "all know their own house. The people scold them when they wander away and address them in very bad language, [and] the animals all seem to understand, especially the pigs. You would be surprised at [their] intelligence."[75]

Lovatt was particularly interested in how "the poorest, [whose numbers] are very large," lived. Indeed, "we have a lot of very poor neighbours round us," including one "poor old woman" who comes out of her house every morning to call the spirit of her dead husband. To ameliorate their plight, Lovatt purchased "rice tickets," entitling the holder to two pints of cooked rice at the kitchens open for two months during the winter and "help a lot of poor people. I find the plan a much better one than giving them cash." Outside the city, the farms are "little larger than a garden patch, for they are the smallest farms in the world. I never saw the land brought to the same high pitch of cultivation anywhere like it is in Szechuen. Literally not an inch of ground is wasted. Everything produced is what will grow rapidly [to] bring in cash at least expense to the cultivator."[76]

The sheer number of the working poor caused them to live on the margins: "Owing to the density of the population, there is a keen competition to get that cent and a half." Water coolies, for example, had to "carry two buckets of water up steps two and three hundred feet above the river and hawk it about the streets for a cent." If unsuccessful, "towards night he will gladly accept a cash or two less." Chair coolies experienced "the same" keen competition.[77]

Others included trackers and beggars, who were "numerous," so Lovatt took an interest in their life as well:

> The beggars look fat and jolly, so to arouse sympathy they go about with hardly any clothes and shiver, howl, and sing. Near our house is a very charitable institution where destitute boys are taken in and looked after to a certain extent, but [who are] sent out every day to beg [and who] are taught the proper begging expressions to use, the way to ask [for] alms, and how to behave. Before starting out, they daub themselves with mud and, when they look dirty and hideous enough, off they go to their proper part of the city. I have seen them

on a holiday, when they are having a day off, as jolly as possible, and playing about as merry as other boys. As soon as they grow up, they fall into the ranks of coolies or boat trackers and earn their own living.

As for the boat trackers, "this summer I have seen hundreds of coolies working upon, and tracking, boats without a vestige of clothing. This is of course outside of the city. The poorest would be obliged to have even an apology for pants if he entered the city. The mildness of the climate puts them to little expense for clothing."[78]

For all four groups—trackers, beggars, chair bearers, and water coolies—the fierce competition robbed people of their inclination toward kindness: "The Chinese are pretty hard on each other. I fear the keen struggle for existence in so densely peopled a province hardens their hearts." In one example of this apparent callousness, "I met a Chinaman who was taken ill on the road. I did what I could for him and left him feeling a little better. He had a relative with him, but could not get a chair. He was going home for the new year. I passed several empty chairs, but the Chinaman would not pay the price the chairmen wanted." The main consideration seems to be, "does man or boy get a sufficient amount of rice? If so, sympathy to a great extent ends there. No place I think are the cash looked as keenly after as here." One mitigating factor is that "living for them fortunately is very cheap. The water supply is abundant, rice is abundant, and about 25 cash will see the coolie through the day." Indeed, "food is very cheap, [for] 1 1/2 cents a coolie can buy a good big bowl of rice, with vegetables, say, and other little tidbits, and makes a capital meal." Many could afford to treat themselves to sugarcane, which "is largely in demand through the winter. The whole population apparently delights to chew it. The cane is not very juicy or sweet, but it is cheap, one cash a cane."[79]

Even when praising Sichuan as "the finest province for fruit and vegetables," he qualified it by finding it "strange how anyone can like hard green fruit, but the Chinese do." He explained this by saying that "no care has been exercised in pruning or improving the fruit or vegetables in any way. Everything is coarse. Flavour or taste little or none. It is the same with the vegetables. What is wanted is quantity, not quality, things that will grow quickly and sell readily to the mass, the rich in China will not give increased price, the rich and poor all alike try to live cheaply."[80]

Many of the poor took advantage of free entertainment and indulged in alcohol, often in excess: "nowhere else do the people go in for more amusement. Unfortunately, it only takes one form—eating and drinking. The native wine is better than usually found in other parts of China, and very cheap, so all classes indulge, and it is said that the ladies take very kindly to it." This was particularly true during holidays such as Chinese New Year, when "the respectable class" strolled through the streets showing off their clothes, while "most of the people remain indoors feasting and a good many get drunk." On the fifth day of the fifth month of the lunar calendar, when the dragon boat races attracted large crowds, Lovatt avoided the event because "the lower classes of Chinamen here are a somewhat drunken and rowdy lot, so it was just as well to keep away." Additionally, the city was "a great place for native theatricals, which are given in the temples and in honor of the gods. Being free, the crowd of Chinese roughs are always present. Each temple appears to have its special day, and as there are very many temples, the performances are very numerous."[81]

Given the dense population and the numerous poor, "diseases of all kinds are in the most flourishing condition." In the spring of 1891, "a good many Chinese are dying [as] there is a peculiar fever here that attacks them and ends fatally." In fact, "one of my chair coolies died yesterday very suddenly." Lovatt himself was not immune, and was laid up for ten days: "I was very ill indeed, and recovered slowly. I could not have left Chung King, I was so weak." Although he initially passed it off as a liver attack brought on by drinking strong tea, he later conceded that it might have been malaria, citing the lack of cleanliness, bad climate, poor food, and damp and airless quarters that "is not conducive to the health of a man who is no longer young." And this extended to his colleagues: "There is nearly always someone sick." The epidemic carried over to the fall when the provincial-level civil service examinations were being held, ten thousand candidates arrived, and "several of the students have died." It flourished despite the fact that "this province is the great medicine producing province of the empire."[82]

LOVATT'S ROUTINE

Lovatt also detailed his own life in Chongqing. He worked six days a week, eight hours a day "on an old Chinese junk passing cargo." While at work, "I have a pot of hot tea alongside of me all day, and have frequent cups. It is certainly a safer, if not so pleasant, a drink as ice water," concluding that "I am becoming a regular old Chinaman." For tiffin every day, he had a sandwich of bread and butter with a slice of Chung King beef, prepared by his *ting chai* who prepared the same lunch for himself. His *ting chai*

> is a very good fellow with a voice like a bear, a low deep growl. He is known by all the foreigners as *The Savage*, but in spite of his roughness, he has many good qualities, one of which is he delights to eat my tiffin and to wear any of my old boots, but woe to the man he hears call me *foreign devil.* He is always wanting to run them in to the nearest yamen.

Lovatt admits that "sometimes he is obstinate, and I think I am now and then, but we each give way when the other is particularly mulish."[83]

One advantage that Lovatt shared with the poor of the city was the low cost of living: "This is a miserable place. It has only one redeeming quality—you can save a large part of your pay"—because "here I have very few expenses but my mess, servant, etc." In fact, "I have lived cheaper here than at any other port in China. No club, no subscriptions, no asking or giving dinners. I often wish this was otherwise, for one would like to see an unfamiliar face sometimes." Since he did not like the quality of the fruit and vegetables available in the local markets, he started his own "splendid" garden, growing lettuce, white turnips, and tomatoes, all tended to by his *ting chai*. And he budgeted carefully: "It takes time to save up enough out of the small allowance I put myself on while at this port. I have allowed myself T[aels] 25 for servant, mess, washing & everything. The balance of my pay goes to Shanghai [to pay off the bank loan]."[84]

Socializing for Lovatt revolved mainly around meals. In Lovatt's communal household, Fulford dined with the customs staff every Saturday night, and on Sunday, Lovatt had tiffin with the other members of the customs. Special occasions called for a break from the routine, such as when a new tidewaiter arrived from New York, "I got a bottle of champagne from Hobson, so we drank prosperity to the *Great Union*. It is seldom we see champagne here." At Christmas, Hobson invited the foreigners to tiffin and fourteen showed up.[85]

After a year and a half in communal living arrangements with the other members of the customs staff, Lovatt finally was able to get a house of his own, renting it from Dr. Davenport of the London Mission "in the dense part of the Chinese city—clean, comfortable, and quiet." The move did not go completely smoothly, however: "I have lost a lot of things. All my Kiukiang chinaware has been stolen. I have had very bad servants, and Hobson's have been worse—opium smokers and thieves. One may safely say opium smokers are all thieves." Nonetheless, "here I am in my own house and enjoying it. Calm quietness." Lovatt's house was in the upper reaches of the hilly city, necessitating a thirty-five-minute chair ride to the office downtown, and a forty-five- to sixty-minute chair ride back uphill to get home. Soon after moving in, Lovatt received an unusual visitor in the person of Frank Lenz who was circling the globe on a bicycle and in the spring of 1893 passed through Sichuan. When he arrived in Chongqing, he stayed with Lovatt for three days: "After a long walk through the city, along the wall and up many steps, we finally reached the comfortably arranged house of Mr. W. Nelson Lovatt. He kindly welcomed me to his home, which seemed an earthly Eden after my long walk over the mountains." Others traversing the mountains to reach Chongqing were the postmen.[86]

Lovatt served as the postal officer for the customs contingent where mail, always important, was even more so there: "imagine how isolated one feels thousands of miles from anywhere, and with what a delightful freshness the news comes to hand." Consequently, "letters are about my only comfort and consolation in this out of the way place." Unlike the other ports that relied on steamers to bring the mail, Lovatt lamented that "the day that steamers will reach Chung King is far distant in my opinion." As a result, "we are solely dependent on the native post hongs, or express companies, for mail," a "rather primitive" courier system that "depend[ed] on some poor old Chinaman traveling 400 miles [from Yichang] on foot with two baskets full of small mail bags for the foreign community of Chung King, through wind and rain, storm and snow. Is it not wonderful that they reach here with the regularity they do?"[87]

Not surprisingly, the mail was often delayed, Lovatt complaining at one point that "the mail is always now five or six days overdue." Others in the community who relied on the same system had similar complaints: "Yesterday I called upon Mr. and Mrs. Lewis of the American Mission [who] told me last year at this time [January] they were two months without mails." In the spring, "I met Dr. McCartney of the [American] Mission the other day and he said their latest news from the States was 31st January." Ironically, he told his wife, "does it not seem strange to think that you will receive Shanghai news before I shall? It will average a month always before Shanghai letters and papers reach us." Some of the reasons for the delays were bad weather, poor infrastructure, weight, and a refusal to succumb to the squeeze: "The weather has been very bad lately, and roads, you know, are not a strong point with the Chinese government, so the poor postman has my sympathy." An additional complicating factor was the volume itself: "The couriers when overloaded quietly leave a few bags of mail in a roadside inn until a courier comes along with a lighter load, and thinks he will pick up the spare bags and bring them on. It is of course pure chance whose bags are left behind." As the postal officer, Lovatt was responsible for the timely arrival of the mail: "I hope to be able to impress on the mail hongs that H. M.'s customs must receive their mails, or his head may be in danger." And he implied that he was not averse to bribing the couriers: "A few extra cash would be more to the point, but Hobson will not pay."[88]

On the other hand, outgoing mail moved much more quickly, carried by two men in a sampan downriver to Yichang, "in four days this time, the river, or rather the current, is so strong." The men then returned to Chongqing as trackers. While the mail and other goods might go downriver easily, the same was not true for goods coming in the other direction, so Lovatt and his fellow expatriates had to lay in their stocks to carry them through: "We shall have no imports until the winter. The junks cannot tug up against the mighty flow of the river in summer. Consequently, if you run out of stores in summer you must wait patiently for the month of November when the junks begin to arrive in numbers." Not infrequently they ran short: "to add to our miseries, our stores are running out, and there is no possibility of replenishing them before the end of October." He added, with some sarcasm, "such is the advantage of being a pioneer in the far west of China."[89]

THE OPENING OF THE CUSTOMS

The main order of business for Lovatt and his colleagues, of course, was to establish a customs office and begin collecting duty. The January 1891 treaty designating the city as a treaty port meant "the opening of the port, and foreigners, if any come here, may send junks down river, flying a foreign, instead of a native, flag." All that remained was for the local *daotai* to open the customs. Initially, Lovatt thought that he would open the customs on the first day of February. That changed to Chinese New Year in mid-February, but that date also slipped. Finally, after all the uncertainty, "the Taotai issued a proclamation yesterday saying the customs would open on the first of March."[90]

On that first day of March, the port officially opened with all the requisite hoopla.

> After breakfast we all got into Chairs and started for the lower city to the old *Guild Hall* belonging to the sugar guild which we had rented for an office and which has been pretty well fitted up. On our arrival we found the place swarming with little officials, all waiting for the arrival of the heavy swells, who soon began to put in an appearance—first the Prefect and soon after the Taotai, who had been down to the far shore to burn incense and bow to the *River God* so that good luck might attend the opening ceremonies. On his arrival at the office all the Officials paid their respects by bowing to him, and after he drank various cups of tea with them, he called to see us, bowed, was pleased to hear we all spoke Chinese and, taking a little more tea, he bowed again and vanished. Hobson sent round a circular saying the Customs was opened for the dispatch of business and that ended the ceremony. Hobson [then] produced several pints of champagne, a very rare and very precious liquid in Chung King, so at tiffin we drank success to the Chung King Customs.[91]

Although the port was now officially open for business, complications arose almost immediately. For one, a permanent location for the customs office had not yet been decided on, and getting one proved to be no easy task. Once again, the *daotai* had the final say. Complicating this process was corruption and the revolving door:

> The old Taotai (a Manchu) vacated his office a few days after our arrival, and consequently his interest in us ceased as soon as he heard he was to rest from his labours. The Viceroy [Liu] of this province had him dismissed from office owing to some irregularity in his accounts. This makes one smile, for we think the whole of the officials are all very regular in their irregularity. The real secret is, he put his relative in, backed by the great Li [Hongzhang], who is also a connection by marriage.[92]

It was left to Hobson to negotiate with the new *daotai* about a permanent location for the customs. Lovatt was able to follow the negotiations and, having been a commissioner himself, was able to critique the process, privately of course. First was the commissioner's negotiating position: "The Taotai has pointed out a place for the Customs below the city, but Hobson says he will not go. He thinks we had better stick where we are for a year and see what the trade amounts to. He does not believe it will amount to much." Lovatt thought Hobson wrong: "I think we ought to go to the place pointed out; it is the most suitable place here, but he will not." Lovatt then critiqued his negotiating style: "There is a possibility of my having to move across the river. Hobson says the Chinese want the examination department on the other side, and the Office on this, a very inconvenient arrangement. I can't understand his way of doing business. One time he is full of suspicion of the Chinese and another time he agrees to everything." Despite his criticism, Lovatt nonetheless praised Hobston as someone who "has a clear head and is a good fellow." Eventually, Hobson accepted the Chinese proposal, important because "the pleasure and happiness of living in Chungking depends on what side of the river you are situated on." Hobson's assent allowed Lovatt to erect a customs pier: "Yesterday I went downtown to one of the great gates to look at a junk suitable for a Customs jetty and found a good one. We can go into business now at any time."[93]

By mid-March, the customs was poised for business: "We are all ready—office and everything in working order"—and translators were "copying journals, regulations, and all sorts of things, all to go by this mail to the I. G., [and] will reach Shanghai in time for the first steamer going north." They awaited only the go-ahead from the IG, but that was not forthcoming because the new (and apparently corrupt) *daotai* had thrown a wrench into the process: "The merchants swear they will not pay the Taotai's squeeze. The Taotai smiles, like all these heathen officials, and says you will—he can wait. The merchant can't [wait], he must ship his goods, so the Taotai is bound to win in the end." To break the logjam, "Hobson has been to call upon the Taotai," but the *daotai* would not budge, meaning that Lovatt still had nothing to do:

> I wish the merchants would begin business so that our time might be more fully occupied, but they will not. The extra tax the Taotai put on (Le Kin tax) [is]

> to pay for soldiers, so he says, but everybody is aware it is to go into his own pocket, [and this] has stopped the trade. I believe a memorial has gone to Peking on the subject.[94]

The stalemate continued into May with no progress: "There has been no despatch from Peking. I presume [Hart] is both disappointed and disgusted with the fiasco of the opening of this port. The Lekin row still goes on and nothing has been shipped or received from the lower river. It is very tedious and tiresome." When Lovatt went down to the office a few days later, "there were a few old fellows quietly dozing and a few coolies having a smoke." When June arrived with still no progress, Lovatt saw a more insidious reason than mere corruption behind the foot-dragging:

> The Taotai is getting anxious over the failure of the merchants to pay the duties and put their cargo through our office, but I am not so sure. There may be a deep-laid scheme by the Chinese high officials to make the opening of the port of no effect, as it was forced upon them, because the Taotai allows all the goods to go through the old native office at less duty than ever, and of course the merchants are not going to pay higher duties at our office.

Whatever the reason, the result was the same for Lovatt: "it is annoying with no regular work."[95]

It was not until June that the logjam was broken when Lovatt received a note from Hobson, who had been given the green light from Hart, telling him to come to the office, as "business began today [June 17]. I have put in a good day's work." Their first customers were two junks that had departed Yichang at the end of May under a foreign flag—the first allowed by the designation of Chongqing as a treaty port. Lovatt worked at the examination department on the large junk that he had converted into a hulk on the south bank opposite the city on the site that Hobson had negotiated with the *daotai*. Lovatt described the scene as "the maddening crowd of Chinese assemble on our Noah's ark of a pontoon, clamouring to have their cargo examined, each one wanting to be first."[96]

Ironically, the *daotai* who had done so much to delay the opening decided to celebrate the occasion by throwing "a great spread tomorrow and has invited Consul, Customs, and Merchants to an entertainment in his Yamen." Here is how Lovatt described it:

> We all turned up at the Taotai's dinner, and an extraordinary dinner it was. It commenced at 3 p.m. and finished at 8 p.m. Only think—sitting, smiling, talking, eating, and drinking [for] five mortal hours. I was tired, very tired, and did not want to sit down again for a month. The courses were endless, well cooked, and fairly well served. All the Chinese officials of Chung King present, about

21 nice civil fellows, and all very courteous and polite. I was careful and only ate things I knew all about. The wine was fairly good. We drank it out of those absurd little cups, warm wine with the thermometer at 90 in the shade, but the tea was delicious and we mostly stuck to the tea. The theatricals were very amusing, a love and fighting story taken from the annals of the *Min* dynasty, but one wearies of the everlasting monotony and noise. A little Chinese theatricals go a long way.[97]

In a short time, the port was humming: "the Chinese are crowding us with cargo [yellow silk, white wax, silk cocoons, refuse silk, and medicine going to Yichang], and our days are now very busy, which I much prefer." By the end of June, even though the customs had been open for less than two weeks, the duty collected amounted to 7,500 taels, "a very good beginning indeed." Seven weeks in, "the trade here appears fairly prosperous, and I think the Customs revenue for last month amounted to over twenty thousand *taels*." By that fall, "we have succeeded admirably in the work." And at year's end, "the revenue collected for little over the six months we have done business will amount to close on 70,000 *taels* in spite of the opposition of the officials who have been very anxious to keep all the trade in the native customs. I can come to the conclusion we have done fairly well in all respects since our arrival."[98]

Although the customs was now up and running, the *daotai*'s corruption remained on full display later that summer, demonstrating "the feebleness of the Government and the unholiness of the officials. It will also show you how very feeble the officials are to protect foreigners, or even themselves, in times of riot and disturbance." When the *daotai* took over soon after Lovatt arrived:

He thought it his duty to disband the fire brigade, and [he] collected and placed in his Yamen some nine hand fire engines that had been placed in different parts of the city, saying he would take care of the engines, and in case of fire his soldiers would take out the engines and attend to putting the fire out. I should also mention that the merchants had been in the habit of paying a small tax for the maintenance of the fire brigade and engines, so when the Taotai did away with the firemen, he did not discontinue the tax but collected it as usual and, as everybody supposes, put it into his own pocket. Things have gone along alright up to two nights ago when a fire broke out in the *Chou fen Kai*, over a hundred houses were destroyed, and many people left homeless. The next morning the Taotai visited the scene of the fire, taking with him 180 strings of cash to help any poor people in need of immediate relief, but on his arrival the people would have none of his cash, upset his Chair, pulled his official hat off, and drove him into the Chen Tai's Yamen where they blockaded him and said he should not leave until he promised to re-establish the fire brigade and to rebuild their houses. This he promised to do, and he was permitted to return to his own Yamen, the Chen Tai furnishing him with a guard of soldiers. The Taotai has a meeting tomorrow with the elders of the district to arrange for the rebuilding

> of the houses and he will have to pay. The Taotai is the son of a former viceroy of Canton. He is very rich, very conceited, and a man of little or no ability. He is a relative of the Viceroy of this province, and also by marriage, of Li Hung Chang, so he is not likely to come to much grief with such very powerful relatives and friends. The Taotai and Magistrate are to pay three hundred taels each to help the poor people re-erect their houses, and this will I think calm the crowd and prevent any row, unless the officials begin to cheat them out of the money, which they are very likely to do.[99]

An incident one month later suggests that the *daotai* had failed to reestablish the fire brigade:

> There was another fire in the city the day before yesterday which destroyed a good many houses. There is a ludicrous side to it, sad, however. The Chinese head of the house died and as the family were pretty well off, the funeral ceremonies were to be conducted in proper style. Priests were sent for, mat sheds erected, altars put in position, paper representation of the Gods were put up in their proper places, and the whole of a large courtyard taken up with matting and made to look as much like a temple as possible. The old gentleman who had lately left this wicked world was brought out from his room and in his nice black lacquered and highly polished coffin was placed in the place of honor to be duly prayed for that his soul might rest in peace. The altar was ablaze with light, enormous red candles were burning, and lanterns were everywhere. The night was very hot and there were a great many friends and relatives present, for a ceremony of this kind is more of the nature of a feast—the soul entering into Paradise. The priests were all assembled and chanting their dull monotonous litanies, horns were sounded at the more important parts, and cymbals clashed when a louder chorus was needed. I have already mentioned we had no rain for a long time, so everything was very dry. The fire was caused by a candle getting lopsided and setting fire to the lantern. This communicated to the matting and the whole place was immediately in a blaze. Everybody had to run, the fire spread so rapidly in such material, and from thence to the house and burnt down three courtyards full of houses. When the fire was over, a search was made for the coffin. Alas, not a vestige of coffin or bones was to be found. The priests say the Gods were so pleased with the good old man and at the piety of his friends in having such a fine and expensive funeral that they caused the fire, and in the midst of it took the old man to heaven. Many people argue otherwise, and say the old man got rich by cheating, and it was the anger of the gods that caused the fire, outraged at his pretense to a holy funeral or entrance to heaven after a long life of roguery. I am inclined to hope the priests are right.[100]

So corrupt was the *daotai* that, despite his connections, he was soon thereafter relieved of his position by the provincial governor who had been apprised of the popular sentiment: "I should not be in the least surprised if we have a riot here, partly owing to the great unpopularity of the Taotai." As for his replacement, "we will be pleased to see him here, for our present Taotai is the most amiable rascal you ever saw, so very polite and so determined to oppose all progress." Lovatt himself was optimistic:

> A couple of gun boats have gone down the river to meet the new Taotai who is reported to have left Ichang yesterday. We are hoping that the new official will be an intelligent man. He has been minister to Japan and, having seen another country besides his own, there is some chance of his having a few extra ideas in his head at least.

When he arrived early in 1892, the new *daotai*, the third since Lovatt had arrived in late 1890, was received with cautious optimism: "The new Taotai . . . is certainly a more intelligent man than the old one who leaves here tomorrow. He is a beast, so we will say no more about him." But a year into his tenure, it appeared that the new *daotai* was little better than his predecessor, if Lovatt's backhanded comment is any indication: "a very good man, very anxious to lead a quiet life and make a few thousand taels."[101]

FINAL DAYS IN CHONGQING

During his time in Chongqing, Lovatt had many occasions to think about his future and that of his family. Nellie, the oldest, worked at a bank; John, the next oldest, had graduated from high school and was casting about for a career; Ida had matriculated at the University of California—Berkeley; Mabel was in junior high school; and Willie was in elementary school. While Lovatt had occasionally thought about getting home leave, he had settled on the idea that Jennie and their two youngest, Mabel and Willie, should join him "when I once more get to a civilized port." He had not brought them to China earlier because he believed they were better off growing up in the States: "Children in China have certain ways and habits from early association with Chinese that are not commendable." On the one hand, "it is true that they have a good deal of self possession, and more of the manners of grown up people, owing to their mixing so much with much older people." On the other hand, "if they had to return to England or America their lives would not fall in very pleasant places, their chances of earning a living would be very small, and things would be very hard for them." He concluded that "we have decidedly done the best for them. They are now growing up American men and women, educated, and with a character of their own, and fitted to go anywhere."[102]

Yet another factor in having Jennie and two youngest children join him was the growing realization that he would probably remain in China for the long term: "No use thinking of my ever leaving the service, too old to learn a new trade or seek fresh employment," adding, "China is bad, but here I have lived 30 years, and feel at home more than anywhere else. [T]here is [no] sense in giving up my position in China to begin anywhere else." And even though his salary had not returned to its previous level of 200 taels, "T[aels] 150 is better in China than hard work and poor pay under the blue sky and below zero of the Northwest." In China, "food is good and plentiful. Servants are very fair, and life is by no means bad or unenjoyable. I feel I am in China and will probably have to stick to my position until old age, disease, or incapacity forces me to resign." That said, he hoped that he could get to a better port where his family could join him. Until then, "I must make the best of Chung King and hope for a change." And when that transfer comes through, "bring Mabel and Willie with you to China, and here we will live and die if necessary."[103]

As Lovatt awaited a transfer, others preceded him. One was the British consul Fulford who had been transferred to Beijing, to be replaced by Hugh Fraser from Yichang: "I am sorry he is to leave us. I shall miss him a good deal, for we have been on the most friendly terms." Another departure was the assistant, Von Rosthorn, who received a two-year leave. "We have been here together from the first. I felt very sorry to see him go away, but he well earned his leave after ten years service. He is a nice fellow in many ways, but with a devil of a temper, which prevents him getting on with his Chiefs. Otherwise, he is remarkably intelligent, well educated, and gentlemanly."[104]

The transfer with the greatest impact was that of Commissioner Herbert Hobson and the arrival of his replacement, Friedrich Hirth, who arrived on June 2, 1893:

> I saw him yesterday morning and met him and Hobson at dinner last night. He is a little German, fair, short and stout, wears gold spectacles, speaks excellent English, is very learned, plays the piano more than well, agreeable manners, and is a friend to Moellendorff. Besides, he takes photographs. The impression he has left on me is very favourable. I like him and think him a very nice fellow. Hobson is busy packing up, and will probably leave about the 8th instant and then I will be the last of the Custom House Invaders.[105]

As the last remaining member of the pioneer Chongqing contingent, his desire for a transfer, evident from when he first arrived ("one might call it being buried alive"), was magnified. Lovatt's friends in better surroundings sympathized with him: "We all keep very well [in Yichang] and hope you will be out of Chung King before it begins to tell on you." Lovatt even asked his former boss to pull some strings with Hart: "I am writing to Commissioner Moorhead [in Yichang], and see if he can't get me out of this," all to no avail.[106]

Lovatt was not the only one looking to get out. His customs colleagues "all hope to get out of this disagreeable station to another where one may enjoy some social life and bracing climate," a sentiment that extended as well as to

> our Chinese servants [who] are equally anxious. They also hate the place, and will probably go anyhow, but knowing the time has arrived for changes, they are holding on, hoping their masters will be transferred to some other port. One boy always asks me, "Master, that Peking letter have got talkee go Shai?" I tell him no, he must wait a little longer. Poor fellow, he has wife and family in Shanghai and wants to get back to them. He has probably done pretty well, and now wants to go home. My sympathies are entirely with him.[107]

Lovatt wanted to be among those "living in the old ports [who] have much to be thankful for in the way of a nice settlement, foreign houses, clean streets lighted with oil, and here and there a policeman, even if he is Chinese." And he hoped that Hart had been impressed by his account of the voyage upriver and would "in a fit of generosity *wire* a promotion, anything to take me out of this awful hole." Jennie, however, was not as optimistic, calling "*Old Bob* a regular old Chinese heathen."[108]

Lovatt had three ports on his wish list. One was the "civilized" port where he had begun his customs career thirty years earlier—Hankou—where he hoped he would replace the current tidesurveyor, but that hope was soon extinguished: "My chance of getting Hankow is ended. A Mr. Patterson has been appointed to Hankow," noting that "I did hope the I. G. would have transferred me to Hankow and give me an increase. I fear, however, I am to remain here." A second desirable port on his wish list was Shanghai: "Whenever I am transferred from here, I intend asking the I. G. for another position, and if possible in Shanghai." But Shanghai also did not materialize. A third desirable port was Yichang. When Chief Examiner Stebbins had earlier been transferred from Chongqing to Yichang as tide-surveyor, "I had a quiet hope that he would be made Tidesurveyor here, [and] nice Lovatt transferred to where the steamboats whistle and carriages roll down electrically lighted streets, but those fond dreams are gone like the visions of the night." So Lovatt, who initially thought he would only be in Chungking for a year or two, entered his third year with no prospects of a transfer in sight.[109]

Whether and where he would be transferred, of course, lay in the hands of the IG: "Here we are likely to remain until that distinguished Irishman nods his head for our removal to some greater sphere of usefulness and an increase of salary. Bob says everything comes to him who waits. I am waiting with a patience that would make dear old Job blush." So Lovatt remained optimistic: "I consider my duty—stick to my post and wait for better times. I feel sure our affairs will take a favorable turn before long." But three years in Chongqing forced Lovatt to reconcile himself to remaining, rationalizing it by noting that "here, my expenses are so few, and if I go to a larger port, I shall not live as cheaply." Nonetheless, Lovatt's preference in that summer of 1893 was to be transferred to one of those three ports downriver. He would have to wait for nearly another year, until the spring of 1894.[110]

NOTES

1. WNL to JSL, August 27, and September 1, 4 and 8, 1890.
2. WNL to JSL, September 1, 4, 8, and 13, 1890. Fulford decided to wait for a later boat to allow the river to fall further.
3. WNL to JSL, September 8, 13, 18, and 22, 1890.
4. WNL to JSL, September 22 and 30, 1890.
5. WNL to JSL, September 18, 22, and 30, and October 1 and 3, 1890. In attendance were those who were staying in Yichang (Mr. and Mrs. D'Arnoux, Dr. Aldridge, and Consul Fraser), and those who were headed for Chongqing (Fulford, Hobson, Dr. Davenport, Strong, Stockwell, Von Rostorn, who was going overland, and Stebbins, who would depart slightly later).
6. WNL to JSL, October 4, 5, 6, 8, 9, 10, 11, 20, 24, and 30, 1890. One hundred cash equals ten cents. On Sunday, October 12th before entering Sichuan, they stopped at Patung [Badong] to give their mail to the local magistrate for forwarding overland back to Yichang, forty miles distant by road.
7. WNL to JSL, October 11 and 12, 1890.
8. WNL to JSL, October 12, 14, 15, and 16, 1890.
9. WNL to JSL, October 16 and 17, 1890.
10. WNL to JSL, October 22, 1890. "Mr. Von Rosthorn was to have joined us here if he got tired of the road, but he has failed to put in an appearance so we presume he is tramping away to Chung Ching all right."
11. WNL to JSL, October 6 and 23, 1890.
12. WNL to JSL, October 29, 1890.
13. WNL to JSL, October 4, 22, and 29, and November 1, 1890.
14. WNL to JSL, October 22, and November 2 and 5, 1890.
15. *North China Herald*, August 22, 1890, 211, and October 3, 1890, 397; WNL to JSL, October 3, and November 5 and 13, 1890. *Service List, 1892*, 22, 89, 123. Second Historical Archives. Nanjing. Wanxian to Chongqing is 214 miles overland and takes 8 to 10 days to walk. Chongqing to Yichang is 539 miles overland and takes 23 days to walk. Missing letter numbers 319 to 380 (May 1892 through February 1893), 382 to 385 (February 25 through March 22, 1893), 387 to 400 (March 24 through June 3, 1893), and 402 to 410 (June 5 through July 22, 1893).
16. WNL to JSL, November 4, 5, and 9, 1890, and January 15, 1891.
17. WNL to JSL, November 5, 9, 13, and 17, 1890.
18. WNL to JSL, November 5, 9, 13, 17, and 22, 1890.
19. WNL to JSL, November 27, 1890. Emphasis in the original.
20. WNL to JSL, November 27, and December 2, 7, and 12, 1890.

21. WNL to JSL, December 8 and 12, 1890, and February 12, October 18, and December 31, 1891; WNL to de Bernieres, December 28, 1890, not sent, enclosure in WNL to JSL, January 15, 1891.

22. WNL to JSL, July 10, 1891.

23. WNL to JSL, November 27, and December 21 and 28, 1890, and January 3 and 15, February 24, and October 3, 1891.

24. WNL to JSL, December 2, 7, and 12, 1890, and February 24, 1891. Emphasis in the original. When two years passed without Hart publishing it, Lovatt turned it into an unpublished guidebook, adding Hobson's name as a second author, and entitling it *Ichang to Chungking: 1890*. *North China Herald*, December 2, 1892, 817. Lovatt also sent a separate journal home to his family in Minnesota: "I shall keep a journal of the trip on letter paper and send it to you." WNL to JSL, September 22, 1890. That journal is preserved at the University of California-Berkeley Bancroft Library. *Journal of Wm. Nelson Lovatt on Board Szechuan Junk from Ichang to Chungking, October 3rd to November 4th, 1890.* Banc Mss Z-Z154 (*Journals of William Nelson Lovatt and Related material, ms.*). He unabashedly compared that journal to published works covering the same terrain:

> I have been reading Capt. Gill's *River of Golden Sand* as the upper portion of the Yangtze is called, and very interesting it is, and Cooper's *Pioneer of Commerce*, but neither of the above works are so full, and if you will permit me to say it, are by any means so accurate as the journal I have sent you, and only it would look very conceited. I would also say my work was by far the most interesting in its account of the mighty river from Ichang to Chung King. Compare it with *Hart, Gill, Cooper, Hanie,* or *Blakiston* and tell me what you think. (WNL to JSL, February 10, 1891)

25. WNL to JSL, November 22, and December 15, 1890, and January 23 and February 8, 1891; WNL to de Bernieres, December 28, 1890 (not sent), enclosure in WNL to JSL, January 15, 1891.

26. WNL to JSL, November 9 and 22, 1890, and June 17 and November 11, 1891. Lovatt enjoyed the company of Fulford, whose predecessor "was glad to get away." Fulford was an Australian and "a very nice fellow [who had gone] to England, competed for a consular studentship, and won, and here he is a remarkably bright smart fellow."

27. WNL to JSL, May 4, 1891.

28. WNL to JSL, January 3, 1891.

29. WNL to JSL, November 17, 1890, and May 24 and 28, 1891. Emphasis in the original.

30. WNL to JSL, January 10, 13, and 29, February 4 and 24, July 16, September 13, and December 21 and 31, 1891. Books he mentioned specifically included William Gill's *The River of Golden Sand: The Narrative of a Journey through China and Eastern Tibet to Burmah* (London: John Murray, 1880; reprinted Cambridge University Press, 2010) and Thomas Cooper's *Travels of a Pioneer of Commerce in Pigtail and Petticoats: Or an Overland Journey from China towards India* (London: John Murray, 1871; reprinted New York: Arno Press, 1967).

31. WNL to JSL, January 29, February 4, June 17, August (n.d.), and September 28, 1891. Rosthorn intended to travel in the western part of Sichuan province and write a book.

32. WNL to JSL, January 8 and 29, and March 6, 10, and 14, 1891.

33. WNL to JSL, April 9 and June 12, 1891.

34. WNL to JSL, June 12, October 13, November 2, and n.d., 1891. Mason eventually pleaded guilty to illegal possession of dynamite under British law and was sentenced to nine months in jail.

See Hart to Campbell, October 1 and 22, and November 1, 1891, in John King Fairbank, Katherine Frost Bruner, and Elizabeth MacLeod Matheson, eds. *The I.G. in Peking: Letters of Robert Hart, Chinese Maritime Customs, 1868–1907.* Two Volumes (Cambridge and London: Belknap Press of Harvard University Press, 1975).

35. WNL to JSL, June 12, October 13, and n.d., 1891.

36. WNL to JSL, November 5, 9, 13, and 27, 1890. He met the Wilsons, Mr. Murtray, and Dr. Davenport at the London Mission, and the Lewises, Mrs. Cady, and Dr. [James] Cameron and his "very nice" wife, son, and daughter at the China Inland Mission.

37. WNL to JSL, November 13 and December 15, 1890, and January 29, June 12, August 14, and December 21, 1891, and January 20 and winter (n.d.), 1892. The Quakers were "Mr. & Mrs. Davidson and child, two Miss Southalls, a Miss Breton, and a Mr. [illegible], all belonging to the Friends' Mission." For more on Hart, see E. I. Hart, *Virgil C. Hart: Missionary Statesman—Founder of the Anerican and Canadian Missions in Central and West China* (Toronto: George H. Doran Company, 1917).

38. WNL to JSL, January 20, 1892.

39. WNL to JSL, June 2 and 27, July 2, 1891, and n. d., winter, 1892.

40. WNL to JSL, December 15, 1890, February 8 and May 28, 1891, and January 20, 1892. Emphasis in the original.

41. WNL to JSL, January 13, and February 4 and 8, 1891.

42. WNL to JSL, May 23 and 24, and June 1 and 2, 1891. The guest list for the first dinner party included "Mr. & Mrs. Wilson, Dr. Davenport, London Mission, Mr. & Mrs. Davidson, Friends (Quakers), Miss Southall, Mr. Dean."

43. WNL to JSL, February 4, April 19 and 24, July 26, and December 11, 1891.

44. WNL to JSL, January 29, February 4, April 28, and May 18, 1891.

45. WNL to JSL, April 19, July 2, and October 3, 1891.

46. WNL to JSL, January 3, 13, and 29, February 8, May 8, and June 27, 1891, and January 20, 1892.

47. WNL to JSL, March 6, May 18, August 14, and October 3, 1891.

48. WNL to JSL, March 23 and September 8, 1891.

49. WNL to JSL, May 31 and November 11, 1891. Emphasis in the original. Other missionaries seemed to lack common sense: "The two sick men in the China Inland Mission are still pretty poorly. Hobson sent down to ask if they would like some port wine. The doctor said it would be just the thing for them, but no, they were strong teetotallers and would not take any—very foolish of them." WNL to JSL, September 8, 1891.

50. WNL to JSL, April 24, July 26, August 14 and 25, and October 3, 1891, and March 23, 1893.

51. WNL to JSL, November 17 and December 11, 1891, and March 23, 1893.

52. WNL to JSL, July 2 and 26, 1891.

53. WNL to JSL, January 29, 1891.

54. WNL to JSL, May 31, 1891. Lovatt obtained this information in a letter from former chief examiner Stebbins, now based in Yichang. The riot in Wuhu occurred on May 12–13.

55. WNL to JSL, April 19, 1891 and March 23, 1893. Emphasis in the original.

56. WNL to JSL, May 23 and 31, June 22 and 27, July 2, 11, and 16, and August 3, 1891.

57. WNL to JSL, June 22 and 27, August 30, and September 23, 1891. The disturbance in Jiujiang occurred on June 7. The incident in Wuxue was chronicled in the *New York Herald*, September 6, 1891.

58. WNL to JSL, September 23, 1891; Irwin Hyatt, "The Chengtu Riots (1895): Myths and Politics." *Papers on China* (Cambridge: East Asian Research Center, Harvard University, 1964), 29.

59. WNL to JSL, August 30, and September 8 and 23, 1891. Emphasis in the original. The incident in Yichang occurred on September 2.

60. WNL to JSL, September 23 and n.d., 1891. The news came in a letter from Count d'Arnoux to Hobson.

61. WNL to JSL, September 15 and 18, 1891.

62. WNL to JSL, June 12, 20, and 27, 1891.

63. WNL to JSL, June 20, 22, and 27, 1891.

64. WNL to JSL, July 11, and September 8, 15, and 23, 1891.

65. WNL to JSL, October 18, 1891; Paul A. Cohen, *China and Christianity: The Missionary Movement and the Growth of Chinese Antiforeignism, 1860–1870* (Cambridge: Harvard University Press, 1963), 45–48, 276–281.

66. WNL to JSL, September 8, 1891.

67. WNL to JSL, September 8, 18, and 28, 1891.

68. WNL to JSL, October 27, and November 2, 1891. For more on antiforeignism in Chongqing, see Judith Wyman, "The Ambiguities of Chinese Antiforeignism: Chongqing, 1870–1900." *Late Imperial China*, 18 (2) (1998), 86–122.

69. WNL to JSL, October 18, November 2 and 5, and December 31, 1891. Emphasis in the original. Of course, paying an indemnity of 50,000 *taels* meant that the rioters went unpunished.

70. Robert Johnson, *The Far China Station: The U. S. Navy in Asian Waters, 1800–1898* (Annapolis: Naval Institute Press, 1979), 228; WNL to JSL, June 12, July 11, September 17, 23, and 28, October 18, and November 2, 1891. For the role of gunboats, see Robert M. Paterno, *The Yangtze Valley Anti-Missionary Rots of 1891*. (PhD Diss., Harvard University, 1967), 256–258.

71. WNL to JSL, September 8, November 5 and 12, and December 31, 1891.

72. WNL to JSL, July 2, 11, and 16, September 8 and 28, November 5, and December 25, 1891; S. M. Meng, *The Tsungli Yamen: Its Organization and Functions* (Cambridge: Harvard East Asia Monographs 13, 1970), 78–79.

73. WNL to JSL, September 28, November 5, 11, and 12, and n.d., 1891, and January 20, 1892. Lovatt's confidence that Western governments were applying sufficient pressure was shaken a year and a half later when he cited "the killing of two Swedish missionaries from America in Hankow province. It is outrageous that foreign Gov'ts tolerate this killing quite an inoffensive people." WNL to JSL, July 28, 1893.

74. WNL to JSL, January 15, May 12, September 3, and December 31, 1891, and January 25 and April 17, 1892.

75. WNL to JSL, June 1, September 3, and November 2, 1891.

76. WNL to JSL, November 2 and December 16, 1891. For more on poorhouses, see Ch'u T'ung-tsu, *Local Government in China under the Ch'ing* (Cambridge: Harvard University Press, 1962), 161.

77. WNL to JSL, May 12 and September 3, 1891, and January 25, 1892.

78. WNL to JSL, May 12, September 3, and November 17, 1891.

79. WNL to JSL, May 12, September 3, and November 17, 1891, and January 25, 1892.

80. WNL to JSL, February 12, July 2 and 21, and September 3, 1891.

81. WNL to JSL, February 14, June 12, August 5, and November 17, 1891.

82. WNL to JSL, WNL to JSL, March 25, May 7, 12, and 31, July 6 and 24, and September 3 and 13, 1891, and n.d., 1892.

83. WNL to JSL, May 31 July 2 and 21, and October 18, and December 31, 1891. Emphasis in the original.

84. WNL to JSL, February 24, April 28, May 31, June 7, July 13, August 30, and December 11, 1891.

85. WNL to JSL, July 2, 6, and 13, and December 21 and 25, 1891. Emphasis in the original.

86. WNL to JSL, April 4, 1891, and June 4 and July 23, 1893. "I enclose a picture of the house I am living in. I give explanation on the back of picture so will not repeat it." The two exceptions to those living conditions were two younger staffers, Strong and Stockwell, who opted to live in the Purple Cloud Mountain temple on the other side of the river. David Herlihy, "Lenz's World Tour Awheel through the Szchuen Province." *Outing*, 24 (February 4, 2008), 432–439. Lenz says he stayed there from April 16 to April 19, but Lovatt says he was there in July of that year (1893). Lenz died before he could complete his trip.

87. WNL to JSL, November 22 and December 12, 1890, and January 3, 1891.

88. *Ibid.* There were sixteen letter agencies [*min xinyu*] in Chongqing in 1891. Ying-wan Cheng, *Postal Communication in China and Its Modernization, 1860–1896*. Harvard East Asia Monographs, 34 (Cambridge: East Asian Research Center, Harvard University, 1970), 44. See also Ch'u T'ung-tsu, *Local Government in China under the Ch'ing*, 154–155.

89. *Ibid;* WNL to JSL, July 21 and 28, 1891. Of course, one could always use the telegraph since there was a line to Beijing and to Shanghai, but "the tariff of charges makes it almost prohibitive to send any but the most important messages."

90. WNL to JSL, January 20, 25, 27, and 29, and February 24, 1891. If the opening had been delayed further to the summer, "junks do not leave here for down river, the freshets in the river being too dangerous to admit of trade being carried on with safety."

91. WNL to JSL, March 2, 1891. Emphasis in the original.

92. WNL to JSL, December 28, 1890.

93. WNL to JSL, September 4 and December 12, 1890, and January 23, February 10, 12, 14, and 24, and March 5, 6, and 10, 1891.

94. WNL to JSL, WNL to JSL, February 12, March 15, April 4, 19, and 24, and May 8, 1891. The *lijin* is a domestic customs levy, an impediment to the free flow of trade. Similar duties in the United States were abolished in the late eighteenth century by the Interstate Commerce Act.

95. WNL to JSL, May 18 and 28, and June 1 and 12, 1891.

96. WNL to JSL, May 28, June 17 and 20, August 5, and November 25, 1891. To get to his post, "it is my disagreeable duty to have to cross the river twice a day . . . in an ordinary sampan, but will soon have a new boat which I have had built with five men to pull it. I shall get backwards and forwards with more comfort." That new "comfortable" boat had a house on it "so I am well protected from the sun and rain."

97. WNL to JSL, June 27 and July 2, 1891. Emphasis in the original.

98. WNL to JSL, June 27, July 2 and 21, August 3, October 3, and December 31, 1891.

99. WNL to JSL, August 12 and 14, 1891. Emphasis in the original.

100. WNL to JSL, September 13, 1891.

101. WNL to JSL, September 18 and 28, December 11, and n. d., 1891, January 20, 1892, and March 23, 1893.

102. WNL to JSL, December 21, 25, and n.d., 1890, April 13, July 10 and 13, October 23, and November 6 and 25, 1891, and April 2 and 22, 1892. If Lovatt were transferred to a post downriver, he could contemplate a leave of between three and six months' duration to get home, something that he could not manage from Chongqing. Making such a trip within a limited window of time gained credence when he noted the latest advances in transportation: "Shanghai to Yokohama four days, Yokohama to Vancouver ten days, and train from Vancouver to St. Paul three days at a cost of $328." WNL to JSL, May 13, July 28, and November 6, 1891.

103. WNL to JSL, July 10, October 18, and December 16 and 21, 1891. Toward the end of his tenure in Chongqing, Lovatt had been sounded out about a postal position in China:

> If I am offered a Province—that is a Superintending postmastership—each province is to have one—I shall accept it. There is no possibility of my going home, and as for looking for employment in America, I am too old. You join me and we will be comfortable enough. The drawbacks to the Post Office positions are you are likely to be buried in some Chinese city, far from everybody and from foreign things, and as I am supposed to get on well with the Chinese, I would be sure to get some awful place. (WNL to JSL, July 28, 1893)

104. WNL to JSL, April 22, 1892, and March 23, 1893. Rostorn had earlier been given a salary increase from 125 to 150 taels. WNL to JSL, September 28, 1891.

105. WNL to JSL, June 4, 1893. In addition to Hirth and Lovatt in 1893 were Second Assistant J. A. Kerr, and Third Class Tidewaiters J. L. McDowall and H. C. W. Court. *Service List, 1893*, 22, 90, 123. Second Historical Archives, Nanjing.

106. WNL to JSL, November 22, and December 8, 21, 25, and n.d., 1890, and January 29, March 6 and 10, June 27, September 28, and November 11, 1891; George Cockburn, in Yichang, to Lovatt, March 5, 1891.

107. WNL to JSL, January 25, 1891 and April 2, 1892. Emphasis in the original.

108. WNL to JSL, April 20, 24, and 26, May 13, July 6 and 10, September 15, and December 11 and 21, 1891. Emphasis in the original.

109. WNL to JSL, November 22, and December 8, 21, and 25, and n.d., 1890, and January 25 and 29, March 6 and 10, April 20, 24, and 26, May 13, June 27, September 28, and November 11, 1891.

110. WNL to JSL, February 24, March 23, and July 23, 1893.

Chapter 13

The Final Decade

Yichang, Guangzhou, Jiujiang, and Hankou, 1894–1904

YICHANG, MAY 1894 TO JUNE 1898

After three and a half years in Chongqing, Lovatt was finally transferred by Hart in May 1894 to Yichang, one of his three preferred ports. Notice of his transfer appeared in the *North China Herald*: "Another friendly face is missing from our midst (Chungking). Mr. Lovatt, the genial head of the outdoor staff of the Customs, has been transferred to Ichang and Mr. Stebbins of the latter place is to come to Chungking." At his new posting, Lovatt, as tidesurveyor and harbormaster, was one of thirteen customs officers, ten outdoor and three indoor, under Norwegian commissioner F. Schjöth, and one of now 735 foreigners in the Customs Service. Before reporting for duty, Lovatt received a short leave to travel to Shanghai to meet Jennie and nine-year-old Willie to accompany them back to Yichang after a six-year separation. But Mabel would not be coming, having died of scarlet fever the previous year at the age of fourteen. Because Lovatt and his wife were now together in China with no need to write to each other, information about his life from this point on is scarce (figures 13.1 and 13.2).[1]

The Lovatts spent four years in Yichang, from 1894 to 1898, living in a large house with four Chinese servants and Willie's pet leopard. Midway through his tenure, a new commissioner arrived, F. E. Woodruff, Lovatt's former commissioner in Wuhu. In that same year of 1896, Willie, now eleven, was sent to the Anglican China Inland Mission School at Chefoo [Yantai]. Back in Minnesota, Nellie, now twenty-six, was married and two years later had a son, making the Lovatts grandparents for the first time. And Ida graduated from the University of California and began working for the *Oakland Tribune*.[2]

Figure 13.1 Lovatt at right doffing hat, Jennie in chair, and Willie in front with walking stick. Yichang. Courtesy: The Bancroft Library, University of California, Berkeley.

Figure 13.2 The Lovatts with four servants in front of their house in Yichang. Courtesy: The Bancroft Library, University of California, Berkeley.

Two years later, in June 1898, Lovatt was transferred to Guangzhou, to the regret of the expatriate community:

> The community (Ichang) suffers a real loss when it says good bye to Mr. and Mrs. Lovatt. They are people who have the happy faculty of making themselves agreeable to everybody they come in contact with. Mr. Lovatt will not only be missed in his office but in the various outside functions that belong to the port that make life less monotonous than it would otherwise be. Mrs. Lovatt always did the nice thing at the right time, whether in anti-footbinding meetings or in the sick chamber. Callers always found the latch string 'on the outside' whenever they called, and years will not make it otherwise with those who know them.[3]

GUANGZHOU (CANTON), JULY 1898 TO OCTOBER 1900

After being granted a four-month leave, Lovatt reported for duty in Guangzhou in November 1898 to his new commissioner Edward B. Drew, becoming one of forty-nine foreigners (forty outdoor and nine indoor) in the customs there. The following year, 1899, found Lovatt and Jennie still in Guangzhou, although there was now a new commissioner, J. F. Schoenicke, and a new second assistant, Onia Tiberii, with whom Lovatt had served in Fuzhou. Lovatt's service in Guangzhou continued into the first four months of 1900, at which point he was granted another leave for six months during which he and Jennie returned to Minnesota, fortuitously taking him out of China just before the outbreak of the Boxer Rebellion.[4]

While in the United States in that summer of 1900, the Boxer Rebellion was making headlines and, not surprisingly, the local newspapers asked Lovatt to comment on the rumors that were circulating. He correctly squelched the rumor that the foreigners surrounded in Beijing had found refuge in the palace because he knew there was no underground connection linking it and the Legation Quarter. But he erroneously confirmed a false rumor that because Hart had not been heard from since the middle of June, he and all the foreigners must have been killed. Although Lovatt was wrong about Hart's fate during the Boxer Rebellion, he was prescient about what Hart's demise would mean for the customs and his legacy:

> China is no longer the country it once was for foreigners, and the Customs future no one can foretell. It at present hangs on Sir R. Hart's life. No future inspector general will hold the strong position he does. In fact, many think there never will be another inspector general a foreigner, and if a Chinaman, the service would soon, as a respectable service, come to an end.[5]

JIUJIANG, NOVEMBER 1900 TO MARCH 1902

When Lovatt's leave expired at the end of October 1900, he and Jennie returned to China to take up his new post once again in Jiujiang, as one of nineteen foreigners in the customs, five indoor and fourteen outdoor, under Commissioner T. F. Hughes and Deputy Commissioner Edmund Grimani, with whom Lovatt had served in Fuzhou. Soon after arriving in Jiujiang, the Lovatts were joined by their daughter Ida, who had been born there twenty-seven years earlier in 1874, and who now went out every morning and rescued infant girls from drowning in the Yangzi River. In that same year of 1901, Willie, now sixteen, graduated from the Anglican mission school in Yantai and enrolled in Kings College in England.[6]

Lovatt's life and activities in Jiujiang surface only briefly, engaged in such routine duties as alerting ship traffic in early 1901 that a buoy light had been placed on an island. And Lovatt was referenced a year later when the newly arrived commissioner William Spinney asked Hart for permission to hire a Eurasian because "he talks Chinese like a Chinaman, so he will be of great assistance to me in this work; he is also a very steady man, and the Tidesurveyor, Mr. Lovatt, has a great opinion of him."[7]

The only document of any interest is an account by Commissioner Hughes on the perennial problem of corruption in which Lovatt plays a supporting role:

> I have visited Kut'ang in company with Yuan Weiyuan, *Mr. Lovatt*, and Chin Pao-ming, our head writer. On arrival at Kut'ang we found chairs awaiting us, but as the distance was so short, I decided to walk and thus give the people who had collected in great numbers a chance of having a good look at me. At the Ch'ang Kuan the [illegible] and chief clerks were awaiting us, and after a good deal of bowing and scraping, we were shown into a very clean reception room where the usual cakes and wine were served. I took the opportunity to reiterate what I had said at Kiukiang, but added that they must not misunderstand me when I said that everything was to go on as before. What I meant was that the old practice, with the exception of "squeezing," was to go on as before! Doubtless, many of them would say, "if we don't squeeze, how are we to live?" And that was just what I wished to talk to them about. I was fully alive to the fact that their salaries were very small, too small in fact to make both ends meet. Now what I wanted them to do was to tell me frankly what they got a month, salaries included. What they told me now would not be considered an offence. I was here to help them, not to oppose them. It was my hope that one of these days they would get salaries which would enable them to do away with "squeezing," to put them, in fact, on a footing with the foreign customs. They had this chance now and they should make the most of it, for if I found later on that they had concealed anything from me, they would only have themselves to blame for being without a billet. They thanked me very much for the interest I took in them

as I said that if their salaries were sufficient they would then not "lose face" by squeezing. They have promised to draw up a report for me giving exactly how much each man got a month, and when I get this there is no reason why we should not give them fixed salaries and take over the whole show ourselves.[8]

HANKOU, APRIL 1902 TO JULY 1904

After a year and a half in Jiujiang, in April 1902, Lovatt was transferred to his final posting, Hankou, where he had begun his customs career forty years earlier and which was another one of his preferred postings. Still not promoted by Hart, he remained at the rank of tidesurveyor and harbormaster, one of forty-two foreigners (thirty-two outdoor and ten indoor) under Commissioner Alfred E. Hippisley. The scant evidence we have on his posting there reveals more routine duties regarding barometers, boat measurements, out-of-position buoys, red and white channel marking lamps, soldering tools to repair lamps, water levels, the tea market, and blowing up sunken lorchas (figures 13.3 and 13.4).[9]

During Lovatt's first year in Hankou only two letters exist that give a glimpse of his life there, both written in the summer of 1902 to his father-in-law, now living in Oregon. In the first, he reports that Will "is getting on in

Figure 13.3 Hankou Bund. Courtesy: The Bancroft Library, University of California, Berkeley.

Figure 13.4 Lovatt in rear doffing hat with local dignitaries in Hankou. Courtesy: Philip Reeser Cuperus.

his studies" in England. In the second letter he recounts a twenty-eight-day leave to escape the July heat, during which he and Jennie went downriver to his former posting of Jiujiang and took chairs up to Kuling where Ida was staying with a member of the China Inland Mission. Returning to Hankou in August, they resumed their usual activities, for example, attending a dinner party hosted by the British consul in honor of the visit of the HMS *Glory*, and throwing a huge garden party for all the resident foreigners at their large house on the Bund.[10]

Perhaps the most important affair for Lovatt and Jennie in Hankou occurred a year after their arrival with the marriage of their daughter Ida, now twenty-nine, in April 1903 at St. Joseph's Church, to twenty-eight-year-old French engineer Jean Michel de Carbonel who was helping to construct the railroad line from Hankou to Beijing. The wedding aroused great interest in the Bay Area of California: Ida's "brilliancy frequently illuminated that special [society] page of *The [Oakland] Tribune*. Personally, she was as genial, womanly, and popular as she was graceful and entertaining as a writer, and when, about three years ago, she was called to the home of her

Figure 13.5 Wedding of Ida Lovatt to Jean Michael de Carbonel, St. Joseph's Church, Hankou, April 3, 1903. Courtesy: de Carbonel Family.

parents beyond the sea, she left a vacancy in social circles which has not since been filled" (figure 13.5).[11]

Other family transitions in 1903 included the death of Jennie's eighty-five-year-old father in Oregon and the marriage of their eldest son John. As the year 1904 dawned, Lovatt and Jennie became grandparents again when Ida gave birth to Henri in Hankou. The last letter we have from Lovatt was to Jennie's brother John and his wife in Oregon in the spring of 1904, to whom he had sent some tea, and who wrote that "Ida, John [Jean], and baby [Henri] are gay and happy. We all met at tiffin today."[12]

In that spring of 1904, in a customs staff that had swelled to forty-eight foreigners, Lovatt, still hoping for a promotion, continued to burnish his credentials, receiving a bonus for having completed Chinese language study Level B. In April of 1904, he was promoted from tidesurveyor to chief tidesurveyor (*zhaodong zongxun*), of which there were only seven in the Service. And he received yet another award from the Chinese government, the Civil Rank of the Fifth Class (*Wupinxian*), making that his sixth medal—three from China, two from England, and one from Austria. Promotion to commissioner still eluded him, however, and three months later he was dead.[13]

William Nelson Lovatt died at 3:20 p.m. in the afternoon of July 9, 1904, at the age of sixty-six, his passing marked by the *North China Herald*:

> It is with very deep regret that we have to announce the untimely death at Hankow of Mr. W. N. Lovatt, Tidesurveyor and Harbour Master there. Although the weather was unusually hot, Mr. Lovatt went for his usual walk round the racecourse, came back, was stricken with heat-apoplexy, and died. Mr. Lovatt had been very many years in the Customs Service, and there was never a man in any walk of life who more deservedly gained and retained the respect and love of all who knew him. He was emphatically a man of a million, everything that an old soldier, as he was, should be. He retired once on competency, which he invested in a farm in America, but he lost his money and had to return to work in the Customs. At the River Ports, and at every port in China where he was known, the greatest sorrow at his loss, and the deepest sympathy with his widow and family will be felt.

Lovatt was buried at the International Cemetery in Hankou, now the site of the Number Eight Hospital.[14]

NOTES

1. *North China Herald*, May 25, 1894, 798; *Service List, 1894*, 22, 92, and 129. Serving with Lovatt in Yichang was Third Assistant E. A. Aldridge, Fourth Assistant J. B. Fitzgibbon, and Tidewaiters Erskine and Hellstrand. Mabel died on March 14, 1893, and was buried in the Lakeview Cemetery in Lakeland along with Jennie's mother, who died four months later at the age of sixty-seven. With Ida in college in California, Jennie was leaving behind their other two children in Minnesota, John and Nellie, as well as her now-widowed seventy-six-year-old father. Before leaving, she was able to attend the wedding of her thirty-seven-year-old younger brother, John, to Ina Letta Hutchins, in June 1894. WNL to JSL, August 2, 1893; *Minnesota State Census Records*: *Washington County*, 1895, Roll 103; Information courtesy of Dorothy Shaw Gillette.

2. *Handlist of the Papers of the China Inland Mission* (London: School of Oriental and African Studies, 1994), 74; *Service List, 1895, 1896, and 1897*, 22, 96. Willie's school had been established in 1880 to provide an education for the children of missionaries and members of the business and diplomatic community, the headmaster being an ex-student at Kings Canterbury. Willie played soccer and cricket, and rowed. Nellie's marriage took place in June 1896 to Charles Beard, thirty-four, a watchmaker from Cincinnati who worked as a jeweler in St. Paul until his retirement in 1932, and who died in 1938. They had four children: William Beard, born in February 1898; Rachel Beard, born in May 1899; Charles Beard, born in July 1902; and John Beard, born in July 1909. Kathryn Beard and Bill Beard to the Author, May 8, 2002.

3. *North China Herald*, July 4, 1898, 17; *Service List, 1898*, 23, 101.

4. *North China Herald*, July 4, 1898, 17; *Service List, 1898*, 172–173; *Service List, 1899*, 23, 109, and 192–193; *Service List, 1900,* 24 and 160; Lovatt (in Hankou) to Captain T. I. Eldridge (in Shanghai), July 5, 1902. *Hankow. Commissioner. Nos. 1 to 62, 1882–1903 and Harbour Master, 1902–1903. Letterbook*. Number Two Historical Archives, Nanjing; *1900 Census*. It is not clear where the Lovatts spent their four months on vacation.

5. "Discredits Conger Message." *The Trenton Times*, July 23, 1900, 2, and *The Wellsboro Agitator*, July 25, 1900, 8; WNL to JSL, October 8, 1891.

6. *Service List, 1900,* 24 and 160; *Service List, 1901*, 24, 116, 171, and 188. Number Two Historical Archives, Nanjing; *Minnesota State Census Records: Washington County, 1895*, Roll 103. Jennie's father, Joseph Shaw, now 82, and his son John (Jennie's brother), his wife Ina, and their three children, moved together to Portland, Oregon in 1905.

7. Lovatt circular, February 17, 1901, in *Kiukiang, Commissioners No. 1 to 132, 1882–1903 and Harbour Master, 1902–1903. Letterbook*; T. F. Hughes to Bredon, October 31, 1901; Spinney to Hart, January 7, 1902, in *Kiukiang, 1901–1910. Letterbook.* Number Two Historical Archives, Nanjing.

8. T. F. Hughes (Commissioner at Kiukiang) to Robert Hart, December 14, 1901. *Kiukiang, 1901–1910. Letterbook.* Number Two Historical Archives, Nanjing. Emphasis added.

9. *Service List, 1902*, 25, 121, 191, and 206; WNL to Captain T. I. Eldridge, Deputy Coast Inspector, May 26 and July 5, 1902, and May 13 and October 20, 1903; WNL to Captain A. Ford Tyler, Coast Inspector, Shanghai, September 5 and 9, November 18 and 20, and December 1, 8, and 10, 1902, and February 2, 1903. *Hankow. Commissioner. Nos. 1 to 62, 1882–1903 and Harbour Master, 1902–1903. Letterbook.* Number Two Historical Archives, Nanjing.

10. WNL to Dear Father Shaw, August 10 and 14, 1902; *North China Herald*, May 14 (1903 or 1904) and May 15 (1903 or 1904).

11. "She Was Married in China." *Oakland Tribune*, May 16, 1903, 10.

12. WNL to John Shaw, March 31, 1904. John and Grace Rowland had two children: William Lovatt was born in 1908 and Lorraine Lovatt was born in 1912. John ran a furniture store and a grocery store in Portland and died in 1934. *Minnesota State Census Records: Washington County, 1895*, Roll 103; information courtesy of Dorothy Shaw Gillette in 2002.

13. Now, there was no rank of Tidesurveyor in Hankou, only Chief Tidesurveyor (Lovatt), followed by Assistant Tidesurveyor. *Service List, 1903*, 24, 122, 211, and 229–230; *Service List, 1904*, 25, 128, 259–260, and 360; *Service List, 1905*, 287. Number Two Historical Archives, Nanjing. Lovatt had received two Silver War medals from the British Government for War Service in India and in China. He had also received the Silver Cross of Merit from Emperor Franz Joseph of Austria.

14. Michael Lovatt to the author, July 3, 1999*; Lovatt Family Genealogy*; *William Nelson Lovatt Death Record*, courtesy of Bill Beard. The doctor who signed the death record was John D. Thomson of Hankou and was registered on July 12, 1904; *North China Herald*, July 11, 1904; Wuhan City Government, *Hankou jujie zhi [Hankou Concession Gazeteer]* (Wuhan: Wuhan Publishing House, 2003), 36. There is no mention of Lovatt's death in any of Hart's correspondence.

Chapter 14

Epilogue

1904–1914

Jennie remained in Hankou after her husband died, having received 2,000 taels that Lovatt was due as a retiring allowance, and sent for Will, who had graduated from King's College and was working for the Hong Kong and Shanghai Bank in London. Upon his return to China, he joined the Hankou branch of the Standard Oil Company with a salary of $150 a month plus a "good" furnished room. According to his mother, "Will is getting on fairly well in the S. O. Co. He is learning Chinese and will get more salary when he can speak Chinese." Jennie now had with her two of her four children, Ida and Will, as well as two of her grandchildren, as Ida's two sons Henri and William (born in June 1905) "come almost every day to see me."[1]

Jennie fell into a routine of spending the winters in Hankou, with her son Will, her daughter Ida, and her son-in-law Jean. She and Ida summered in the cooler scenic mountain retreat of Chi Kung Shan, the railroad that Jean had helped to construct giving them easy access. Even in that seemingly idyllic setting, anti-Western sentiment persisted six years after the Boxer Rebellion:

> There has been some trouble about foreigners going there [Chi Kung Shan] this spring, the Chinese governor of that province objecting to the foreigners going there and insisting on their leaving. But the viceroy of Hupaih [Hubei] is willing foreigners should go there and go with his passport. The people are all friendly and like the foreigners because they are giving them a good market for their produce. So it will all be settled peaceably. We are not far from the [illegible] Station so if [illegible] are unfriendly we will be able to leave on short notice. But as the Japanese consuls and the Italian consuls families are going there in houses they have had built for themselves, the Chinese will think twice before making trouble. We think and [have] no doubt in time it will be all settled. To keep the good will of the foreigners they will not disturb the foreign settlements.[2]

In February 1907, Jennie and Ida made their first and only trip to the capital, having received a free train pass from Jean:

> I had never been there [Beijing] before and I liked seeing the places my dear Will had told me so much about, and also to see the old location of the besieged people in 1900 [the Boxer Rebellion], and I met quite a number of old friends there. The Customs House people were also very kind to me and invited [me] to picnics and to visit temples and places of interest in Peking. Sir Robert Hart I did not see as he was not going out in the cold weather, but Sir Robert Bredon [Hart's brother-in-law] called and invited [us] to a tiffin party, then to a reception at the American legation. I met Mr. and Mrs. [William W.] Rockhill at the [US] Consulate, and also went to the British Legation. So if it is in China, one can hardly go anywhere without meeting someone they have known before.[3]

Although the family seemed to be settling into a comfortable routine in China, they were about to take separate paths. Jennie wanted to return to America, and Ida, Jean, and their two children wanted to visit Jean's homeland of France. So in May 1908, they all sailed down the Yangzi to Shanghai along with Will who helped Jennie purchase her Pacific Mail Steamship ticket, but who could not go because he had not worked long enough for Standard Oil to qualify for a leave. At the same time, Ida and Jean with their children left for France. Just as the Lovatts were departing China in 1908, Robert Hart was also leaving China for the last time for England, succeeded by Francis Aglen, who would serve as inspector general for the next thirty years.[4]

After a "very pleasant" trip across the Pacific, Jennie arrived in Victoria, British Columbia, in June, and traveled to Ellensburg, Washington, where her younger sister Bessie and her husband lived. The change had done Jennie good, writing that "I am feeling much better than when I left Hankow." After visiting her sister, Jennie returned to Minnesota, clearly missing her two children: "Ida may visit me in St. Paul in the autumn and wishes me to go back to China with them. Will hopes to be in position to have his own little home in a year or two, and wants me to come back [to China] and keep house for him, and if I am well and strong I should like to do so." But Jennie would never return to China or see Ida and Will again.[5]

Jennie Shaw Lovatt died in St. Paul at 8:00 p.m. on December 28, 1911, and was buried in the Lakeview Cemetery in Lakeland next to her daughter Mabel. The newspaper in Stillwater, where she had lived, noted that "many friends of the Lovatt family in Washington County will be pained to learn of the passing of this good woman." Her obituary read:

> A lovely soul, of rare charm and beauty, went from us into the sunshine of Paradise on the evening of the day dedicated to purity and innocence, Holy

> Innocents' Day, December 28. Mrs. Lovatt was not only a remarkable woman but she had lived a remarkable life, with the romance which is usually written in fiction. The girl from a Minnesota farm married, after a charming courtship of unusual incident, the Lieutenant Colonel under Chinese Gordon, and was taken from the quiet of the St. Croix into the atmosphere of court and public life. She met the greatest men in the Orient, saw the world at its best, and gave it something which only a woman of the sweetest Christian spirit can impart. She was in the world but not of the world. With vivid and fascinating powers of description, she has made the Orient real to us who have had the inestimable privilege of knowing her. Such a life is the earnest of immortality and the sympathy of the parish goes out to a family who found in the life of their mother the reality of the gracious promises of Christ.

In the same year that Jennie died, 1911, Robert Hart died and the Qing dynasty for whom he and Lovatt had worked for decades was overthrown in the Xinhai Rebellion and replaced by the Republic of China.[6]

Ida, Jean, and their two boys returned to China after their 1908 trip to France, but five years later, in 1913, Jean died in Shanghai of food poisoning and was buried there. Ida then took her two sons to France and then to the United States, arriving in New York City on the *Louisane* in May 1914, and then to Minnesota for a family reunion. From Minnesota, Ida and her two sons moved to Berkeley, California, where Ida had lived previously, and she died there in 1951.[7]

Ida's son Henri donated his grandfather's journal and photo album to the Bancroft Library of the University of California at Berkeley in 1963 and died three years later in California. Ida's other son William graduated from the University of California in 1928 in engineering, his career taking him to the Philippines, where, like his uncle Will, he also worked for Standard Oil. After the Second World War, William returned to California and died there in 1965.[8]

Will Lovatt remained in China working for Standard Oil until the outbreak of the First World War when he returned to England and joined the Royal Artillery, the same branch of service that his father had served in. After the war, he married Jane Budd and returned with her to Hankou, where they had four sons. In a semi-fictional account of the Standard Oil Company in China by Alice Tisdale Hobart entitled *Oil for the Lamps of China*, Will is one of the four Bills depicted in the book. It became a best-selling novel when it was first published in 1933, just two years after Pearl Buck's *The Good Earth*, about a man who wants to bring progress to China but who is caught between Chinese nationalism and a heartless American corporation. The title became a catchphrase for the "myth of the China market." Upon the outbreak of the Second World War, Will Lovatt rejoined the Royal Artillery. He died in 1955 and is buried in Cambridge.[9]

NOTES

1. WNL to JSL, January 10, 1878; JSL to John and Ina Shaw, June 2, 1906.

2. JSL to John and Ina Shaw, June 2, 1906; JSL (in Chi Kung Shan) to Arline Shaw (her niece, daughter of her brother John), August 21, 1906; JSL to John and Ina Shaw, October 24, 1906. Among Lovatt's papers is the printed menu of a dinner that Jennie, Ida, Jean, and Will attended: "Caviar, Consomme choux-fleuris, Poisson Bouilli, Filet Jardineiere, Snipes (for a change), Gigot di mouton, Chicories au Jus, Gateau, Glace a le crème, Fruits, Dessert, Café." May 12, 1906.

3. JSL to John and Ina Shaw, October 24, 1906; JSL to Ina Shaw, March 24, 1907; JSL to Arline Shaw, February 8, 1908. Hart had married Hester Jane Bredon. Her brother Robert would serve as Acting IG between 1908 and 1910 after Hart returned to England.

4. JSL to Ina Shaw, March 24, 1907; JSL to John Shaw, June 29, 1908. Jennie Shaw Lovatt May 16, 1908, diary entry in the *Imperial English and Chinese Diary and Almanac for 1908.* Aglen was succeeded by Frederick Maze, who was in turn succeeded by the last Western IG, the American Lester Little, who served from 1944 to 1950.

5. JSL to Ina Shaw, March 24, 1907; JSL to John Shaw, June 29, 1908; Jennie Shaw Lovatt diary entry, June 24, 1908 in *Ibid.* Bessie Shaw, born on February 2, 1863, married James Nesbitt, a teacher, in December 1884 in Lakeland. They had two sons and one daughter. The family moved to Ellensburg, Washington, in 1905 where he became superintendent of schools in 1910 and Bessie was elected city treasurer in 1915. She died in November 1923.

6. *Stillwater Daily Gazette*, December 29, 1911, and December 30, 1911.

7. Helen (Nellie) Lovatt Beard to Aunt Bessie, no date; Marge' de Carbonel to the author, December 5, 2001; Michael Lovatt to the author, July 3, 1999; Dorothy Shaw Gillette to the author, March 15, 2002.

8. *Buffalo Courier Express*, March 15, 1945; Marge' de Carbonel to the author, December 5, 2001; Michael Lovatt to the author, July 3, 1999.

9. Michael Lovatt to the author, July 3, 1999, and March 5, 2015; *Oil for the Lamps of China* (Indianapolis: Bobbs-Merrill, 1933, reprinted by Norwalk, CT: Eastbridge, 2002). Hobart (1882–1967) first went to China in 1908 and there met her future husband, an executive in the Standard Oil Company. Will Lovatt's four sons were Anthony Lovatt, who died in infancy and was buried in Hankou with his grandfather William Nelson Lovatt; John Budd Lovatt, who died in 1979 and is buried in Cincinnati; William Lovatt, who died in 1954 and is buried in Cambridge with his parents; and Michael Alexander Hugh Lovatt, born on November 15, 1926 and died in England on July 15, 2019.

Conclusion

William Nelson Lovatt spent most of the last two-thirds of his life in China, 44 years from 1860 until his death in 1904. He had first come to China in the British army during the Second Opium War. After participating in the siege of Beijing, his deployment to Shanghai transformed him from an enemy of the Qing dynasty into a supporter, helping to suppress the Taiping Rebellion from 1860 through 1862 and training Chinese soldiers to fire Western artillery. He thus became an integral part of the Cooperative Policy between the West and China during that decade, much like his more famous contemporaries, the Frenchman Prosper Giquel and the British Colonel Charles "Chinese" Gordon. His eyewitness accounts of the taking of the Dagu forts, the march on Beijing, and the campaigns against the Taiping are revealed here for the first time. During those early years in China, he became enamored with the country, and when the young sergeant mustered out of the army, instead of returning to his native England he took employment in the Chinese Imperial Maritime Customs Service in 1863 under the new inspector general, Sir Robert Hart, yet another manifestation of the Cooperative Policy. His first post, and ironically his last, forty years later, was Hankou.

Lovatt and the Customs Service operated within a semicolonial or "informal imperialism" framework that bound together Western nations and China in the late nineteenth century. As a British American citizen, Lovatt enjoyed extraterritorial immunity and his treaty port residences and workplaces represented carved-out spaces that reflected Western privilege. At the same time Lovatt, Hart, and the Customs Service operated as adjuncts of the Qing government to provide a stable income from maritime trade. In short, defining Lovatt's role is problematic at best. One example of this is his role in two of China's conflicts after joining the Customs Service.

Although he was now a tidesurveyor, Lovatt's military exploits were far from over, as his experience and background gave rise to two instances when Hart reassigned him to assist the Chinese military again. The first came in the late 1860s when for three years he trained the Qing cavalry in Tianjin, and at one point actually led his cadets against the Nian rebels, representing yet another aspect of the Cooperative Policy. By all accounts his service was exemplary, and he received a decoration and honorary rank from the Chinese government that allowed him to refer to himself from then on as "Colonel." While his efforts in military training did not go unnoticed, the larger program of military Self-Strengthening of which he was a part did not result in the rejuvenation of the Chinese military, as the loss to Japan in 1895 dramatically illustrated.

Several years later, Lovatt was tapped again by Hart to assist the Chinese military when Japan invaded Taiwan in 1874. Although Lovatt did not see action, his temporary duty in Taiwan became embroiled in the vagaries of international politics. Because Britain was a mediator in the conflict, Lovatt's assistance to the Chinese military was seen as a violation of British neutrality, and the British Consul in Jiujiang arrested British Commissioner Kopsch for transmitting Hart's order to Lovatt to go to Taiwan, Lovatt himself barely escaping arrest. The incident raised the question of whether Kopsch and Lovatt were British subjects subject to British jurisdiction or civil servants of China immune from such sanctions. Ultimately, the latter perspective prevailed, with Hart, Kopsch, and Lovatt representing penultimate Chinese civil servants and the Maritime Customs a purely Chinese institution.

Lovatt served in nine different treaty ports, some of them more than once, mostly on the Yangzi River. He enjoyed his job and most of his postings, with the possible exception of remote Chongqing, and became a keen observer of treaty port society. Like many other Westerner expatriates in China, although he had married the American Jennie Shaw in 1869, he was alone for most of the first quarter century of his married life, so much of his socializing was with other Westerners, many of whom were missionaries. Because Lovatt was a Christian, one might think that he would give an unvarnished view of missionaries and their activities. Yet his observations of missionaries, mostly British and American, male and female, good and bad, were surprisingly objective. His accounts of their evangelizing efforts allowed him to generalize about the Christian enterprise in China in a no less critical way.

His socializing with Western diplomats in the treaty ports allowed him a window into the diplomatic world and the rumors and gossip associated with it. Because international events like the murder of Augustus Margary in 1876 and the war scare with Russia in 1880 might affect his position specifically and more generally the Customs itself, he was alert to every report of possible conflict. Consequently, his keen analyses of Chinese diplomatic behavior are instructive. At the same time, he was able to poke fun at the foibles of some of the diplomats he interacted with, such as the love-smitten consul in Tianjin or the completely out-of-touch diplomat in Jiujiang.

Because Lovatt had mastered Chinese, and because it was his habit to escape the narrow confines of the treaty ports at every opportunity, he was able to get a view of Chinese life and society during the late Qing available to few others. Unlike most Westerners whose interactions with Chinese, if any, were severely restricted, Lovatt observed, met, and spoke not only with Chinese officials both honest (few) and corrupt (many) but also with a wide array of characters, such as opium smokers, beggars old and young, chair bearers, water coolies, junk crews, boat trackers, tea merchants, Buddhist monks, mail carriers, and gamblers, to name but a few. So varied were his encounters and his observations that they defy easy categorization. Some of his comments on Chinese society would suggest that he was a cultural imperialist, reflecting Western superiority and the need to introduce liberal Western values to a backward civilization. To that extent, Lovatt was probably no different than most of the Westerners living and working in China in the late nineteenth century. At the same time, many of his comments show an understanding of China and an empathy for the Chinese people in those four decades. Suffice it to say that the window on Chinese society that Lovatt provides has few parallels.

While treaty ports, diplomats, and missionaries were key staples of the Western presence in late Qing China, they also represented obvious targets for rising antiforeign nationalism. Lovatt encountered many incidents both large and small during his sojourn in China. While the 1870 Tianjin Massacre was perhaps the best known worldwide early in his career while he was in Jiujiang with his new bride, a multitude of lesser-known instances are documented by Lovatt. His forty years of dealing with antiforeignism in China made him a seasoned observer and analyst of the phenomenon that began to peak in the 1890s when Lovatt was in Chongqing. The antiforeign incidents of this decade served as a prelude to the Boxer Rebellion at the end of the decade, in which several hundred foreigners, including many missionaries, were killed. Lovatt avoided becoming a victim himself only because he was on leave in the United States.

Finally, Lovatt gives us an inside look at the workings of the Chinese Imperial Maritime Customs Service and its inspector general Robert Hart. Like all in the Customs, he participated in the gossip and speculation regarding transfers and promotions. He was also ambitious, wanting to be a commissioner eventually, and to that end he did everything possible to win Hart's favor to advance his career. Lovatt was a competent and hardworking tidesurveyor who had never been disciplined or put on report. He had also mastered

Chinese, a skill that Hart had identified as a *sine qua non* for advancement in the Service. But he was never promoted by Hart to commissioner, and Lovatt was left wondering why, particularly when others rose so rapidly to that rank.

One reason for his lack of advancement may have been that Lovatt did not go to university but rather was self-taught, in contrast to someone like Hosea Morse, who had graduated from Harvard as a Classics (Greek and Latin) major at the age of nineteen, the same age and major as Hart at Queens University. Hart favored men of this background because he believed them better able to deal with Chinese mandarins trained in their own classical tradition. But the main reason probably lay elsewhere.

The evidence suggests that the main stumbling block was that Lovatt had been disloyal to Hart and the Customs first by resigning in 1883 to take a commissionership in Korea. He then compounded that misstep three years later by blackmailing Hart for a more generous severance package to leave Korea quietly by implying that he would publicly reveal Hart's secret plan to annex the Korean customs service. Although Lovatt would never know, Hart had determined never to promote Lovatt to comissioner as early as 1885, saying that he was "not the stamp of a man to run a port," despite the fact that Hart was aware that he was the most efficient of the three customs commissioners in Korea. Lovatt's advancement would be stalled at the rank of tidesurveyor for the remainder of his customs career.

Lovatt's view of Hart was decidedly mixed. At times he praised Hart and acknowledged the difficult job he had. And Lovatt had to be grateful to Hart for taking him back when he swallowed his pride and asked to return to the Chinese Customs Service after his stint in Korea, something that Hart did not have to do. Although Hart brought him back as assistant tidesurveyor, Lovatt acknowledged that Hart had acted with a sense of equity because he had after all opted for $6,000 in retirement hush money rather than $1,500 and a return to his former rank of tidesurveyor. And Hart did eventually promote him back to his former rank. While it is probably fair to say that Hart held a grudge against Lovatt for his disloyalty and his blackmailing, Lovatt himself acknowledged that loyalty was one of the criteria for advancement in the Service, that he had run afoul of that benchmark, and that he might never again be promoted as a result.

On the other hand, Lovatt had good reason to dislike Hart, telling his wife (on October 21, 1891) that "I have long thought Bob Hart a bad fellow." After all, it had been Hart who had unfairly forced him out of his commissionership in Korea in 1886. And despite his exemplary record as a trainer of the Qing military at Hart's bidding, as the best commissioner in Korea, as a hardworking and competent tidesurveyor, and his mastery of the Chinese language, Hart never promoted him to commissioner. Although Lovatt suspected that he would never attain that rank, he never stopped trying, continuing his study of Chinese and in the last year of his life passing a language examination. He died in 1904 without reaching the pinnacle in the Customs.

An undated poem by Lovatt entitled "Depreciation" that appeared in *The North China Herald* perhaps aptly sums up his attitude toward Hart and the Customs. To protect himself from possible retaliation by Hart, Lovatt signed it simply, "A Victim."

When in this great Celestial land
The Allied armies held command,
They called from every Western nation
For men to form a combination,
To help the inexpert Chinese
In getting in their Customs fees.
To this end men from every clime
Freely gave up their youthful prime,
Believing they would be repaid
For the great sacrifices made;
Alas! the hopes were doomed to fail
Of those who clung to the Chinese tael!
Their mighty chief who rules in Pekin
Controlling fees and dues and lekin,
With brains and courage to command,
And wisely guide his trusty band,
Now for his work can justly claim
High honours, titles, wealth, and fame.
To most promotion comes too late;
Those silver shoes for which they wait
Poor Duty's slaves may never wear
Until they climb the golden stair.
The kudos, too, for which they strive
May never find them while alive!

Bibliography

Banno, Masataka. *China and the West, 1858–1861: The Origins of the Tsungli Yamen*. Cambridge: Harvard University Press, 1964.

Bays, Dan. *A New History of Christianity in China*. Oxford and New York: Wiley and Blackwell, 2011.

Bennett, Adrian Arthur. *Missionary Journalist in China: Young J. Allen and His Magazines, 1860–1883*. Athens: University of Georgia Press, 1982.

Bickers, Robert A. *Britain in China: Community, Culture and Colonialism, 1900–1949*. Manchester: Manchester University Press, 1999.

———. "Purloined Letters: History and the Chinese Maritime Customs Service," *Modern Asian Studies*, 40, 3 (2006), 691–723.

———. *The Scramble for China: Foreign Devils in the Qing Empire, 1832–1911*. London: Allen Lane, 2011.

Bohr, Paul Richard. *Famine in China and the Missionary: Timothy Richard as Relief Administrator and Advocate of National Reform, 1876–1884*. Cambridge: Harvard East Asian Monograph 48, 1972.

Bredon, Juliet. *Sir Robert Hart: The Romance of a Great Career*. London: Hutchinson, 1910.

Broomhall, Alfred J. *Hudson Taylor and China's Open Century. Book Three: If I Had a Thousand Lives*. London: Hodder and Stoughton and the Overseas Missionary Fellowship, 1982.

———. *Hudson Taylor and China's Open Century. Book Five: Refiner's Fire*. London: Hodder and Stoughton and the Overseas Missionary Fellowship, 1985.

———. *Hudson Taylor and China's Open Century. Book Six: Assault on the Nine*. London: Hodder and Stoughton and the Overseas Missionary Fellowship, 1988.

Brunero, Donna. *Britain's Imperial Cornerstone in China: The Chinese Maritime Customs Service, 1854–1949*. New York: Routledge, 2006.

Buffalo Courier Express, March 15, 1945.

Carr, Caleb. *The Devil Soldier: The American Soldier of Fortune Who Became a God in China*. New York: Random House, 1992.

Cassel, Par. *Grounds of Judgement: Extraterritoriality and Imperial Power in Nineteenth Century China and Japan.* Oxford: Oxford University Press, 2012.

Chen Shiqi. *Zhongguo jindai haiguan shi [China's Modern Maritime Customs History].* Beijing: Renmin Chubanshe, 2002.

Chen Xiafei and Han Rongfang, eds. *Archives of China's Imperial Maritime Customs Confidential Correspondence between Robert Hart and James Duncan Campbell, 1874–1907.* Comp. The Second Historical Archives of China and the Institute of Modern History of the Chinese Academy of Social Sciences. Two Volumes. Beijing: Foreign Languages Press, 1990.

Cheng Ying-wan. *Postal Communication in China and Its Modernization, 1860–1896.* Harvard East Asia Monographs, 34. Cambridge: East Asian Research Center, Harvard University, 1970.

The China Directory for 1874. Hong Kong: China Mail, 1874; reprinted Taipei: Ch'eng-Wen Publishing Company, 1971.

Chouban yiwu shimo. Tongzhi zhao [Complete Record of the Management of Barbarian Affairs. Vol. 6. The Tongzhi Period]. Taipei: Kuofeng ch'upanshe, 1965.

Ch'u, T'ung-tsu. *Local Government in China under the Ch'ing.* Cambridge: Harvard University Press, 1962.

Cohen, Paul A. *China and Christianity: The Missionary Movement and the Growth of Chinese Antiforeignism, 1860–1870.* Cambridge: Harvard University Press, 1963.

Cooper, Thomas T. *Travels of a Pioneer of Commerce in Pigtail and Petticoats: Or an Overland Journey from China towards India.* London: John Murray, 1871; reprinted New York: Arno Press, 1967.

Correspondence with descendants of William Nelson Lovatt, Jennie Shaw Lovatt, and others in the Chinese Customs Service:

———. Dorothy Shaw Gillette to the Author, March 15, 2002.

———. Kathryn Beard and Bill Beard to the Author, May 8, 2002.

———. Marge' de Carbonel to the Author, December 5, 2001.

———. Michael Lovatt (grandson) to the Author, July 3, 1999.

———. Peter Hodge (great-grandson of William F. Stevenson) to the Author, December 18, 2014.

———. Susan Tropeano (Mrs. John N. Lovatt) to the Author, June 10, 1999.

Dai Yifeng, *Zhongguo haiguan yu Zhongguo jindai shehui: Chen Shiqi jiaoshou jiuzhu huadan zhushou wenji [The Chinese Maritime Customs and Modern Chinese Society: Essays Commemorating the 90th Birthday of Professor Chen Shiqi].* Xiamen: Xiamen University Press, 2005.

Dean, Britten. "Sino-British Diplomacy in the 1860s: The Establishment of the British Concession at Hankow," *Harvard Journal of Asiatic Studies*, 32 (1972), 71–96.

"Discredits Conger Message," *The Trenton Times*, July 23, 1900, and *The Wellsboro Agitator*, July 25, 1900.

Doolittle, Justus. *Social Life of the Chinese*. London: P. Hood, 1868.

Erickson, Caroline S. "Romance, Courage in the Story of a Tiny Red Shoe; Milwaukee Woman Writes Most Vivid Recollection; It Takes Us to Old China," *Milwaukee Journal*, June 17, 1942.

Esherick, Joseph. "Harvard on China: The Apologetics of Imperialism," *Bulletin of Concerned Asian Scholars,* 4 (1972), 9–16.

Eskildsen, Robert. "Of Civilization and Savages: The Memetic Imperialism of Japan's 1874 Expedition to Taiwan," *American Historical Review*, April 2002.

Fairbank, John King. *Trade and Diplomacy on the China Coast: The Opening of the Treaty Ports, 1842–1854*. Cambridge: Harvard University Press, 1953.

———, Katherine Frost Bruner, and Elizabeth MacLeod Matheson, eds. *The I.G. in Peking: Letters of Robert Hart, Chinese Maritime Customs, 1868–1907*. Two Volumes. Cambridge and London: Belknap Press of Harvard University Press, 1975.

———, Martha Henderson Coolidge, and Richard J. Smith. *H. B. Morse: Customs Commissioner and Historian of China*. Lexington: University Press of Kentucky, 1995.

———, Richard J. Smith, and Katherine Frost Bruner, eds. *Entering China's Service: Robert Hart's Journals, 1854–1863*. Cambridge: Harvard East Asian Monographs, 1986.

———, Richard J. Smith, and Katherine Frost Bruner, eds. *Robert Hart and China's Early Modernization: His Journals, 1863–1866*. Cambridge: Harvard East Asian Monographs, 1991.

Gill, William John. *The River of Golden Sand: The Narrative of a Journey through China and Eastern Tibet to Burmah*. London: John Murray, 1880; reprinted Cambridge University Press, 2010.

Handlist of the Papers of the China Inland Mission. London: School of Oriental and African Studies, University of London, 1994.

Hankow. Commissioner. Nos. 1 to 62, 1882–1903 and Harbour Master, 1902–1903. Letterbook. Number Two Historical Archives, Nanjing.

Hart, E. I. *Virgil C. Hart: Missionary Statesman – Founder of the American and Canadian Missions in Central and West China*. Toronto: George H. Doran Company, 1917.

Hart, Robert. *Diaries*. Hart Collection. MS 15/1. Special Collections. Library, Queens University, Belfast. Cited as *Hart Diaries*.

———. *Letter Series Z (1868–1906)*. PP MS 67. University of London, School of Oriental and African Studies Library.

———. *Letters, 1865–1910: Letters to Various Westerners in the Chinese Customs Service*. MS Chinese 4.1. Houghton Library, Harvard University. Cited as *Hart Letters*.

———. *Papers Concerning the Chinese Inspectorate General of Customs, 1885–1909*. bMS Chinese 4. Houghton Library, Harvard University. Cited as *Hart Papers*.

Herlihy, David. "Lenz's World Tour Awheel through the Szchuen Province," *Outing*, 24 (February 4, 2008), 432–439.

Hobart, Alice Tisdale. *Oil for the Lamps of China*. Indianapolis: Bobbs-Merrill, 1933; reprinted Norwalk, CT: Eastbridge, 2002.

Hsu, Immanuel. *China's Entrance into the Family of Nations: The Diplomatic Phase, 1858–1880*. Cambridge: Harvard University Press, 1960.

Huc, Evariste Regis. *A Journey through the Chinese Empire*. Two Volumes. New York: Harper Brothers, 1857.

Hucker, Charles O. *A Dictionary of Official Titles in Imperial China*. Stanford: Stanford University Press, 1985.

Hunter, Jane. *The Gospel of Gentility: American Women Missionaries in Turn-of-the-Century China.* New Haven: Yale University Press, 1989.

Hyatt, Irwin T. "The Chengtu Riots (1895): Myths and Politics," *Papers on China.* Cambridge: East Asian Research Center, Harvard University, 1964, 26–54.

———. *Our Ordered Lives Confess: Three Nineteenth-Century American Missionaries in East Shantung*. Cambridge: Harvard University Press, 1976.

Imperial Maritime Customs Service. *Service Lists, 1878, 1880–1883, 1888–1889,* and *1891–1905*. Shanghai: Statistical Department of the Inspectorate General of Customs. Number Two Historical Archives, Nanjing.

Jarman, Robert L. ed. *Taiwan: Political and Economic Reports, 1861–1960.* Volume One. Slough: Archive Editions, 1997.

Johnson, Robert. *The Far China Station: The U. S. Navy in Asian Waters, 1800–1898.* Annapolis: Naval Institute Press, 1979.

King, Charles, Nicholas Belfield Dennys, and William Frederick Mayers. *The Treaty Ports of China and Japan: A Complete Guide to the Open Ports of Those Countries, Together with Peking, Yedo, Hongkong, and Macao, Forming a Guide Book and Vade Mecum for Travellers, Merchants, and Residents in General.* London: Trubner and Company; Hongkong: A. Shortrede and Company, 1867.

King, Paul. *In the Chinese Customs Service: A Personal Record of Forty-Seven Years.* London: Heath Cranton Ltd., 1930.

Kiukiang, 1901–1910. Letterbook. Number Two Historical Archives, Nanjing.

Kiukiang. Commissioners No. 1 to 132, 1882–1903 and Harbour Master, 1902–1903. Letterbook. Number Two Historical Archives, Nanjing.

Ladds, Catherine. *Empire Careers: Working for the Chinese Customs Service, 1854–1949.* Manchester: Manchester University Press, 2013.

Little, Archibald, ed. *The Anti-Foreign Riots in China in 1891.* Shanghai: The North China Herald, 1892.

Liu, Kwang-Ching. *Anglo-American Steamship Rivalry in China, 1862–1874.* Cambridge: Harvard University Press, 1962.

Loch, Henry B. *Personal Narrative of Occurrences during Lord Elgins's Second Embassy to China in 1860.* Third Edition. London: John Murray, 1900.

Lodwick, Kathleen. *The Chinese Recorder Index: A Guide to Christian Missions in Asia, 1867–1941.* Two Volumes. Wilmington: Scholarly Resources, 1986.

Lovatt, William Nelson. *Papers:*

———. *Biographical Sketch*, April 21, 1901.

———. *Correspondence* (letters from and to William Nelson Lovatt).

———. *Correspondence* (letters from Jennie Shaw Lovatt).

———. *Correspondence* (letters to and from Lovatt children).

———. *Death Record, William Nelson Lovatt.*

———. *Depreciation (*Poem*)* (undated).

———. *Family Genealogy, Lovatt.*

———. *Imperial English and Chinese Diary and Almanac for 1908* (Jennie Shaw Lovatt's Diary).

———. *Journal, 1853–1868.* Banc Mss Z-Z154. *Journals of William Nelson Lovatt and Related Material, ms.* Bancroft Library. University of California-Berkeley.

———. *Journal of Wm. Nelson Lovatt on Board Szechuan Junk from Ichang to Chungking, October 3rd to November 4th, 1890*. Banc Mss Z-Z154. *Journals of William Nelson Lovatt and Related Material, ms.* Bancroft Library. University of California-Berkeley.

Lovatt, William Nelson and Herbert E. Hobson, "Ichang to Chungking: 1890," *The North China Herald*, December 2, 1892, 817.

Meng S. M. *The Tsungli Yamen: Its Organization and Functions*. Cambridge: Harvard East Asia Monographs 13, 1970.

Merrill, Henry F. *Letters to Sir Robert Hart and Others in the Chinese Customs Service, 1884–1913*. 2 Boxes. Ms Chinese 5. Houghton Library, Harvard University.

Merrill Letterbook, October 1884–October 1887.

Merrill Letterbook, November 1887–1913.

Mesny, William. *Mesny's Chinese Miscellany: A Textbook of Notes on China and the Chinese*. Volume One and Volume Two. Shanghai: China Gazette Office, 1896.

———. *Mesny's Chinese Miscellany: A Textbook of Notes on China and the Chinese*. Volume Four. Shanghai: E. Lee Printing Office, 1905.

Minnesota Genealogical Journal, 6.

Minnesota Genealogist, Vol. 12, No. 1.

Minnesota State Census Records: Washington County. Stillwater Public Library.

1865 Census, Roll 17.

1885 Census, Roll 45.

1895 Census, Roll 103.

1900 Census.

Möllendorff, Rosalie. *P. G. von Möllendorff: Ein Lebensbild*. Leipzig: Otto Harrassowitz, 1930.

Morse, Hosea Ballou. *The International Relations of the Chinese Empire. Volume Two. The Period of Submission, 1861–1893*. London and New York: Longmans, Green, and Co., 1910–1918.

———. *In the Days of the Taipings: Being the Recollections of Ting Kienchang, Otherwise Meisun, Sometime Scoutmaster and Captain in the Ever-Victorious Army and Interpreter-in-Chief to General Ward and General Gordon: An Historical Retrospect*. Salem: The Essex Institute, 1927.

Neill, Edward D. *History of Washington County and the St. Croix Valley*. Minneapolis: North Star Publishing Company, 1881.

New York Herald, September 6, 1891.

Nield, Robert. *China's Foreign Places: The Foreign Presence in China in the Treaty Port Era, 1840–1943*. Hong Kong: Hong Kong University Press, 2015.

The North China Herald:

November 29, 1871.

July 10, 1875.

March 14, 1878.

August 22, 1890.

October 3, 1890.

May 25, 1894.

July 4, 1898.

May 14, 1903(?).
May 15, 1903(?).
July 11, 1904.

Ocko, Jonathan K. *Bureaucratic Reform in Provincial China: Ting Jih-ch'ang in Restoration Kiangsu, 1867–1870*. Cambridge: Council on East Asian Studies, Harvard University, 1983.

Osterhammel, Jurgen. "Semi-Colonialism and Informal Empire in Twentieth-Century China: Towards a Framework of Analysis," in W. J. Mommsen and Jurgen Osterhammel, eds. *Imperialism and After: Continuities and Discontinuities.* London: Allen and Unwin, 1986.

Paterno, Robert M. *The Yangtze Valley Anti-Missionary Riots of 1891*. PhD Diss., Harvard University, 1967.

Patterson, Wayne. *In the Service of His Korean Majesty: William Nelson Lovatt, the Pusan Customs, and Sino-Korean Relations, 1876–1888*. Berkeley: University of California Institute of East Asian Studies Korea Research Monograph 35, 2012.

Plat Book of Washington County, Minnesota. Minneapolis: Northwest Publishing Company, 1901.

Platt, Steven R. *Autumn in the Heavenly Kingdom: China, the West, and the Epic Story of the Taiping Civil War*. New York: Knopf, 2012.

Rapp, John. "Clashing Dilemmas: Hong Rengan, Issachar Roberts, and a Taiping 'Murder Mystery,'" *Journal of Historical Biography*, 4 (Autumn 2008), 27–58.

Reinhardt, Anne. *Navigating Semi-Colonialism: Shipping, Sovereignty, and Nation-Building in China, 1860–1937*. Cambridge: Harvard Asia Center, 2018.

Rosenfelt, Willard E. ed. *Washington: A History of the Minnesota County: Fifty-Six Vignettes of the Past*. Stillwater: The Croixside Press, 1977.

Rowe, William T. *Hankow: Conflict and Community in a Chinese City, 1796–1895*. Stanford: Stanford University Press, 1989.

Seligman, Scott D. *The First Chinese American: The Remarkable Life of Wong Chin Foo*. Hong Kong: Hong Kong University Press, 2013.

Shaw, Joseph. Papers, 1857–1889. Minnesota State Historical Society, Minnesota Historical Society Research Center, Folder P710.

Shemo, Connie A. *The Chinese Medical Ministries of Kang Cheng and Shi Meiyu, 1872–1937: On a Cross-Cultural Frontier of Gender, Race, and Nation*. Bethlehem: Lehigh University Press, 2011.

"She Was Married in China," *Oakland Tribune*, May 16, 1903.

Smith, Richard J. "The Employment of Foreign Military Talent: Chinese Tradition and Late Ch'ing Practice," *Journal of the Hong Kong Branch of the Royal Asiatic Society*, 15 (1975), 113–138.

———. "Foreign Training and China's Self-Strengthening: The Case of Feng-Huang-Shan, 1864–1873," *Modern Asian Studies*, 10, 2 (1976), 195–223.

———. *Mercenaries and Mandarins: The Ever-Victorious Army in 19th Century China*. Millwood, NY: KTO Press, 1978.

Stillwater Daily Gazette, December 29, 1911 and December 30, 1911.

Sykes, William Henry. *The Taeping Rebellion in China, Its Origins, Progress and Present Condition*. London: Warren Hall and Co., 1863.

Tianjin. Correspondence to and from Outposts, Number 679. Number Two Historical Archives, Nanjing.

Tiffen, Mary. *Friends of Sir Robert Hart: Three Generations of Carrall Women in China*. Crewkerne, UK: Tiffania Books in Association with Queen's University, Belfast, 2012.

Van de Ven, Hans. *Breaking with the Past: The Maritime Customs Service and the Global Origins of Modernity in China*. New York: Columbia University Press, 2014.

Washington County Marriage Records, Record A500.

Weale, B. L. Putnam. *The Re-Shaping of the Far East*. London: Macmillan and Co., 1905.

Wilson, Andrew. *The Ever-Victorious Army: A History of the Chinese Campaign Under Lt.-Col. C. G. Gordon, C.B. R.E. and of the Suppression of the Tai-Ping Rebellion*. Arlington: University Publications of America, Inc., 1976.

Woodworth, Elijah Burghardt. *Descendants of William Woodworth of Scituate, Mass.* Boston: Elijah B. Woodworth, 1901.

Wright, Mary. *The Last Stand of Chinese Conservatism: The T'ung-chih Restoration, 1862–1874*. Stanford: Stanford University Press, 1967.

Wright, Stanley F. *Hart and the Chinese Customs*. Belfast: Wm. Mullan and Son, 1950.

Wuhan City Government. *Hankou jujie zhi [Hankou Concession Gazeteer]*. Wuhan: Wuhan Publishing House, 2003.

Wyman, Judith. "The Ambiguities of Chinese Antiforeignism: Chongqing, 1870–1900," *Late Imperial China*, 18, 2 (1998), 86–122.

Yangwu Yundong [The Foreign Affairs Movement], III Shanghai: Renmin Chubanshe, 1961. Comp. Chungkuo shihhsuehhui chupien.

Zhan Qinghua. *Quanqiuhua shiye: Zhongguo haiguan yangyuan yu ZhongXi wenhua chuanbo [A Globalization Perspective of Foreign Staffs in the Chinese Maritime Customs Service and Trans-Cultural Communication between East and West (1854–1950)]*. Beijing: Zhongguo Haiguan Chubanshe, 2008.

Zhang Zhiyong. *Hade yu wanQing ZhongYing waijiao [Hart between China and England in the Late Qing]*. Shanghai: Shanghai Shudian Chubanshe, 2012.

Index

Page references for figures are italicized

About the Author

Wayne Patterson is Professor of modern East Asian history at St. Norbert College in Wisconsin. He received his undergraduate degree in history from Swarthmore College and two master's degrees and a PhD in history and international relations from the University of Pennsylvania. He has been a visiting professor at Harvard University, the University of Chicago, the University of Pennsylvania, the University of California at Berkeley, Vanderbilt University, the University of Kansas, the University of Wisconsin-Madison, the University of South Carolina, and the University of Hawaii at Manoa. Abroad, he has been a visiting professor at universities in Korea, the Philippines, and Hong Kong. He has held four Fulbright fellowships. He is the author or editor of sixteen books, including *In the Service of His Korean Majesty: William Nelson Lovatt, the Pusan Customs, and Sino-Korean Relations, 1876–1888* (Berkeley, 2012), *The Korean Frontier in America: Immigration to Hawaii, 1896–1910* (Honolulu, 1994), and *The Ilse: First-Generation Korean Immigrants in Hawaii, 1903–1973* (Honolulu, 2000). The 2003 Annual Meeting of the American Historical Association in Chicago devoted an entire panel to a discussion of his research.

www.ingramcontent.com/pod-product-compliance
Lightning Source LLC
LaVergne TN
LVHW100353290926
849146LV00001B/5
9781498566469